VEGETARIAN DINNER PARTIES

150 MEATLESS MEALS GOOD ENOUGH TO SERVE TO COMPANY

BRUCE
WEINSTEIN

& MARK
SCARBROUGH

Photographs by ERIC MEDSKER

RODALE

Rodale books may be purchased for business or promotional use or for special sales. For information, please write to: Special Markets Department, Rodale Inc., 733 Third Avenue, New York, NY 10017.

Printed in the United States of America

Rodale Inc. makes every effort to use acid-free ∞, recycled paper ♻.

Book design by Christina Gaugler

Photographs by Eric Medsker

Kamut® is the registered trademark of Kamut brand khorasan wheat.

Library of Congress Cataloging-in-Publication Data is on file with the publisher.

ISBN-13: 978–1–60961–501–7   hardcover

Distributed to the trade by Macmillan

2 4 6 8 10 9 7 5 3 1   hardcover

🌱 RODALE.

We inspire and enable people to improve their lives and the world around them.

rodalebooks.com

CONTENTS

INTRODUCTION

The culinary powers-that-be say dinner parties are staging a comeback. Pardon us if we snicker. We've read that headline too often during the many years that we've been full-time food writers. There's no *comeback* because there was never a *go away*. Good cooks have been having friends over for dinner all along. What's better than a night at the table, a couple of bottles of wine, great camaraderie, and lots of laughs?

But since there's always room for improvement, we'd like to raise the bar and make a plea for dinner parties like the ones that have long been a part of our lives together. At least once a month, we brush off the stemware, pull together a collection of recipes, and put on a plated affair. The meal's pace is accomplished with discrete servings offered in several courses. The flavors are intense within a single dish, but each helping is small enough that your palate doesn't get exhausted before you move on to the next course. The cooking then becomes the canvas for the real masterpiece: a long, gorgeous evening together. Eyes sparkle in the candlelight. Time is measured in plates, not minutes. And people find themselves in the warmth of each other's affections. So, okay, *that* sort of dinner party may well be due for a comeback.

Yes, we plate the courses. You needn't. We find it a beautiful experience, a chance to be artistic with food and to offer our friends a delicious present. We've also become adept at certain tricks for throwing a successful dinner party; we'll want to share those with you. But almost every dish in this book could be set in the center of the table for a family-style meal. Just bring the roasting pan or big platter to the table and pour some more wine while everyone helps themselves.

However, we should also be honest about what this book doesn't have. We don't offer options for putting together a buffet. The courses don't do well jammed together on a single plate. They were developed to be focused and balanced—in other words, to stand on their own. As you'll see, the drama will happen *between* the plates—that is, both in the juxtaposition of one dish to the next and in the narrative arc of the longer meal, beginning to end. Don't worry: We'll give you lots of help putting it all together. But it's that arc, that movement between plates, that will create a memorable evening at your table.

And there are no side dishes here. For us, dinner parties are a way to re-create modern-day, four-star dining at home. When you arrive at one of these new French Laundry–inspired restaurants, these critically acclaimed temples of cuisine, you're presented with a menu that offers the evening's flavors in small bits: a bowl of soup with gingered carrots and miso, a plate of cold-smoked romaine lettuce with a candied walnut dressing, another plate of pickled shiso leaves and caramelized shallots with a dusting of ground green tea. You spend your time moving from plate to plate, experience to experience. That is our vision of the dinner parties we're about to lay out for you.

Let's face it: A vegetarian dinner party is not an everyday affair. And that's too bad. A vegetarian meal can be more satisfying than that big hunk of roasted meat that has held court on our tables for too long. So here's to an old-fashioned concept in a new-fashioned medium: the (truly) vegetarian (honest-to-God) dinner party.

Truly means no fakes. We're just not into tofurkey or fakin' bacon. We don't need to be. Vegetables can carry the day without doing a meatish drag show. After writing 22 cookbooks and developing almost 12,000 original recipes, we've come to the countercultural conclusion that asparagus, morels, sweet potatoes, tomatoes, peaches, pears, figs, and the rest of their plantish kin are more flavorful and offer more textural satisfaction than anything else in the larder—more than even the most über-grass-fed, über-grass-finished beef. A decade ago, our dinner parties were notorious for roasts; but our menus have shifted dramatically. These days, we're more interested in expanding the taste and texture range at the table, moving away from the mostly savory flavors of a hunk of meat and into the sour, sweet, bitter, herbaceous, and (yes) larger spectrum that fruits, vegetables, and grains provide. Over the course of hundreds of dinner parties, we've crafted vegetarian and vegan rec-

ipes that meet those demands—and now make up this book.

Every writer has a hidden agenda. Here's ours: When we embrace the modern, fine-dining scheme of carefully crafted courses, we can begin to see vegetables for their true worth. They're no longer relegated to the rim of the plate, a lost mound of steamed greens or roasted potatoes. They become more than main-course handmaids, a position they've held for too long in Western culture. No wonder so few of us understand that the produce section holds a more astounding array of culinary delights than the meat and fish cases combined. We're just not used to noticing vegetables, fruits, and grains. So it's high time we liberated them to the center of the plate. Our dinner parties do that. Yours can, too.

We want to encourage you to throw a five-star dinner party once in a while *and* to give vegetables, fruits, and grains their rightful due, even if you're the type who wants a steak the next night. You may have underestimated the bounty you're about to witness. Even some of our vegetarian friends seem stymied when it comes to preparing dinner parties—sometimes because they haven't realized the *culinary* potential of their plantish fare. They know the health benefits, they may be able to talk about the ethics, but they haven't explored the full gourmet potential of what's at hand. In this book,

we'd like to make a subtle plea for more heart and less head. Or to put it another way, more pleasure and less theory. No matter your tradition, carnivore or pescatarian, vegan or omnivore, come discover that plants are truly matchless when it comes to creating dishes good enough to serve to company.

Truth be told, neither one of us is a vegetarian. We're both *lapsed* vegetarians. Earlier in life, we both had sworn off meat: one for political reasons (aka he was in grad school in the humanities) and one for personal reasons (in chef school, he witnessed one too many broken-down animal carcasses). But hard-and-fast rules don't fit creative lives. We're both driven explorers (in life, in music, in art, in travel, and at the table). We take pleasure in pushing the boundaries. A strict set of thou-shalt-nots never sits well. By our thirties, just as our culinary careers began to flourish, we were getting pretty restless. One of us had a steak at a backyard barbecue; one of us ordered Chinese takeout. Soon, we were setting an omnivore's table again. A few years later, we'd written tomes on goat and ham. We were officially lapsed.

But as we were writing our seven-step plan to get off processed food, and even more so as we were developing a collection of savory main courses for our whole-grain book, *Grain Mains*, we again started eating more and more vegetarian meals. We were amazed at what we'd missed! At subsequent dinner parties, side dishes looked like a lackluster take on vegetables and grains. What exactly were we doing with all that glorious produce? Not much. Sliced almonds are not a garnish; a pat of butter is not a sauce. Ever wanting to push the boundaries, we needed to remedy that. But how?

Our past offered few clues. Back in the days when we were vegetarians, there weren't many role models for the sorts of dinner parties we like to throw. Vegetarian meals were, well, pretty lifeless, a horrid mash-up of tofu and steamed greens. Many fine restaurants back then shared our dilemma, too. When we would order the vegetarian or vegan option, we'd just get all the side dishes lumped together on a plate. That's not what we had in mind! (Maybe that lack of creativity explains the steak and the Chinese takeout.)

Just as we found ourselves newly interested in the culinary prospects of vegetables for their own sakes, we noticed better options on menus, thanks in large part to new, high-end vegetarian restaurants that weren't just patchouli-soaked 1970s holdovers with folk music in the background and an ice cream scoop of overcooked brown rice on the plate. Chefs Yotam Ottolenghi and Amanda Cohen led the way just as our own table was becoming a place where vegetables got

top billing. We, too, were soon serving multiple courses of vegetarian food, nuanced and balanced.

But I don't want to run a restaurant! you might say. Don't worry: We've got some ways to get you in the swing of it all (and to spread the word about vegetarian cooking, whether you make the full lifestyle choice or not). First off, our recipes are not restaurant fare; they were designed for our kitchen at home. We don't have a battalion of sous-chefs or a cleanup crew. We've made sure that most of the recipes can be made ahead or in parts and simply assembled at the last minute. We're not going to stand in the kitchen for an hour while our friends sit at the table. We'd be missing too much fun. Dinner parties needn't be stuffy. They can be—and should be—loud, hilarious, affectionate affairs.

RECIPE GIVENS

- Vegetables are properly washed and often dried (some greens need water to adhere to the leaves for proper cooking—as stated).

- Onions, shallots, and garlic cloves are peeled unless otherwise stated.

- Bell peppers are first stemmed, cored, and seeded if chopped, diced, or minced.

- Fresh ginger is peeled if minced.

- Scallions and leeks are trimmed of rooty bits as well as any large, tough, fibrous leaves.

- Carrots, turnips, beets, and other root vegetables are trimmed of their greens unless otherwise stated. Carrots need not be peeled after carefully washing for use in braises, soups, or stews.

- Olive oil is moderately priced, sturdy, and first cold-pressed. A fine, costly, finishing olive oil is so listed, usually as a garnish.

- Vegetable broth is reduced-sodium where possible; it's certainly free of MSG, often labeled as "natural flavorings."

- Skillets and saucepans are heavy, preferably stainless steel. They need not be nonstick unless requested.

INTRODUCTION

About two years ago, one of us had a birthday. It wasn't a significant digit flip (thank God), but we still invited friends over for several courses. The whole thing morphed into one of the best evenings we've ever had. A friend wanted to bring one dish—which turned into a disaster, a flambéed ceiling narrowly averted. It all ended with two lemon meringue pies in the center of the table and a veritable food fight to divide the slices among a passel of otherwise mature adults. Our closest neighbors are far enough away that we can't see another house from ours in the New England hills. The next day, one of them said the laughter rang up our narrow valley. "What in the world were you doing over there?" he asked. "Eating," we replied. (A case of champagne may have been an accessory to the good-humored mêlée.) Now, years later, it's still a glorious memory, a deep well of good feeling, and a chance to have found ourselves more fully

woven into the fabric of our friends, to have cheated the sorrow out of life one more time.

If dinner parties needn't be stuffy, dinner-party *dishes* needn't be fussy either. You might be surprised to find some pretty fine sliders among our recipes. And tacos. And arepas. And a vegan version of mac and cheese. Yes, there's chic, modernist fare here. But sometimes it's great fun to bring out old-fashioned comfort food, even with the stemware. Or to stick a shepherd's pie in among more innovative flavor pairings.

Come along and see the advantage of a vegetarian dinner party as we do it: individual courses, few to no side dishes, each plate a little work of art, some rustic but many elegant, some reimagined throwbacks but most decidedly modern. (With no molecular gastronomy. Whatever its value, we don't allow chemical warfare at our table.) In so doing, you, too, will begin to see that

vegetarian fare carries more possibilities than you might have imagined. Try a few of our small plates—maybe one or two on your own with your spouse or partner some evening. Then try a couple more. Try putting some together for friends. Soon enough, three things will happen. One, you, too, will put together a meal with plated courses. Two, you will learn that formal food doesn't mean a stuffy evening. And three, you'll see that vegetables deserve the center of the plate in ways that you might not yet have imagined, no matter if you're a committed vegetarian or a long-time carnivore who's just experimenting in the plant kingdom on the down low. Your friends will begin to covet invitations to your table. They'll soon become the very reason for your table. You'll be a master at this craft. Our only hope is that you, too, can avoid the flambéed ceiling. (Hint: Do the cooking yourself.)

How This Book *and* Our Dinner Parties Work

First off, we've divided the recipes into seven chapters that follow the arc of a dinner party: cocktails, nibbles to go with them, small plates, salads and soups, pastas, large plates, and desserts. No, you don't need to choose a recipe from each chapter. In fact, you shouldn't. A good dinner party

isn't a jigsaw puzzle with a set number of interlocking pieces. Rather, as you'll see, it needs some sort of narrative, a story with food. Would you like to offer two larger courses back to back or a couple of small plates followed by a warm soup and a crunchy salad? Or maybe just a collection of elegant

small plates, one after another? Or maybe a more traditional setup of a pasta, a salad, and a main course, followed by dessert? This book is designed to help establish the flow without determining the exact story.

As we've said, we have a hidden agenda. Whether you're

already a vegetarian or are just intrigued by the concept, we have a sneaking suspicion that all of us need to get better at what cookbook author Deborah Madison has called "vegetable literacy." Sure, the produce section is the most gorgeous part of the supermarket, bright and colorful. But it's also the loss leader for that store, the place where profits suffer an acute downgrade because, well, the pretty produce doesn't move fast enough to avoid spoilage. It's mostly eye candy: fresh food without high sales. Many of us walk in, see the bounty, and pass right by. Yes, even we two long-term food writers have brought home containers of hummus and baba ganoush, some salad bar olives, and a bag of pita chips when we're too tired to cook.

In the end, many of us lack the knowledge of how vegetables operate in a culinary landscape: how their more intense flavors can balance and complement each other and how their textures offer the best contrasts in any recipe collection. Even if you've picked up this book without ever wanting to put on a dinner party, don't worry. We've filled it with what we've learned over the years working with this bounty. We hope to advance not only vegetables but our literacy of them.

Inside the chapters, the recipes have some individual compo-

OUR BEST ADVICE

Don't panic. Sure, there's a lot to plan. And plan you must. But don't get bound by those plans. Go family-style if plating seems onerous. Skip the dinner party altogether and cook a couple of these recipes for friends one night. Or pull out all the stops and put on the shindigs we're proposing. What's the worst that could happen? You ruin a dish, make scrambled eggs, and crack open another bottle of red wine? Or call in takeout? Your friends won't mind. In fact, it'll be even more of an adventure. Relax. It's just dinner. And a nuanced, balanced vegetarian one at that.

nents to help you make your meal a success.

1. To start, each recipe is *vegetarian* unless specifically marked *vegan*. In fact, about half the recipes are vegan, which means that there are absolutely no animal products in the mix: no eggs, honey, dairy, or cheese. (We do understand that some vegans will not eat yeast, but we have let it stay in our notion of vegan fare.) In truth, we did not set out to include so many vegan recipes. But the more we've worked with fruits, grains, and vegetables, the more we've realized that their flavor combinations can be unduly or unwittingly muted by ingredients from the dairy case, despite the ubiquitous pat of butter on corn or sweet potatoes. So for culinary reasons

alone, our vegetarian recipes have skewed more and more vegan.

2. Next comes the matter of *servings*. Unlike most cookbooks, these recipes are calibrated for a larger number—mostly eight, occasionally six. Indeed, we have come to think of eight as the perfect dinner party. The noise level stays below a roar; the conversation can break into smaller groups without needing to. You're not trapped talking over your left and right shoulders but can still carry on a conversation with someone across the table. Yes, we've done 12, even 16. But those meals become more and more a professional production.

However, our portion sizes are often restrained; they're geared for a multicourse meal.

If you want to test out a recipe on your family some weeknight, the small plates that serve eight will probably serve four. Some of the main courses will likewise feed about four—although others will leave you with leftovers (provided you don't have teenagers). And by the way, if you want to turn one of the small plates into a larger course for eight or ten, choose a recipe that serves six and double it.

3. Almost all the recipes include a note called *Ahead*, which refers to the pieces or steps that can be made in advance as well as a tip about how to store those parts in anticipation of the evening. We have long made it a policy that the host must not vacate the table for endless stretches to pull together a course. Sure, we violate that policy occasionally—when the fare is so extraordinary that it warrants a last-minute push. (Donuts for dessert, anyone?) But for the most part, we want our last-minute kitchen work to be a small set of simple tasks that bring a dish together in minutes. In the end, dinner is *not* the most important part of a dinner party. It's the party.

4. Many recipes include ways to take the dish over the top (*More*) and/or ways to pull it back from the brink if you want an easier evening (*Less*). The former are most likely the ways the dish appears at our table, although its fussiness may be a tad excessive for some; the latter are simple steps to cut down the work—perhaps by using freshly made (but purchased) pasta rather than making your own or by using prechopped vegetables from the produce case or the salad bar.

5. Many recipes have a *Garnish* option. In truth, we often feel that this small detail is essential to a dish. No one in a ball gown skips the jewelry. Thus, the garnishes are tasty decorations to take the plate to another level. But they're admittedly not essential to the inherent flavor pairings. Angelina Jolie in a ball gown is still Angelina Jolie, jewelry or not.

6. The *Notes* that follow the recipes explain some quirky ingredient, or offer a tip about how to accomplish a task required, or help you hone your technique to make the dish even more successful. They're explanatory but also perhaps necessary, particularly if you've got opening-night jitters.

7. The vast majority of the recipes include a selection of other dishes that would make a *Menu* for the evening: our thoughts on what works with what. Sometimes you'll find three courses; sometimes, five; sometimes they're all small plates; sometimes, a small plate followed by two larger offerings. All end with some sort of dessert—sometimes a recipe in this book, but sometimes just a simple suggestion for fruit, chocolate, or cheese. Of course, these menus represent our tastes; you should more fully explore your own. Swap something out, nix a course, offer more, offer less, and build your own menu.

8. Finally, most of the recipes offer a *Pour*—that is, our idea of the wine, beer, or other beverage that best highlights the flavors. After years of writing travel articles for a prestigious wine magazine without ever being allowed to comment directly on the wine served at any restaurant, we had great fun here. Pairing wine and other drinks with vegetables is something of a new frontier. We felt the freedom of the expanse. But that said, one man's Syrah is another woman's swill. Treat these like stoplights in Manhattan: mere suggestions. If our pour doesn't strike your fancy, bring the recipe to your favorite wine shop and ask what they would recommend.

The Eight Things You Need Before You Start Cooking

1. A recipe list

Don't start figuring out what you'll cook on the same day as a dinner party. Although we've written countless articles that urge us all to walk to a farmers' market and see what's fresh for dinner on a weeknight, such advice has *no* merit when we're hosting a coursed fête on the weekend. Sure, we've occasionally morphed courses to match food finds. But more often than not, we plan the menu well in advance, knowing exactly what we'll serve and in what order.

We've also learned—the hard way—to read through recipes before we make them a part of our menu. We had a notable disaster one evening when we chose a recipe, looked at the ingredient list, and didn't turn the page to read the rest of the tale. Four o'clock in the afternoon was not the right moment to read "Refrigerate for 24 hours."

While you're at it, choose recipes that highlight your strengths. If you hate chopping, biryani is probably not for you. If you love grilling, set up your meal so that at least one course shows off your skills as a pit master.

2. A guest list

As Epicurus wrote, "To eat and drink without a friend is to devour like an animal." There are few things more redemptive than a meal shared with those we love. But it's also never a good idea to form a tight circle and breathe our own air all evening. Consider mixing it up. Invite that new couple on the block, that interesting guy at work you've been wanting to talk to, or that summer renter who's moved to town. Make the Upper East Side touch Brooklyn, Hollywood rub shoulders with the Valley, downtown discover the 'burbs.

However, your own dinner party is not—repeat, *not*—a good time to go on a first date. Or a second. Or a third. Your attention will frankly be elsewhere.

And remember that we live in

PLAYLIST SUGGESTIONS

For a mellow but modern evening, queue up some of today's torch singers: Jane Monheit, Patricia Barber (particularly *The Cole Porter Mix*), Pamela Luss, Robin McKelle, Melody Gardot, Emilie-Claire Barlow, and Stacey Kent.

For a downtown vibe, go with the fabulous duets between Carla Bley and Steve Swallow, as well as cuts by Geoff Gascoyne, Marian McPartland, and the Serge Forté Trio.

If you want to slip abroad while at your table, mix up the Gotan Project with some of the old recordings by Gilberto and Getz as well as cuts by Venissa Santí, Cesária Évora, and the Karim Baggili Quartet.

Try a night of old-school pop in French: France Gall, Liane Foly, Isabelle Boulay, Mireille Mathieu, and the très cool Paris Combo.

To go with classical piano, offer Bach's *Goldberg Variations* with Chopin's *Nocturnes* and Debussy's *Préludes*. Since these are full works in their own right, it's best not to put them on shuffle.

And for oldies but besties, you can't beat a mix of Blossom Dearie, Margaret Whiting, Rosemary Clooney, and June Christy. Toss in some Xavier Cugat to make these old girls swoon.

polarized times. If you've got a friend who can't stop posting left or right wingnut bilge on Facebook, consider who else will be at your table. While friction makes heat, you don't want a forest fire.

As you're building a list of dinner-party companions, make sure you ask about any known food issues among the ranks. If you find a cow's milk allergy or a distinct dislike of, oh, turnips, you'll want to reconsider your menu. It's your job to offer everyone a fine, fun evening. You can always make that selected recipe another time.

3. A task list

As we'll write again and again, bring out your inner OCD for a dinner party. One of us makes a list on paper; one, in his head. But we both *make lists*. We figure out what needs to be done—and the order in which it needs to be done. Our goal is to be reading a novel 30 minutes before everyone arrives. You might not be able to pull off such insouciance the first time you host a multicourse meal, but you certainly don't want to be stepping into the shower when the doorbell rings—unless that's the kind of party you're throwing. In which case, you've bought the wrong book.

4. A playlist

Think about the food you're serving—and make your music selections accordingly. Are you highlighting fresh, bright flavors?

Then try some cool, downtown torch singers for contrast. Are you offering casseroles and comfort food? Then put on some Chopin nocturnes to bring darker tones into the dining room.

And think about your guests. Someone in the middle of a nasty divorce probably doesn't want to hear sentimental love songs. Almost no dinner party needs Wagner. And professional musicians often find background music thoroughly distracting, even irritating.

Also think about the time of year, the proximity to certain holidays. We refuse to put on Christmas music for a December dinner party, not because one of us is Jewish, but mostly because we don't want our table to sound like the mall. Instead, we might put together a collection of 1940s standards. Doris Day and Frank Sinatra are perennial guests. Or we might put together an evening of 1970s European pop. A good playlist will send subtle cues about the mood and the pace. Save the metal for another time.

5. A seating order

Although long a go-to requirement, this one's actually optional at our table. We rarely use place cards. We find them stuffy. Besides, we have no clue if the couple who's showed up at our door just got out of the car in the middle of a fight. So we always make this announcement: "We're at either end of the table and you

may sit wherever you like." There's rarely any awkwardness. Those starkly left- or right-handed can take the appropriate corner. And catfights can be duly avoided by mature adults. If not, you need new friends, not a dinner party.

But we often think about seating in terms of who's new at our table. If we did invite that summer renter in our New England community, one of us is apt to say, "Come sit by me." Graciousness is its own reward.

That said, we recently added an outdoor dining porch onto our home and we have occasionally used place cards out there because the table is smaller and we want to make sure each guest is comfortable, not squeezed tight, depending on, well, girths. That may sound catty, but we're just trying to make sure everyone is content. You may find the same advice holds true for those with alternate political positions or even former spouses who end up at your table together. Frankly, we wouldn't put together those sorts of guest lists. So don't say we didn't warn you.

6. A well-set table

We've never once run out and purchased new stuff for a dinner party. We mix and match silver and stainless, this set for this course and that one for the next. We put fine crystal with everyday glasses, tall with short. And we gleefully employ a host of plates.

The many combos set a relaxed tone.

Look around your house. There are objects that can be turned into lovely centerpieces, some a little surprising. For the first dinner party we ever threw together, back in our apartment in Manhattan, we stacked bricks on the table, wrapped some in bits of gold ribbon, and made them the levels for candles and salt cellars. We've used rhubarb stalks to good effect in the early summer. And we recently snagged a set of scuffed-up billiard balls at a flea market. They're terrific alongside the cut crystal.

In the end, your table should reflect you. If you're not a cut-flower person, don't sweat it. Try vegetables or little pots of herbs. If you're earthy rather than ethereal, skip the lace and scatter some apples among the candles. Your table functions like the food you prepare: It's the platform for the love and goodwill you want to share with your friends and fam-ily. It should never get in the way of the conversation. Unless you're gunning to be the next Queen of Versailles, forgo the candelabras.

7. Good lighting

Even without candelabras, candles are the lighting choice for us—and not solely tea lights. Those are just tiny accents. Instead, we've got pillars and posts that we group on the table for a warm, soft glow. Our outdoor dining porch isn't even electrified! If you're going with traditional lightbulbs in the fixtures, knock them down a notch. Some entertaining mavens insist that a dining room should never have a bulb over 15 watts. We'll go with 25, but not much more.

8. A chat list

We once went to a dinner party where we were actually handed a list of topics to be discussed for the evening—and the order in which they were to be discussed. Needless to say, we haven't been back. While we don't have topics in hand for conversation, we want to keep the evening flowing, particularly when we've got new guests who may not know all the other players. Sure, the wine will take care of some of the silence, but we look for unobtrusive, friendly ways to keep momentum building for the courses ahead.

For example, we say something about each guest to the newbies when they're introduced around. We don't want them to leave at the end of the evening and later say, "You mean he invented texting?" However, we also don't proffer pedigrees: "She graduated from Oxford at the top of her class." This is not an interview; nobody's impressed. Instead, we make a small introduction, then move on to light conversation: a local festival, a new restaurant, someone's recent vacation. And don't forget, you've always got the best opener in hand: "I'm trying something new: a vegetarian dinner party."

1

TWELVE WAYS TO SAY "WELCOME"

Doyens of dinner parties past intoned that guests shouldn't be in your house more than 10 minutes before a drink was in hand. We don't lash our evenings to the clock, but we do feel that *Can I take your coat?* should be soon followed by *What are you drinking?*

Most guests stumble over that second question. Gone are the days of simple cocktails. With the advent of celebrity bartenders, with more drink offerings on restaurant menus than entrée choices, and with nagging remnants of our Puritan past, the cocktail hour remains a minefield. Some people don't want to put you on the spot: *You mean you don't have that new cashew aperitif?* Others just lack imagination: *A margarita, I guess.*

To thwart any awkwardness, we often offer a signature cocktail. Yes, we've got beer and wine on hand, as well as some basic liquors (vodka, gin, blended scotch) with their mixers (club soda, tonic, bitter lemon). But there's almost always a planned offering in the mixology department.

A cocktail is the stealth first course, the first preparation your guests will enjoy. As such, it should reflect the care and attention you bring to food. We find the modern, slapdash ethic of cocktails a bit depressing: melting ice and half-open bottles strewn across a kitchen counter. Don't start a dinner party out by pointing to the bar, shrugging, and walking away. Such actions scream *You're on your own*. If that's the case, everyone could have stayed home.

Of course, cocktails often come with some little nibbles—which we'll get to in the next chapter. But we should say up front that eating something will not keep you from getting tipsy. Eating a lot will keep you from getting tipsy *immediately*. A heavy meal slows down the absorption of the brain-impairing ethanol, thus delaying the slur. But food does not somehow alter basic chemistry in your stomach. You'll just get potted later. A thoughtful host offers a cocktail to start the evening, some nibbles to go with it—and then clams up. If someone wants another drink, they can always ask.

When you plan a signature cocktail, think about the meal and pair the first drink to it. Your evening is a romance of flavors: starting quietly, getting bigger as it moves along, and finally morphing into something sweet. You want to vary *and* underscore the full range you'll establish over the meal. For example, if you're starting out with a chile-laced first course, go with a rather sweet cocktail, something with lots of fruit in the mix. A million Tex-Mex restaurants can't be wrong! If dinner starts with more elemental flavors, begin with a cocktail that has less fruit zing and more simple warmth. And if you're skipping the starter and jumping right to a salad, go even simpler. Fruit-laced alcohol concoctions and vinegary greens are rarely a good match. Forgo the signature cocktail gambit and offer G&Ts. But make them for your guests; don't just set them off on their own.

Finally, here's rule #1 of bartending: You will always use more ice than you think. Buy a bag. Or two. Or start making and storing cubes in plastic bags in the freezer up to 3 days before the party starts. You want your evening to go smoothly, launched from a cocktail shaker: the click of the lid, the slow pour into a highball or martini glass. It's been the standard for generations. It's hard to argue with success.

A RANT ABOUT PAPER NAPKINS

Sure, they're easy on the host. In fact, they scream *easy*. They cling to cocktail glasses, a rank mess. They don't save your furniture or your clothes. Listen, we're not completely opposed to them. Whenever we have friends over for burgers on the deck, we've always got a stack of paper napkins on hand. But a dinner party is a different sort of event, more Hollywood romance than Facebook hook-up. Would a leading man start out a love affair in shoddy clothes? We think not. Nix the paper napkins. Offer cloth.

BAR TOOLS

A proper bar has the right gear: a cocktail shaker (or two), a strainer, a muddler (for crushing items in the bottom of a glass or shaker), good glassware, and a jigger—that is, a little, two-sided measuring device with a larger side that usually holds $1\frac{1}{2}$ ounces and a smaller side for either 1 or $\frac{3}{4}$ ounce. But while a jigger is handy, keep this in mind: 1 fluid ounce = 2 tablespoons. No, it's not cool to measure cocktails with tablespoons. But it's more accurate than eyeballing it.

Two Bartending Staples

These two syrups are go-to bar accoutrements. Both can be made months in advance and squirreled away in the fridge for your next dinner party—or maybe just for a Wednesday evening after work.

Simple Syrup

MAKES ABOUT 2 ¼ CUPS

Don't just keep this sweet syrup on hand for cocktails. Use it in iced tea or coffee—it dissolves instantly.

    2 cups sugar
    1 cup water

Stir the sugar and water together in a medium saucepan over medium heat until the sugar dissolves. Boil for 1 minute. Remove the pan from the heat and cool to room temperature. Pour into a glass jar or container, seal, and store in the fridge for up to 2 months.

Caramel Syrup

MAKES ABOUT 1 ¾ CUPS

Beyond cocktails, drizzle tiny amounts of this intense syrup on pineapple chunks, ice cream scoops, frozen yogurt, or even into a very spicy, black pepper–laced stir-fry still in the wok over heat.

    2 cups sugar
    1 cup boiling water

1. Melt the sugar in a large, high-sided saucepan over medium heat. Stir only after you see good melting at the edges and continue to cook until amber brown.

2. Stirring all the while, pour in the boiling water. The syrup will froth and foam—be careful! Keep stirring over the heat until the sugar melts again. Remove the pan from the heat and cool to room temperature. Pour into a glass jar or container, seal, and refrigerate for up to 2 months.

Twelve Signature Cocktails

Here's the splash that starts the party. Most of these recipes are torqued versions of standard cocktails, something familiar morphed into something new. Many are made in a shaker, one drink at a time. But some are pitcher punches, just the thing for a more informal evening. We like to say that a handmade cocktail is followed by plated food; a pitcher punch, by family-style platters. But we break that rule as often as we keep it. And we've certainly been known to whip up a pitcher of Stone Fruit Daiquiris when there's no dinner party in sight.

Watermelon Punch

8 SERVINGS

Here's summer sophistication in a glass. Since the cocktail packs a punch, serve it in champagne flutes or relatively small glasses.

- 6 cups watermelon chunks, seeded and rinds removed
- 1 cup gin
- 1 cup Simple Syrup (page 4)
- ¾ cup fresh lemon juice
- 2 tablespoons grenadine
- Chilled prosecco or cava

1. Puree the watermelon in a large blender until smooth. Strain into a large pitcher.

2. Stir in the gin, simple syrup, lemon juice, and grenadine. Chill in the fridge for at least 4 hours or up to 1 day.

3. Pour into glasses (without ice) and top with a splash of prosecco or cava.

Caramel Lemon Drop

1 COCKTAIL

The caramel is the twist on this classic, but the drink's still all about the spiky sour lemon juice. Avoid the bottled, reconstituted stuff; squeeze the real deal for your guests.

- Small ice cubes for the shaker and the glass
- 1½ ounces vodka
- 1 ounce limoncello liqueur
- 1 ounce fresh lemon juice, preferably Meyer lemon juice
- 1 ounce Caramel Syrup (page 4)
- Fresh raspberries, for garnish

1. Fill a cocktail shaker with ice. Add the vodka, limoncello, lemon juice, and caramel syrup. Cover and shake well, until the shaker is fogged with cold moisture.

2. Strain over fresh ice in a highball glass. Garnish with a raspberry or two.

Passion Pisco Sour (opposite)
Elderflower Spritz (opposite)
Tequila Punch (opposite)

Elderflower Spritz

1 COCKTAIL

This may be the first time you've put wine in a cocktail shaker. Use a wine you'd drink on its own, straight up. Don't cheap out—but also don't insult your guests by opening the nice white wine they brought and pouring it into a cocktail shaker.

>   Small ice cubes for the shaker
> 3 ounces medium-dry white wine, such as Grüner Veltliner
> ½ ounce St-Germain elderflower liqueur
> 2 ounces bottled bitter lemon mixer

1. Put ice cubes in a cocktail shaker. Pour in the wine and liqueur. Shake well, until the shaker is fogged with cold moisture.

2. Strain into a highball glass (without ice). Top with the bitter lemon and stir.

Tequila Punch

1 COCKTAIL

Pink or white grapefruit juice? It won't matter with this big twist on the more standard margarita. There's no need to put a salt rim on the glasses.

>   Small ice cubes for the shaker and the glass
> 2 ounces reposado tequila
> 2 ounces grapefruit juice
> 1 ounce Aperol
>   Thin rhubarb stalks, for garnish

1. Put ice cubes in a cocktail shaker. Add the tequila, grapefruit juice, and Aperol. Cover and shake well, until the shaker is fogged with cold moisture.

2. Strain into a tall glass filled with fresh ice. Garnish with rhubarb.

Passion Pisco Sour

1 COCKTAIL

Don't skimp on the pisco. Better bottlings simply cost more. There's not much in this cocktail to hide the taste of the rotgut stuff. (And don't use an aged Chilean pisco, more like aged rum, too dark a taste for this simple libation.)

>   Small ice cubes for the shaker
> 2 ounces pisco (South American sugarcane rum)
> 1 ounce Simple Syrup (page 4)
> 1 ounce fresh lemon juice
> 1 large egg white
>   Juice from 1 small passion fruit, strained
>   Bitters, for garnish

1. Fill a cocktail shaker with ice. Pour in the pisco, simple syrup, lemon juice, egg white, and passion fruit juice. Cover and shake well, until the shaker is fogged with cold moisture.

2. Strain into a martini glass; sprinkle a few drops of bitters on the foamy top.

Stone Fruit Daiquiris

8 SERVINGS

Don't fill the glasses with ice cubes in advance; they'll melt and water down this very flavorful concoction. Choose the most fragrant nectarines and plums at the market.

>   2 large ripe nectarines, quartered and pitted
>   2 large ripe yellow plums, quartered and pitted
>   ¾ cup Simple Syrup (page 4)
>   1 cup white rum
>   1 cup umeshu (a Japanese stone-fruit wine)
>   ¾ cup fresh lime juice
>   6 cups small ice cubes, plus more for the glasses

1. Puree the nectarines, plums, and simple syrup in a large blender. Strain into a large pitcher, discarding any skin and pulp solids.

2. Stir in the rum, umeshu, and lime juice. Add the ice and stir well. Strain into tall glasses filled with fresh ice.

Vanilla Orange Martini

1 COCKTAIL

The use of the word *martini* here will be sacrilege to the cocktail purist. But we're willing to take the risk for a drink that tastes like an old-fashioned, orange-and-vanilla frozen dessert.

>   Small ice cubes for the shaker
>   1½ ounces vanilla vodka
>   1 ounce Caramel Syrup (page 4)
>   ½ ounce orange liqueur, such as Cointreau
>   Demerara sugar, for garnish
>   Orange wedges, for garnish

1. Fill a cocktail shaker with ice. Pour in the vanilla vodka, caramel syrup, and orange liqueur. Cover and shake well, until the shaker is fogged with cold moisture.

2. Spread a little demerara sugar on a small plate. Wash and dry your hands; dip your finger in water and use it to wet the rim of a martini glass. Run an orange wedge around the rim of the glass. Roll the rim in the sugar, coating it lightly.

3. Strain the cocktail into the glass, taking care to keep the sugar rim in place.

BARTENDING WITHOUT BOOZE

Too often the choices for those who don't imbibe are canned soda and tap water. It's not fair. People who don't drink alcohol shouldn't be left out. Start their choices with bottles of bubbly water and an array of fruit syrups like black currant, sour cherry, or raspberry from which you can make fizzy sodas. Consider serving up a pitcher of iced tea, laced with a little pomegranate juice for zip. Or make a pitcher of your own signature lemonade from 6 cups water, 1½ cups sugar, 1½ cups lemon juice, and 2 cups of any one of these: coconut milk, watermelon juice, strawberry puree, or pear nectar. Or offer individual maple sodas: put about ½ inch of maple syrup in a tall glass, add a tiny drip of vanilla extract, and top with club soda or seltzer, stirring as little as possible, just to dissolve the syrup, before adding lots of small ice cubes.

The Caramel Pear

1 COCKTAIL

Sweet and mellow, this may well be the perfect cocktail for a winter evening.

  Small ice cubes for the shaker and the glass
2 ounces pear vodka
1 ounce Caramel Syrup (page 4)
  A dash of bitters, preferably fig or orange bitters
  Ginger ale

1. Put ice cubes in a cocktail shaker. Add the pear vodka and caramel syrup. Cover and shake well, until the shaker is fogged with cold moisture.

2. Strain into a highball glass filled with fresh ice. Top with ginger ale. Serve with a swizzle stick.

Pink Sangria

8 SERVINGS

This fruit-filled punch is light and refreshing, probably best before a spice-heavy meal.

1 bottle (750ml) sweet white wine, such as Riesling
¾ cup raspberry vodka
¾ cup pomegranate juice
¼ cup fresh lime juice
¼ cup Simple Syrup (page 4)
2 cups small ice cubes, plus more for the glasses
½ cup raspberries
1 lime, thinly sliced
  Club soda

1. Stir the wine, raspberry vodka, pomegranate juice, lime juice, and simple syrup in a large pitcher. Add the 2 cups ice, raspberries, and lime slices. Stir well.

2. Strain into tall glasses filled with fresh ice. Top each with a splash of club soda.

Ginger Cosmopolitan

1 COCKTAIL

If you've got some Asian-inspired courses ahead, particularly on a fall evening, you'll want to start with this lemon/pear/ginger take on a favorite bar drink.

    Small ice cubes for the shaker
1½ ounces vodka
  ½ ounce orange liqueur, such as Cointreau
  ½ ounce fresh lemon juice
  ½ ounce pear nectar
  1 teaspoon sugar
  1 teaspoon ginger juice

Put ice cubes in a cocktail shaker. Add the vodka, orange liqueur, lemon juice, pear nectar, sugar, and ginger juice. Cover and shake well, until the shaker is fogged with cold moisture. Strain into a martini glass.

Coconut Lime Cooler

1 COCKTAIL

Call this one an adult limeade from the tropics. Because the coconut milk isn't sweetened, the drink is more savory than you might imagine. (Don't use cream of coconut, which has added sugar.)

  1 small lime, cut into quarters
  1 tablespoon fresh cilantro leaves
  1 tablespoon sugar
    Small ice cubes for the shaker and the glass
1½ ounces vodka
  1 ounce regular or light coconut milk

1. Crush and grind the lime quarters, cilantro leaves, and sugar in the bottom of a cocktail shaker with a cocktail muddler or the handle of a wooden spoon.

2. Fill the shaker with ice, then add the vodka and coconut milk. Cover and shake until the shaker is fogged with cold moisture. Strain into a tall glass filled with fresh ice.

Pineapple Margarita Punch

8 SERVINGS

There are so many fruit flavors going on in this pitcher drink that you probably shouldn't use the finest aged tequila around. Use a floral, full-flavored silver or reposado tequila such as Jose Cuervo Tradicional.

  6 cups small ice cubes, plus more for the glasses
2½ cups pineapple juice
1¼ cups tequila
  1 cup orange liqueur, such as Grand Marnier
  1 cup fresh lime juice
  1 cup fresh orange juice
  ½ cup Simple Syrup (page 4)

Place the 6 cups ice cubes in a large pitcher. Add the pineapple juice, tequila, orange liqueur, lime juice, orange juice, and simple syrup. Stir well and strain into iced-tea glasses filled with lots of fresh ice.

Ginger Cosmopolitan (opposite)
Pineapple Margarita Punch (opposite)

NO PLATES

Francophiles know these as *amuse-bouches,* as if they tickle your mouth and keep it jolly. Better, think of them as the first kiss of our meal-long romance. Nobody wants anything too dramatic, overstated, or (ugh) wet. In the movies, lovers kiss for the first time, a light touch, then back up, look at each other, before they go at it in earnest. And thus these: the faintest touch with the excitement locked behind it. They'll stand out, although none is a show-off. The more complicated techniques are to come; the first flavors must be present, identifiable, and concentrated. In other words, promise without complication, like a good romance.

To that end, none needs a plate. Each is finger food, a tidbit for bringing people together and starting the evening. Sure, we often put out plates and forks. Somebody might not want to snarf up a bruschetta without a shelf to catch the crumbs. But the tableware just as often ends up back in the cabinet, as clean as when it first appeared.

Many of these are fried tidbits of salty crunch that'll make your mouth water just thinking about them. As such, they may be the last thing you prepare, finished as the doorbell rings. Deep-frying requires good nerves and some precautions: Kids and pets should stay out from underfoot. Guests should stand clear of the stove. You shouldn't have taken a sip of the wine yet. And once you're done, push the pot with the oil to the back of the stove and turn the handle away from any overhangs.

Most of these servings are small, meant as no more than a hint of what's to come. We've all been to that dinner party where we've gorged on chip-and-dip, or made our way through a platter of shrimp, or doggedly attacked an array of cheeses, only to discover that we're full before we sit down. It's just irritating, much like a first date that won't end. So don't overwhelm your guests. Keep the flavors big and the portions small. Less is more at this point.

SOLVING AN INEVITABLE PROBLEM

Since these small bites are not served at the table, your guests will tend to congregate in the kitchen. You're trying to finish up, you've prepared an appetizer or two, yet you're dodging a crowd as you make that last-minute addition to the main course. Modern, open-concept homes exacerbate this dilemma. How do you get people to move on without being rude?

1. **Be prepared.** If your friends walk in and you're flying around, still cutting this and searing that, they'll feel obligated to watch, some to be nice, some to offer culinary triage ("Can I help?"), and a few to try to witness a train wreck. Do your prep earlier in the day. Run the dishwasher, clean the counters, and be ready.

2. **Show them the way away.** When guests arrive, lead them into the living room and sit down. Have enough prep done that you actually have the luxury of a little conversation. Besides, your influence over the first 30 minutes will set the tone for the whole evening.

3. **Instigate conversation.** If you've got guests who don't know each other, appoint a spouse, partner, or friend as the "host-in-waiting." Make sure this person stays with your guests as you sneak back to the kitchen for last-minute ops.

4. **Move the food.** Get the appetizers out of the kitchen. If possible, put the bar in another room, too. If you're serving beer, put the bottles in a big bowl of ice, not in the fridge right next to the stove.

5. **Make another room friendlier than the kitchen.** Drop the lighting, put on a lounge playlist, and build a fire over there. Everyone will soon leave the kitchen without feeling displaced.

Fried Olives, Caramelized Garlic

16 FRIED OLIVES

High-quality, juicy olives are a go-to nibble in our house. But when more elaborate gestures are called for at dinner parties, we stuff green olives with roasted garlic for a wonderful treat—then batter those olives and fry them for the sheer pleasure of this soft/crunchy, sweet/briny mash-up.

1 or 2 garlic heads (unpeeled but to yield 16 cloves)

16 pitted large green olives, such as Jumbo Gordals

¼ cup all-purpose flour

1 large egg, well beaten in a small bowl

½ cup unseasoned dried breadcrumbs

Olive oil, for deep-frying (about 4 cups)

1. Position the rack in the center of the oven and heat to 400°F.

2. Cut about the top quarter off each garlic head to expose most of the cloves. Wrap the heads tightly in foil (use one packet for 2 heads). Set the packet on a baking sheet and roast until the garlic cloves are very soft, about 45 minutes.

3. Cool on a wire rack for 10 minutes, then open the packet and cool until you can handle the garlic easily, at least another 15 minutes. Gently squeeze the soft cloves from their skins and stuff them into the pitted olives.

4. Set up a three-stage dipping process: a plate with the flour spread on it, a shallow bowl with the beaten egg in it, and a second plate with the breadcrumbs spread across it.

5. Pour about 1½ inches oil into a large, high-sided sauté pan or skillet. Clip a deep-frying thermometer to the inside of the pan and heat the oil over medium heat to 350°F.

6. Roll a stuffed olive in the flour, then in the egg, then in the breadcrumbs, shaking off any excess at each stage but coating the olive completely. Slip into the oil, then coat several more olives and add them to the pan as well. Fry until browned, about 1 minute, turning the olives on all sides and adjusting the heat so that the oil's temperature remains constant. Use a slotted spoon or kitchen tongs to transfer the olives to a fine-mesh wire rack set over paper towels to catch the drips. Continue coating and frying more olives until you're done. Serve warm or at room temperature (but within 30 minutes of their coming out of the oil).

LESS

Look for roasted garlic cloves on the salad bar at the supermarket. But avoid the garlic-stuffed olives—that garlic is raw, not roasted, and will overpower this preparation.

NOTES

- Go slowly at first: Fry a few olives, just to get the hang of it. Then add more in the second and third batch. But never crowd the pan or skillet. There should be plenty of real estate around each olive.

- For a more economical (if less aromatic) starter, substitute canola oil for the olive oil.

POUR

Passion Pisco Sours (page 7) or an amber lager to amplify the briny notes

Wrinkled Cherry Tomatoes, Crunchy Panko, Fresh Herbs

16 CHERRY TOMATOES

If the best sort of appetizer is a simple, single bite with straightforward flavors, these roasted tomatoes fit the bill. They're vernally herbaceous: Make sure the first course to come isn't too floral or aromatic so you can get a good contrast among the flavors. In fact, these are such a powerful pop, we'd advise swearing off tomatoes for the rest of the meal.

½ cup panko breadcrumbs

2 tablespoons minced pitted black olives

2 tablespoons minced dried currants

½ tablespoon minced fresh oregano leaves

½ tablespoon minced fresh rosemary leaves

½ teaspoon minced garlic

⅛ teaspoon red pepper flakes

2 tablespoons olive oil

16 cherry tomatoes (about ¾ pound)

1. Mix the panko, olives, currants, oregano, rosemary, garlic, and red pepper flakes in a small bowl. Stir in the olive oil until well moistened.

2. Cut the tops off the cherry tomatoes and use a melon baller or a very small spoon to hollow out the insides of each without breaking its walls.

3. Position the rack in the center of the oven and heat to 400°F. Line a large rimmed baking sheet with parchment paper or a silicone baking mat.

4. Fill each tomato with about 2 teaspoons breadcrumb stuffing, then line them up on the baking sheet.

5. Bake until hot and tender, the stuffing even browned a bit on top, about 20 minutes. Cool for at least 10 minutes before serving.

AHEAD

● The stuffing can be made up to 4 hours in advance. Store, covered, at room temperature.

● The tomatoes can be stuffed and placed on the baking sheet up to 2 hours in advance. Seal in plastic wrap and store at room temperature before baking.

● Although the dish can be served at room temperature, the tomatoes are best if still warm—say, up to 30 minutes after coming out of the oven.

NOTES

● Panko breadcrumbs, once a Japanese specialty but now available across North America, are made from bread cooked with electric currents passed through it, creating a loaf that is airy and light without any crust. Its lacy crumbs cook to extreme crunchiness. Some versions are vegan; some are not. The latter can have eggs, milk, or even just an animal-derived enzyme in the production process. If that's a concern, search out vegan panko breadcrumbs (such as those from Edward and Sons) at specialty markets and health food stores.

● If the tomatoes are perfectly round, they may not stand up on the baking sheet. Slice off a very thin bit off the ends opposite where you've hollowed them out to give them a small flat surface to stand on.

POUR

Elderflower Spritzes (page 7) or a blanc de blancs champagne to spark sweet notes against the herbs

Parmesan Crisps, Lots of Black Pepper

18 TO 20 CRISPS

These crunchy tidbits couldn't be simpler: Bake, cool, and serve for a savory and spicy combo that goes perfectly with cocktails. The crisps will look lacy and bubbly when you take them out of the oven—and are indeed too gooey to move. Don't despair: They'll soon harden to perfection.

6 ounces Parmigiano-Reggiano cheese, finely grated (about 1½ cups)

Up to 2½ teaspoons freshly ground black pepper

1. Position the racks at the top and bottom third of the oven (or do the best you can dividing your oven into thirds) and heat to 400°F. Line 2 large baking sheets with parchment paper or silicone baking mats.

2. Drop heaping tablespoonfuls of the cheese onto the prepared baking sheets, spacing them ½ inch apart. Sprinkle each with ⅛ teaspoon pepper.

3. Bake for 4 minutes. Reverse the sheets top to bottom and rotate them back to front, then continue baking until golden and bubbling, 3 to 6 minutes longer. Transfer the sheets to wire racks to cool until the crisps harden, then transfer the crisps to a serving platter.

▶ AHEAD

● Bake up to 1 hour in advance, storing the crisps on the baking sheets, uncovered, at room temperature.

▶ MORE

Grind more interesting versions of the black pepper onto the rounds: a peppercorn blend, Aleppo pepper, or even Urfa biber, a dried pepper from Turkey that has a smoky, raisiny flavor.

▶ NOTE

● You'll need to watch the crisps carefully in the oven. Because of varying degrees of moisture content in the cheese, as well as normal temperature fluctuations in any oven, the little rounds may be done in a comparatively wide range of timing.

▶ POUR

A sweet cocktail like Caramel Lemon Drop (page 5)—or better yet, brut champagne, because nothing pairs with black pepper like those bubbles

Creamy Cashew Dip, Garlic, White Balsamic Vinegar

8 SERVINGS

We love this sweet-but-savory, slightly musky dip, a creamy starter before a meal that should probably include more vinegary and spicy flavors among the offerings. Have water crackers, baked vegan pita chips, or baby carrots at the ready. But maybe not too many. Leftovers are a dream when spread on toasted rye for a sandwich with lettuce, tomato, and Dijon mustard.

1½ cups raw, unsalted cashews

2 tablespoons nutritional yeast flakes

2 tablespoons dry vermouth

2 teaspoons white balsamic vinegar

2 medium garlic cloves

½ teaspoon salt

½ teaspoon freshly ground black pepper

1. Soak the cashews in a big bowl of water on the counter overnight, at least 12 hours but not more than 24 hours.

2. Drain the cashews and transfer to a large food processor. Add the nutritional yeast, vermouth, vinegar, garlic, salt, and pepper. Process until smooth, adding water 1 tablespoon at a time through the tube and scraping down the inside of the bowl occasionally, just until the mixture is a thick paste, a little stiffer than fresh ricotta. Spoon into a bowl to serve.

▶ MORE

Split raw snow peas along the curve of the concave edge, then spread them open and pipe or smear the dip inside them, about ½ tablespoon in each. (You'll need about 1 pound snow peas for this much dip.) When arrayed on a serving platter, top each snow pea with a sprinkle of white sesame seeds and a drizzle of rice vinegar.

▶ GARNISH

Drizzle the dip in its bowl with toasted pumpkin seed oil.

▶ NOTE

● Nutritional yeast is a deactivated yeast, prized for its musky, cheesy flavor. It's sold in flakes or as a powder, the former used here. Look for it in the refrigerated section of health food stores. Once opened, it can be resealed and stored in your refrigerator for up to 1 year (but check the expiration date on the package). Mixed with dried herbs, nutritional yeast can make a savory topping for popcorn.

▶ POUR

Stone Fruit Daiquiris (page 8) to bring the floral notes of the fruit to bear on the creamy, very savory dip

Fried Artichokes, Ginger Aioli

8 SERVINGS

Artichokes naturally offer an unsurpassed but well har-monized blend of sweet and herbaceous notes. Given that, crunchy artichoke bits are one of the best starters, a dis-tinctly grassy and floral flavor that's set off by this gingery dip. These nibbles can be followed by almost any dish in this book except for the most fiery.

1 large egg yolk, at room temperature

1 medium garlic clove, minced

2 teaspoons minced fresh ginger

½ teaspoon ground ginger

½ teaspoon sugar

1 teaspoon salt, divided

⅔ cup almond oil

8 cups frozen artichoke heart quarters, thawed (about four 9-ounce packages)

¼ cup all-purpose flour

Vegetable oil, for deep-frying (about 4 cups)

1. Whisk the egg yolk, garlic, fresh ginger, ground ginger, sugar, and ½ teaspoon of the salt in a large bowl until creamy. Whisk in the almond oil in a thin, slow stream until thick, like a slightly looser version of mayonnaise. Set the ginger aioli aside.

2. Squeeze the artichoke heart quarters by the handfuls over the sink to get rid of excess moisture, dropping them in a second large bowl as you do. Add the flour to the bowl and toss well to coat the artichokes evenly.

3. Position the rack in the center of the oven, set a rimmed baking sheet on the rack, and heat the oven to 200°F.

4. Pour about 3 inches oil into a large, high-sided sauté pan. Clip a deep-frying thermometer to the inside of the pan and heat the oil over medium heat to 350°F. Adjust the heat so that the oil's temperature stays constant through the next step.

5. Add about one-fourth of the artichoke heart quarters to the hot oil and fry until golden brown, about 8 minutes, turning occasionally. Use a slotted spoon to scoop them out, letting them drip a bit before transferring to the baking sheet in the oven. Fry more artichoke heart quarters until you've done the lot.

6. To serve, fill a small bowl with the ginger aioli, set the bowl on a platter, and surround it with the fried artichoke bits.

AHEAD

● Make the ginger aioli up to 1 day in advance. Cover and store in the refrig-erator but allow to come to room tem-perature for 1 hour before serving.

MORE

Buy 4 to 6 pounds of baby artichokes. Trim them down by removing the leaves and the choke, then quarter the hearts. Fry as directed.

NOTES

● Don't be tempted to use jarred arti-choke hearts for this more substantial *amuse-bouche*. They'll be too wet, even squishy.

● It's for recipes like this one that God invented aprons, especially since this is a last-minute appetizer and you'll already have your party duds on.

POUR

Ginger Cosmopolitans (page 10) to double the gingery bite that'll set up the appetite for the evening to come

Gouda Gougères, Smoked Paprika, Thyme

ABOUT 24 GOUGÈRES

We morphed the traditional French tidbit toward an American backyard barbecue by swapping the traditional Gruyère for smoked Gouda—and knocking those pit-master flavors up one more step with smoked paprika. Since ambient humidity is the sworn enemy of gougères, these won't last long, even at room temperature and even on the driest evenings. But that won't be a problem. They're irresistible.

½ cup water

3 tablespoons unsalted butter

½ teaspoon sweet smoked paprika

¼ teaspoon salt

¼ teaspoon freshly ground black pepper

½ cup all-purpose flour

2 large eggs, at room temperature

1 teaspoon thyme leaves

¾ cup shredded smoked Gouda cheese (about 3 ounces), divided

1. Position the rack in the center of the oven and heat to 400°F. Line a large rimmed baking sheet with parchment paper.

2. Combine the water, butter, smoked paprika, salt, and pepper in a medium saucepan and bring to a boil over medium-high heat.

3. Reduce the heat to medium-low. Add the flour and stir constantly until a dough forms, the pan dries out, and a fine, milky skin forms around the interior of the pan, 4 to 5 minutes. Scrape the paste into a bowl and cool for 10 minutes.

4. Use an electric mixer at medium speed to beat in the eggs one at a time until smooth, then beat in the thyme to make a sticky, pasty batter. Scrape down and remove the beaters; stir in about three-fourths of the smoked Gouda with a wooden spoon.

5. Drop by heaping teaspoonfuls into small mounds onto the prepared baking sheet. Sprinkle the mounds with the remaining cheese. Let stand at room temperature for 20 to 30 minutes.

6. Bake until puffed and browned, about 30 minutes. Cool the baking sheet on a wire rack for 5 minutes, before transferring the gougères to a serving platter.

▶ NOTES

● Although this recipe requires good timing, you have a little leeway, given that the dough mounds need to sit at room temperature for at least 20 minutes before baking.

● Gougères are all about technique. Stir the batter over the heat until that light, white film appears in the pan. The dough will then become a coherent, seemingly oily mass that is nonetheless dry to the touch.

● Use parchment paper to line the baking sheet. A silicone baking mat will provide a small amount of insulation that can keep the balls from puffing up correctly.

▶ POUR

The Caramel Pear (page 9), because smoke and pears are a perfect match

Green Bean Spring Rolls, Honey Mustard Dip

33 SPRING ROLLS

We're fans of tempura green beans, a crisp snap under a crunchy batter. We've even been known to order a side of them as our appetizer in restaurants. But let's face it: They can be a pain to prepare at home. And even more of a pain at the last minute. Here's a simplified version with spring roll wrappers standing in for the more temperamental, ice-laced tempura batter. Better yet, the wrappers stay crisp longer than the traditional batter. (And by the way, once you make this very spiky honey mustard dip, you'll never go back to the bottled stuff.)

1¾ cups Dijon mustard

⅓ cup honey

¼ cup soy sauce

1½ tablespoons sambal oelek

¼ teaspoon wasabi powder

11 square (8-inch) spring roll wrappers

33 green beans

Canola oil, for deep-frying (about 2 cups)

1. Whisk the mustard, honey, soy sauce, sambal, and wasabi powder in a small saucepan over medium-low heat until the honey melts and the mixture is warm. Cool to room temperature before serving, about 1 hour.

2. Cut a spring roll wrapper into three even strips, each a rectangle about 2⅔ × 8 inches. Separate the strips and set one green bean in the center of each rectangle. Wet a clean finger and run it along the long edge of the wrapper. Roll up, starting with the dry edge and rolling to the wet, to enclose the green bean. Press to seal. Continue making more strips and rolling them around the green beans.

3. Pour about 1 inch oil into a large, high-sided sauté pan or skillet. Clip a deep-frying thermometer to the inside of the pan and heat the oil over medium heat to 350°F. Add one-fourth of the wrapped beans and fry until browned, turning occasionally and adjusting the heat so the oil stays at a fairly constant 350°F. Transfer the green beans to a wire rack set over paper towels to catch the drips.

4. Continue frying the remaining wrapped beans in batches, adjusting the heat to keep the oil's temperature constant and transferring the crisp brown beans to the wire rack.

5. Serve warm with the dipping sauce on the side.

AHEAD

- The dip can be made up to 6 hours in advance. Cover and store at room temperature.

- The green beans can be fried up to 30 minutes in advance. Store on the rack at room temperature.

NOTE

- Look for the straightest green beans at the supermarket; any curve will put a kink in the wrappers. And you'll want fairly thick green beans that will stand up to the deep-frying and still have some crunch afterwards.

POUR

Pink Sangria (page 9) or a sweet Riesling to take some of the sting out of the dip

Pea Samosas, Warm Spices

32 SAMOSAS

Although samosas are often fried, these baked ones will be easier on your nerves before a dinner party. Besides, the flavors have a better chance of melding in the oven's gentle heat. And the results stay crisper longer. *And* you can make them well in advance and freeze them. Given all that, they're the best sort of dinner-party nibbles we can imagine.

1 medium russet (baking) potato (about 8 ounces), peeled and quartered

1 cup shelled fresh peas or thawed frozen peas

1½ teaspoons salt

½ teaspoon ground coriander

¼ teaspoon ground cinnamon

¼ teaspoon ground cloves

¼ teaspoon ground cumin

¼ teaspoon ground ginger

¼ teaspoon cayenne pepper

Peanut oil, for greasing and brushing

16 sheets vegan frozen phyllo, thawed (see Note)

1. Bring a large saucepan of water to a boil over high heat. Add the potato and boil just until tender, about 10 minutes. Add the peas and cook for 1 minute from the time they hit the water. Drain everything in a colander set in the sink.

2. Scoop the still-hot potato and peas into a large bowl. Add the salt, coriander, cinnamon, cloves, cumin, ginger, and cayenne. Mash with a potato masher or a fork until the potato is smooth but the peas are only flattened a bit. Cool to room temperature, about 1 hour.

3. Position the rack in the center of the oven and heat to 375°F. Oil a large rimmed baking sheet.

4. Lay a phyllo sheet on a clean, dry work surface. Brush it with oil, then fold it in half lengthwise. Turn it so a short end faces you and brush again with oil. Place a heaping tablespoon of filling in the right corner nearest you. Fold it up like a flag in triangles: Fold the lower left corner over the filling sitting on its lower right corner, lining the left corner against the opposite edge just above the filling and thereby making an angled end at the bottom of the sheet. Then keep folding this newly made end up the sheet to meet the opposite side each time, repeatedly making triangular ends, points to opposite sides. Brush the samosa with oil and set it on the prepared baking sheet. Continue making the remaining samosas.

5. Bake until crisp and browned, about 18 minutes. Cool on the baking sheet for a couple of minutes, then transfer to a wire rack to continue cooling. Serve warm or at room temperature.

AHEAD

● Make the filling up to 24 hours in advance. Store, covered, in the refrigerator.

● Fill the samosas and place them on a baking sheet. Seal tightly in plastic wrap and refrigerate for up to 8 hours. Or freeze for up to 1 month, sealing them in a plastic bag once they're firm. Bake the frozen samosas straight from the freezer until crisp and browned, 20 to 22 minutes.

● Bake the samosas 30 minutes in advance. Store on the wire rack at room temperature.

MORE

Thin out mango, tomato, or other fruit chutney with coconut vinegar to make a dip. Or make this cilantro dipping sauce: Whir 2 cups packed cilantro leaves, 2 tablespoons minced seeded jalapeño chile, 2 tablespoons fresh lemon juice, 1 tablespoon minced fresh ginger, ½ teaspoon ground cumin, ½ teaspoon sugar, and ½ teaspoon salt in a large food processor. Drizzle in water in teaspoon increments through the tube until you create a thin, pestolike texture.

NOTES

● Phyllo dough dries out quickly and unforgivingly. Without pulling them apart, lay the *unfolded* sheets in a stack on your work surface, then lay a sheet of plastic wrap over them, followed by a clean kitchen towel. Peel off a sheet and keep the rest covered. Always have more sheets on hand than you think you'll need since they can tear and break.

● Phyllo dough is not necessarily vegan. If this matters to you, check the labeling.

POUR

Watermelon Punch (page 5) or homemade sour cherry sodas to brighten the contrasts among the spices

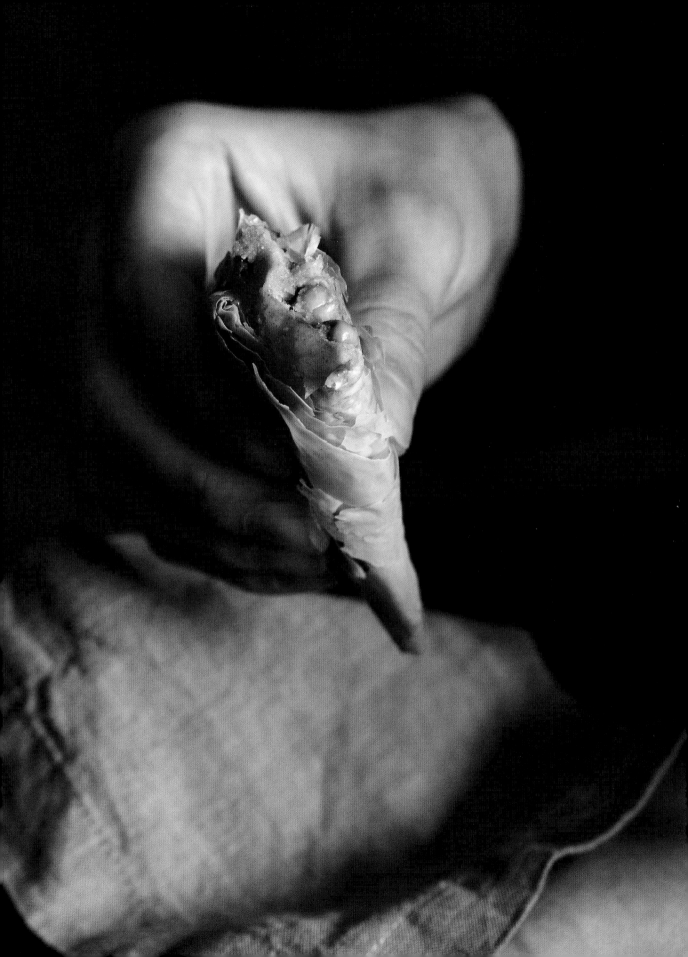

Gaufrettes, Parmesan Fondue

8 SERVINGS

Call these *French nachos*: waffle-cut potato chips, topped with a cheese sauce and sprinkled with chives. Suffice it to say, they're an elaborate opening for a dinner party, so you might consider making these after you've become a little more practiced at the art of throwing one of these affairs. But be fair warned—you won't get a soul to come to the table until the last crunchy-but-gooey chip has been eaten.

Olive oil, for greasing

3 medium russet (baking) potatoes (about 8 ounces each), peeled, halved crosswise, and soaked in cool tap water for 15 minutes

⅓ cup dry white wine, such as Pinot Gris

1 teaspoon minced garlic

1 teaspoon all-purpose flour

2 ounces Parmigiano-Reggiano cheese, finely grated (about ½ cup)

2 tablespoons minced fresh chives

1. Position the rack in the center of the oven and heat to 400°F. Oil 2 large rimmed baking sheets.

2. Fit a mandoline with the waffle blade at a ¹⁄₁₆-inch cutting depth. Grip a potato half with the food guard and run the cut side over the blade. Discard the first slice, which is not fully ridged. Rotate the potato 90 degrees and run it over the blade again. Now a waffle-cut slice will fall out of the bottom of the mandoline. Continue making more slices, rotating the potato and grip by 90 degrees after each pass. Line the slices up on one of the prepared baking sheets. Lightly brush the tops of the potato slices with oil.

3. Bake the first sheet until browned, about 15 minutes. Some slices will brown faster than others and will thus need to be transferred from the sheet to a wire rack. Once all are browned, transfer them to the wire rack and set the baking sheet aside. Continue making more slices and placing them on the second prepared baking sheet. Bake as directed. If you find you need a third baking sheet, you'll need to oil the first sheet again.

4. To make the sauce, put the wine and garlic in a small saucepan set over medium heat. Whisk in the flour until smooth and continue whisking over the heat until bubbling and thickened. Remove the pan from the heat and whisk in the Parmesan until melted.

5. When the potato chips have cooled, pile them on a serving plate or platter. Drizzle with the sauce; sprinkle with the chives.

▌ AHEAD

● Make the gaufrettes up to 8 hours in advance. Cool completely, then store in an airtight container at room temperature.

▌ NOTES

● You should see the crosshatch pattern on both sides of the potato slice with some holes throughout; if not, adjust the blade for a thinner cut.

● To get the proper coverage on the chips, spread them on a large platter, almost a single layer with little overlap. If you only have a smaller serving platter, overlap some of the chips, drizzle on the fondue, sprinkle on some chives, make another layer, and repeat, working your way through the batch.

▌ POUR

A fairly dense Oregon Pinot Noir to bring jammy fruit notes to bear on the cheese sauce

Three Bruschette

8 SERVINGS

At our table, bruschette are cocktail nibbles that sometimes become the first course. Each of these sauces is dolloped on small serving plates, then we pass around slices of this hearty bread. We have to thank Jim Lahey for introducing us to his technique for no-knead bread; we started making it with Kamut flour because of its buttery, nutty flavor and we haven't ever looked back. If you're smart, you'll hold some of the loaf back for toast the next morning.

3 cups (400 grams) bread flour

1½ cups (200 grams) Kamut flour, plus more for dusting

2 teaspoons salt

1 teaspoon instant active dry yeast

2 cups (450 grams) cool water

One or more toppings (recipes on page 29)

1. Mix both flours, the salt, and yeast in a big bowl. Stir in the water until a sticky dough forms. Cover the bowl with plastic wrap and set aside at room temperature for 24 hours, or until risen more than halfway up the bowl; the surface of the dough will be flat and bubbly.

2. Dust a clean, dry work surface with flour, then scrape the dough out onto it. Fold all the sides of the dough toward the middle, turn the whole thing over, and shape it into a squat ball.

3. Sprinkle a clean kitchen towel with flour and place the dough ball on it. Sprinkle the dough with flour, then cover with a second towel. Set aside at room temperature until doubled in bulk, about 2 hours.

4. Position the rack in the center of the oven and heat to 475°F. Once the oven is at the proper temperature, place a 5- to 6-quart, *covered*, cast iron pot in the oven for 30 minutes.

5. When the pot is hot and the dough has risen, remove the lid and turn the dough into the pot. Cover and bake for 30 minutes. Uncover and continue baking until golden brown and cracked, 15 to 20 minutes. Remove the (hot!) pot from the oven and turn the bread onto a wire rack to cool for at least 30 minutes.

6. To make the bruschetta, slice the bread into thick lengths, then slice the longer of these in half. You can either toast the slices or leave them au naturel. Arrange one or more of the toppings in bowls so your guests can spread the bread as they like.

AHEAD

- The toppings can be made up to 3 days in advance. Store, covered, in the refrigerator but allow them to come back to room temperature before serving.

- The bread can be baked up to 1 day in advance. Once cooled to room temperature, wrap in a plastic bag to store overnight.

LESS

You can substitute store-bought bread, but we recommend a crunchy, whole-grain loaf to stand up to these assertive toppings.

NOTES

- Kamut is a trademarked strain of khorasan wheat that by law must be grown organically. Although much of the world's production takes place in North America, most of the Kamut grown is shipped off to Italy where it is highly revered in pasta- and bread-making. You can find the flour from several whole-grain producers, whether in their packages at high-end stores and health food stores or from their online outlets. The flour yields a decidedly wheaty bread with excellent, tender texture.

- Although we haven't insisted on grams in other recipes, those measurements are more necessary in this more exacting recipe. Set a large bowl on a kitchen scale, then zero out the weight of the bowl. Add the flours to the right weight, zeroing the reading out between them. Then zero it out again before adding the water.

POUR

An uncomplicated, unoaked California Chardonnay or just bourbon on the rocks, so that the complex flavors of the toppings are not competing with much besides the sweet notes in the glass

Three Toppings

YELLOW BELL PEPPER, ALMOND, CUMIN

Toast 2 medium yellow bell peppers over an open flame until blackened on all sides, turning often. Place the peppers in a bag and seal or set them in a large bowl and cover with plastic wrap. Set aside for 20 minutes. Peel the peppers as well as you can, then core and seed them. Place them in a large food processor with 1 cup tamari-roasted almonds, 1 tablespoon white balsamic vinegar, ½ teaspoon ground cumin, ½ teaspoon ground fenugreek, ½ teaspoon salt, ½ teaspoon freshly ground black pepper, and 1 medium garlic clove. Process until smooth, then spread on the bread slices.

WHITE BEAN, LEMON, PINK PEPPERCORN

Boil a large lemon in a covered saucepan of water until soft, about 45 minutes. Drain in a colander set in the sink, then cool for 30 minutes. Split the lemon open; scrape out and discard the pulp, pith, and seeds. Chop the rind, then add it to a large food processor with 1¾ cups drained and rinsed canned cannellini beans, ¼ cup olive oil, 2 tablespoons fresh lemon juice, ½ teaspoon ground cinnamon, ½ teaspoon pink peppercorns, and ½ teaspoon salt. Process until smooth, then spread on the bread slices.

BUTTERNUT SQUASH, ONION, ESPRESSO

Toss 2 cups cubed and seeded butternut squash, 1 quartered small onion, and 3 tablespoons olive oil in a large roasting pan. Bake in a 375°F oven until soft and golden, stirring occasionally, about 45 minutes. Cool on a wire rack for 10 minutes, then scrape the contents of the roasting pan into a large food processor. Add ½ teaspoon ground cumin, ½ teaspoon salt, ¼ teaspoon ground cinnamon, ¼ teaspoon dried oregano, and ¼ teaspoon cayenne pepper. Process until smooth, spread on the bread slices, and sprinkle each with a pinch of instant espresso powder.

SMALL PLATES

To sit down at a dinner party is to feel the physical warmth of your companions. Everyone's been at arm's length during the cocktail hour. Now they're closer, nearer. It's all intensely human—and a fine corrective to our mechanized, wired, online culture. Yes, you also feel that little bump in your stomach. Anticipation? Hunger? Everyone's laughing, talking. The conversation drifts back to where it was during cocktails—if louder, more glowing. You're about to settle in to a full meal, one of the best rituals we've invented.

In truth, we humans could eat any time of the day: midmorning, late at night. The natural world outside our dining rooms is made up of opportunistic eaters. When it's available, chow down. But we've condensed our habits to eat larger portions at set times. And we've synchronized those habits, eating in the morning, at midday, and in the cool of the evening within a fairly narrow time range across vast swaths of global culture. We've also made eating a communal activity, a group event, one that's a long way from animal opportunism. Sure, we might grab a slice of pizza on the run. But for a meal, families

gather. Friends come near. And we share what sustains us.

A dinner party makes it all even more civilized. First comes a small portion, or maybe two plates in sequence, no more than a few bites each. These openers are supposed to settle the stomach, stanch the more pressing urge to eat so that the main course will be savored, not devoured. It's also the first time your host can show you the breadth of her or his skills. You've already gotten the scope and promise of the production from the overture: the cocktails and the *amuse-bouche*. Now it's the first act.

Fine restaurants know that what comes first controls the aura of what comes thereafter. A great starter means that a gaffe later on may be more easily forgotten. So most chefs offer elemental fare first. These dishes highlight brighter flavors through juxtaposition rather than marriage. The dishes are ingredient-focused rather than technique-based.

With that in mind, we've clarified the palette of these small plates. Yes, many are simple in technique; most are simpler in their flavors. In fact, many are straightforward: roasted vegetables, flavorful oils, pleasurable if unusual pairings. As the chapter goes forward, the recipes become more complicated—but still not the flavors. Even when we end up with some amazing pot stickers or Chinese buns, we keep the overall play fairly elementary.

Here is where your vegetarian cooking will begin to take off. Working with this fare, you'll see that there's a greater promise of new flavor and texture combinations than in most omnivore recipes. Because of the range of complex sugars as well as the vast multitude of natural flavor esters in plants, sour notes are more pronounced; sweet, more intense. Even bitter notes, those rarely found in a hunk of meat, come to the fore. It's all a boon to us innovative cooks, yet it also means we have to work hard at balancing those ingredients to make sure they don't turn the dish into the culinary equivalent of a barroom brawl. It's important to add small accents, garnishes, and secret touches tucked inside the larger flavors to make sure one flavor isn't given undue force.

We suspect that the basic technique of starters—the juxtaposition of flavors rather than their marriage—explains why many people can make a meal out of several in a fine restaurant rather than one and then a main course. There's something so understandable, uncomplicated, and satisfying about small plates. You could even highlight them at your dinner party. You could match up three or four of these recipes and call them dinner—not tapas really, but savory bits of this and that to add up to a celebration.

The pacing rule among small plates—which can be broken at will—is that the first offering should be less ornate, more straightforward than any subsequent. Think of it as a symphony from Brahms or Beethoven. The melody is first stated simply, then it begins to build in complexity, more instruments entering and morphing the line. In other words, make your courses crescendo, quiet to loud. Even if you put together a dinner party of three or four smaller offerings, let the bigger, bolder tastes come later, once the wine's flowing and the conversation's blooming. A dinner party should have a narrative arc. It should move to a climax—from the first plate, yes; but also from that moment you feel the nearer warmth of someone sitting next to you.

PLATING RULES

We plate a course only after everyone's at the table. We get our guests settled, one of us pours the wine, and the other stays back in the kitchen. We line the small plates or bowls up on our counter and make an assembly line, working down the row with each component of the dish until we've completed the set, a layer at a time. Somebody inevitably wants to help us carry the plates into the dining room. We respond with a polite "No." Managing a waitstaff just breaks our concentration.

Roasted Radishes, Their Greens, Browned Butter

8 SERVINGS

Radishes calm down considerably when heated, becoming appealingly sweet while still peppery—and therefore an intriguing first course, way beyond the '60s relish tray. Their greens are surprisingly spicy, even sour; they offer the basic contrast to the sweetened vegetable that the nutty butter then balances. This simple dish needs only crunchy bread or crackers to set it off. It's like summer-tipping-into-fall in one spoonful.

32 medium red radishes with their greens attached

¼ cup olive oil

2 teaspoons salt, preferably kosher salt or coarse sea salt

1 teaspoon coarsely ground black pepper

2 tablespoons fresh lemon juice

4 tablespoons (½ stick) unsalted butter, cut into small pieces

1. Position the rack in the center of the oven and heat to 425°F.

2. Remove the sandy greens from the radishes. Wash the greens well. Dry completely between paper towels.

3. Halve the radishes, then toss with the oil, salt, and pepper in a large roasting pan. Roast until softened and lightly browned, stirring once or twice, about 10 minutes. Toss with the lemon juice while hot and divide among 8 serving plates.

4. Melt the butter in a large skillet over medium heat. Continue cooking until the butter begins to brown in spots. Add the greens and toss until wilted and tender, about 30 seconds. Spoon the greens and butter over the radishes before serving.

AHEAD

- Remove the greens (but do not wash them) up to 2 hours in advance. Wrap in paper towels and store in the refrigerator.

- Clean the greens up to 1 hour in advance; leave them at room temperature between paper towels until you're ready to cook them.

- Roast the radishes up to 2 hours in advance. Store, uncovered, at room temperature.

GARNISH

Sprinkle chopped, toasted walnuts over the servings.

NOTE

- Radish greens are notoriously gritty. To wash them, fill a stoppered, clean sink about a third of the way with water. Submerge the greens, agitate gently, and leave them alone for 10 minutes while the sand sifts out. Skim them out of the water, taking care not to disturb the gunk below, then unstop the sink.

A MENU

FIRST SMALL PLATE: Roasted Radishes, Their Greens, Browned Butter

SOUP: Garlic Soup, Gruyère, Cognac (page 130)

SECOND SMALL PLATE: Fiddlehead Tacos, Almond Romesco (page 70)

SALAD: Brussels Sprout/Fennel Salad, Kumquats (page 102)

DESSERT: Roasted cashews and a cup of green tea

POUR

A chilled Chilean rosé to ground this rather bold first course with a mellow, acidic earthiness

Roasted Grapes/Olives

8 SERVINGS

Roasting grapes intensifies their natural sweetness—which then means they'll pair gloriously with the briny green olives in this aromatic starter. That simple flavor alignment is balanced by earthy walnuts and fragrant rosemary. In other words, this dish is an elegant start for a meal, something beyond mere finger food, simple but appealing.

- 2⅔ cups (about 1 pound) seedless red globe grapes
- 2½ cups pitted large green olives, such as cracked Sicilian olives
- 4 teaspoons balsamic vinegar
- ½ tablespoon honey
- 4 teaspoons olive oil

- 1⅓ cups chopped walnuts
- 4 teaspoons minced fresh rosemary
- ½ teaspoon freshly ground black pepper
- 5 tablespoons finely grated Parmigiano-Reggiano cheese

1. Position the rack in the center of the oven and heat to 400°F.

2. Stir the grapes, olives, vinegar, and honey in a roasting pan. Bake until the fruit is hot and any sauce in the pan is a tad syrupy, stirring once or twice, about 25 minutes.

3. Just as the grapes and olives are finishing up, warm the oil in a medium skillet over medium-high heat. Add the walnuts, rosemary, and pepper and stir until the nuts are lightly toasted, about 5 minutes.

4. Transfer the roasting pan to a cooling rack, then scrape the contents of the skillet into the roasting pan. Stir well, scatter the cheese over everything, and stir again before spooning the mixture, along with the pan sauce, onto small plates.

> GARNISH

Sprinkle the servings with freshly grated orange zest.

> NOTES

● Choose an aromatic honey, one beyond the standard clover or wildflower.

● If you can't find seedless red grapes, use black or dark purple, as opposed to green. Don't substitute Concord grapes; their flavor will be too aggressive.

> A MENU

FIRST SMALL PLATE: Roasted Grapes/Olives

SECOND SMALL PLATE: Parsnip Flans (page 64)

THIRD SMALL PLATE: Cauliflower Grains, Cucumber, Parsley (page 53)

FOURTH SMALL PLATE: Stewed Giant Lima Beans, Dandelion Greens, Feta (page 60)

SOUP/DESSERT: Plum Soup, Cinnamon, Cloves (page 121)

> POUR

Blanc de blancs champagne with sweet notes that will underline the natural flavors of the grapes while balancing the olives and rosemary

Grilled Leeks, Hazelnuts, Lemon

8 SERVINGS

Although ramps rule the culinary cosmos in early spring, their bulked-up cousins, leeks, deserve a shot at glory during the rest of the year. Once blanched, then grilled, their pugnacious flavor mellows beautifully. They morph into a starter that's still pretty elemental, if more fall than spring, although the lemon will brighten the dish considerably. Crunchy bread seems a natural on the side, but we actually prefer baked pita chips for a cleaner, nonyeasty flavor with this fairly simple small plate.

8 small leeks, about 1 inch in diameter at the base

3 tablespoons olive oil

½ medium lemon, preferably a Meyer lemon

½ cup toasted, skinned hazelnuts, finely chopped

1 teaspoon salt, preferably flaked sea salt

1. Trim the leeks by cutting off *just* the hairy roots, thereby leaving the end intact so that the vegetable will stay together. Trim off and discard all the tough, green leaves, leaving only the white and pale green parts. Slice in half lengthwise, then rinse under cool water to remove the grit in the inside layers.

2. Fill a large bowl about two-thirds with water and add some ice cubes. Fill a large, high-sided skillet or sauté pan halfway with water and bring to a boil over high heat. Slip the leeks into the boiling water, reduce the heat so the water bubbles slowly, and blanch for 4 minutes from the time they enter the water. Use a wide spatula to transfer the leeks to the ice water. Cool completely, then transfer the leeks to paper towels. Dry well but gently.

3. Set a large grill pan over medium-high heat for a couple of minutes. Smear the oil on the leeks, then grill on both sides until marked and warm, about 4 minutes, turning once.

4. Transfer the leeks to small serving plates, two halves on each. Squeeze just a smattering of lemon juice over the leeks, then sprinkle them with hazelnuts and salt to serve.

AHEAD

- Blanch and grill the leeks up to 8 hours in advance. Leave them uncovered at room temperature.

GARNISH

For a vegetarian version, crumble bits of blue cheese over each serving.

NOTES

- Once blanched, the leeks are very fragile. They'll slip right through the grate of a grill—which is why a grill pan is the tool of choice. Oil them well and use a large spatula to turn them carefully over the heat.

- Skinned hazelnuts may be available at the supermarket, but they may not be toasted. Drop them into a dry skillet over medium-low heat and cook about 5 minutes, stirring occasionally. If the hazelnuts are not skinned (that is, they have a papery brown scrim), scatter them on a large rimmed baking sheet and roast in a 325°F oven until fragrant, about 8 minutes, stirring occasionally. Cool a few minutes, then wrap in a clean kitchen towel, gather it together, and rub the nuts against one another as well as against the towel to remove as much of the papery skin as possible.

A MENU

SMALL PLATE: Grilled Leeks, Hazelnuts, Lemon

FIRST LARGE PLATE: Zucchini Pancakes, Yellow Pepper Relish (page 192)

SECOND LARGE PLATE: Stuffed Escarole, Agrodolce Sauce (page 223)

DESSERT: Apricot No-Cheese Cake (page 262)

POUR

A white Trebbiano wine, made from an Italian (even Tuscan) grape known for its citrus overtones.

Warm Buffalo Mozzarella, Yellow Tomato Sauce

6 SERVINGS

Cheese as a first course? It often seems too heavy. Still, it's hard to argue with this warm, decadent starter, perfect any time of year, even for a little more heft in a summer meal. You first create an aromatic and penetrating tomato sauce from lower-acid yellow tomatoes, then "poach" little balls of buffalo mozzarella in it until they're warm and soft. A fork and spoon is the best way to tackle the dish.

3 tablespoons olive oil	½ teaspoon salt
1 tablespoon minced garlic	½ teaspoon freshly ground black pepper
2 pounds yellow cherry tomatoes, halved	¼ teaspoon red pepper flakes
½ teaspoon fennel seeds	18 baby bocconcini, drained

1. Set a large skillet over medium heat for a few minutes. Swirl in the oil, then add the garlic. Cook for 1 minute, stirring often, until aromatic.

2. Add the tomatoes, fennel seeds, salt, black pepper, and red pepper flakes. Continue cooking, stirring occasionally, until the tomatoes fully soften, about 30 minutes.

3. Puree the tomato mixture by using an immersion blender right in the skillet. (Be careful of the electric cord around the burner!) Or process in a blender or food processer and then pour the puree back into the skillet.

4. Bring the mixture to a slow simmer. Drop in the baby bocconcini, turn off the heat, and let stand for 5 minutes. Use a large, shallow spoon to transfer the balls and sauce to small serving plates.

AHEAD
• Prepare the tomato sauce up to 2 hours in advance. Leave it covered in its skillet on the stove.

GARNISH
Sprinkle plates with minced basil leaves.

NOTE
• Baby bocconcini are very small buffalo mozzarella balls, about the size of large grapes. If you can't find these, buy regular bocconcini and cut them in half—or larger mozzarella balls and cut them into quarters. However, beware of imitators. There are all too often small, rubbery balls of cow's milk cheese that are passed off as bocconcini in the United States, particularly at large supermarket salad bars. You'll probably need to go to an Italian market or grocery store to find the real thing.

A MENU
FIRST SMALL PLATE: Walnuts, Peas, Daikon, Butter, Tomatoes (page 52)

SECOND SMALL PLATE: Warm Buffalo Mozzarella, Yellow Tomato Sauce

LARGE PLATE: Stuffed Pears, Wild Rice, Mushrooms (page 228)

DESSERT: Fig Galette, Honey Cream (page 248)

POUR
A sturdy, white Vouvray to tame the mild acidity in the tomato sauce and bring the luxurious seduction of the cheese forward

Asparagus Spears, Pickled Radicchio

8 SERVINGS

Ever the side dish, never the meal: Asparagus is the bridesmaid of vegetables, despite being one of the best harbingers of spring. So we've gussied up those (dare we say it?) lackluster spears with radicchio poached in wine and two kinds of vinegar for extra spike. Pickling the leaves in this way softens their bitterness and brings out a rather unexpected sweetness amid the sour notes. We then wrap those leaves around the asparagus, morphing its essential grassiness into better elegance. Perhaps best of all, this spiky but straightforward starter can be made well in advance.

2 large round radicchio heads (radicchio di Chioggia, about 10 ounces each)

1 cup dry but fruit-forward red wine, such as Zinfandel

½ cup red wine vinegar

½ cup balsamic vinegar

½ cup olive oil

1 pound thin asparagus spears

3 ounces Parmigiano-Reggiano cheese, shaved (about ¾ cup)

1. Core the radicchio heads and carefully separate the leaves. Use the 25 largest leaves and reserve the remainder for a salad later in the week.

2. Bring the wine and both vinegars to a boil in a small saucepan over high heat. Add 5 radicchio leaves, push them under the bubbling liquid with a wooden spoon or kitchen tongs, and keep them there, simmering until wilted and tender, about 3 minutes. Transfer the leaves to a bowl and drizzle them with 1½ tablespoons olive oil. Repeat this process 3 more times. You'll then have 2 tablespoons oil for a last batch—and you'll make one extra leaf, a safeguard against any tearing. Let the radicchio leaves cool completely, about 1 hour at room temperature.

3. Fill a large bowl with ice and water. Bring a large skillet of water to a boil over high heat. Add the asparagus to the skillet and blanch for 1 minute from the time the spears hit the water. Use a slotted spoon to transfer them to the ice water. Cool to room temperature, then drain and dry completely.

4. Roll each asparagus spear tightly in a radicchio leaf. Set 3 on each serving plate. Top each serving with the shaved cheese.

▶ **AHEAD**

● Pickle the radicchio leaves up to 2 days in advance. Once cooled, store, covered, in the fridge.

● Blanch the asparagus spears up to 1 day in advance. Store, covered, in the fridge as well.

● Wrap the asparagus spears up to 4 hours in advance. Store, covered, at room temperature.

▶ **GARNISH**

Sprinkle coarsely ground black pepper or cracked black peppercorns over each serving.

▶ **NOTES**

● To core radicchio heads, use a paring knife to make a conical incision around that core, pulling it out in one piece. Peel the leaves off from this indentation rather than by their fragile, leafy edges.

● Blanching the radicchio leaves is truly a matter of timing. It might be best to blanch a few extra leaves in case any don't come out right.

● The asparagus spears should be thin but not too thin—say, a little larger than a #2 pencil. If they're too thick, shave them down with a vegetable peeler.

▶ **A MENU**

FIRST SMALL PLATE: Asparagus Spears, Pickled Radicchio

SECOND SMALL PLATE: Chickpea Blini, Curried Sweet Potatoes (page 74)

PASTA: Ziti, Chard, Beans, Poached Eggs (page 138)

DESSERT: Porter Pie, Graham Cracker Crust, Meringue (page 260)

▶ **POUR**

A creamy red ale to tame the sour spark in the leaves and add a floral mellowness the dish admittedly lacks

Steamed Artichokes, Red Peppers, Basil

6 SERVINGS

A bit of a luxury—mostly because you discard a great deal of an artichoke before grilling it—this starter is best at an early summery dinner party to celebrate the burgeoning green in the world around you. Jarred roasted red peppers make easy work of the sauce—which is a bit sour, muting the low-grade earthiness of the artichokes and thereby bringing out their natural sweetness.

1 cup drained, jarred, roasted red bell peppers or pimientos

5 tablespoons olive oil, divided

2 tablespoons balsamic vinegar

¼ cup packed fresh basil leaves

¼ teaspoon salt

6 medium globe artichokes

1. Puree the roasted peppers or pimientos, 2 tablespoons of the olive oil, the vinegar, basil, and salt in a blender or a large food processor until smooth. Set aside.

2. Trim the artichokes by pulling off all the outer leaves until you reach the leaves that have changed both color and texture, becoming pale and thinner. Slice off the top of each artichoke to the heart. Peel the stalk with a vegetable peeler; cut the artichoke in half and scrape out the hairy choke, preferably with a serrated grapefruit spoon.

3. Set up a vegetable steamer over 2 inches of simmering water. Steam the artichokes, covered, until tender, about 20 minutes.

4. Prepare the grill for high-heat, direct cooking (or heat a grill pan over medium-high heat until smoking). Coat the artichokes in the remaining 3 tablespoons olive oil and grill cut side down until well marked, 4 to 5 minutes.

5. Spoon the sauce onto small plates and set the artichokes in the middle of the sauce.

AHEAD

- Make the red pepper sauce up to 2 days in advance. Store, covered, in the refrigerator but allow to come back to room temperature before serving.

- Grill the artichokes up to 4 hours in advance. Store them at room temperature.

MORE

Add smoke by 1) putting soaked and drained smoking chips in the grill's smoker box, 2) using smoked olive oil to coat the artichokes, or 3) putting the grilled artichokes in a large baking dish, covering it with plastic wrap, and using the very esoteric, gourmet tool of a smoking gun to pipe an intense burst of smoke into the pan before tightly sealing it.

NOTE

- If you don't work quickly and efficiently, or if this is the first time you've made this dish, set up a large bowl of water combined with the juice of 1 lemon. Drop the prepped artichokes in that water as you finish them to keep them from oxidizing (and thus browning).

A MENU

SALAD: Roasted Pears, Fig Caponata (page 110)

SMALL PLATE: Steamed Artichokes, Red Peppers, Basil

LARGE PLATE: Zucchini Casserole, Mashed Potatoes (page 216)

DESSERT: Chocolate Chip Cookies, Maple, Tahini, Dates (page 236)

POUR

Since artichokes are notoriously difficult to pair with wine, a dry sherry with its woody fragrance to balance the sweetness in the dish

Crunchy Runner Beans, Pickled Shallots

8 SERVINGS

A real treat, runner beans make a flashy midsummer appearance at our farmers' markets, only to disappear too quickly. Yes, you can sometimes find them in larger, high-end supermarkets in the off-seasons. Although a little stringier by that point in the year, they're still worth the splurge, a perfect vegetable balance between sweet and savory—and mellower than either green beans or sugar snaps without the starchiness of wax beans. Here, we've pickled shallots to round out those natural sugars, giving the beans complexity through juxtaposition rather than a more technique-driven marriage of flavors in a baked or sautéed preparation. In some ways, this dish represents our theory of small-plate first courses in its purest form.

¾ cup red wine vinegar

½ cup water

¼ cup honey, preferably orange blossom honey

1 teaspoon salt

1 teaspoon black peppercorns

4 fresh sprigs thyme

1 bay leaf

6 medium shallots, peeled and sliced into thin rings

1½ pounds runner beans, trimmed and cut into 1-inch pieces on the diagonal

1¾ ounces Pecorino Romano cheese, shaved (about ⅓ cup)

½ teaspoon freshly ground black pepper

1. Stir the vinegar, water, honey, salt, peppercorns, thyme sprigs, and bay leaf in a medium saucepan over medium-high heat until the honey dissolves.

2. Place the shallot rings in a large heatproof bowl or a large glass canning jar. When the mixture in the saucepan comes to a boil, remove it from the heat, cool for 1 minute, then pour over the shallot rings. Cover and refrigerate for at least 24 hours.

3. Bring a large saucepan of water to a boil over high heat. Add the runner bean pieces and blanch for 1 minute from the time they enter the water. Drain in a colander set in the sink. Run cool water over the beans to stop the cooking. Drain thoroughly.

4. Drain the shallots in a fine-mesh sieve. Pick out the peppercorns, bay leaf, and thyme sprigs and discard. Toss the beans with the shallots, then spoon onto small plates. Top with the Pecorino and ground black pepper.

AHEAD

• Prepare and refrigerate the shallots up to 3 days in advance.

• Blanch and drain the runner beans up to 2 hours in advance. Store, covered, at room temperature.

• Toss the beans with the shallots, plate the course, cover lightly with plastic wrap, and leave at room temperature up to 30 minutes in advance. Add the cheese and pepper just before serving.

MORE

Add toasted croutons, preferably croutons you've toasted from cubes of day-old pumpernickel bread. Toss them with the beans and shallots in step 4 so they're lightly dressed.

NOTES

• We do not mean the dried runner bean seeds also called "runner beans." Rather, we mean the fresh, long pods, seeds and all. For more color, search out scarlet runner beans, often available at farmers' markets.

• Save the marinade from the shallots. Use it to marinate firm tofu steaks for up to 24 hours in the fridge before grilling.

A MENU

FIRST SMALL PLATE: Roasted Cipollini Onions, Fava Beans Two Ways (page 56)

LARGE PLATE: Basmati Rice, Cashews, Spring Vegetables (page 218)

SECOND SMALL PLATE: Crunchy Runner Beans, Pickled Shallots

DESSERT: Dried apple slices and cups of Earl Grey tea

POUR

A somewhat acidic Soave with its characteristic bitter almond notes to form a balance point between the sweet and sour in the dish

Squash Noodles, Almond Chimichurri

6 SERVINGS

Raw and fresh, the essence of summer, this starter is so simple, it might become a signature at your table, welcome even during the winter holidays. The flavor of the crunchy squash "noodles" is surprisingly complex with a characteristic funky sweetness that glints off the more complex sour and herbal notes in this twisted version of the classic South American sauce. Make sure you have a sliced (or even torn) baguette on hand. Everyone will want to sop up every last drop.

½ cup whole roasted, unsalted almonds

½ cup olive oil

¼ cup packed fresh parsley leaves

¼ cup packed fresh cilantro leaves

3 tablespoons fresh lemon juice

1 tablespoon capers, rinsed

2 teaspoons minced garlic

1 teaspoon salt

1 teaspoon freshly ground black pepper

2 large yellow or summer squash

1. Place the almonds, oil, parsley, cilantro, lemon juice, capers, garlic, salt, and pepper in a large food processor. Pulse and process a bit, scraping down the inside of the bowl several times, until the mixture is a coarse paste. Scrape into a bowl and set aside.

2. Run a vegetable peeler down the squash to make thin, long, waggly "noodles." Rotate the squash after every few swipes so that the noodles remain evenly sized as you work your way around the vegetable. Stop when you reach the seed core on all sides. Discard that core and soldier on with the second squash.

3. Add the almond and herb paste to the bowl with the squash noodles. Toss gently to coat before mounding onto small plates.

> **AHEAD**
> - Make the almond sauce up to 4 hours in advance. Store, covered, at room temperature.

> **MORE**
> Substitute tamari-roasted almonds for the whole almonds.

> **GARNISH**
> A sprinkling of minced parsley leaves might seem a natural addition, but you might also consider red pepper flakes, just to spice things up.

> **NOTE**
> - Chimichurri is a South American herb and oil sauce. We've added almonds for heft, since there won't be a piece of beef in sight, and tweaked it a bit toward the Mediterranean to better match the raw vegetable.

> **A MENU**
> FIRST SMALL PLATE: Squash Noodles, Almond Chimichurri
>
> SECOND SMALL PLATE: Wilted Chard, Pistachios, Lovage (page 47)
>
> LARGE PLATE: Brie Arepas, Asparagus Salsa (page 200)
>
> DESSERT: Lightly chilled maple syrup shots (preferably dark amber maple syrup), followed by a single-malt whisky

> **POUR**
> A big, white Burgundy, particularly a Chassagne-Montrachet, for a smooth, almost velvety softness against this full-flavored starter

Blistered Butter Beans, Pecans, Fennel

8 SERVINGS

Despite their natural muskiness, dried butter beans make an intriguingly sophisticated start to a dinner party—mostly because they're ridiculously creamy. When blistered in a hot skillet with lots of aromatic vegetables and a fairly aggressive palette of spices, the beans come to offer a terrific mash-up of their natural sugars *and* inherent earthiness. If you pair this dish with, say, a heavy casserole to follow, make sure there's an intervening course with acidic notes to lighten things up—like the Gazpacho Shooters (page 126). Or perhaps whisk softened lemon sorbet into a little Aperol in tall glasses, then top with chilled prosecco for a bright, palate-cleansing spark.

1 pound dried butter beans

6 tablespoons olive oil

1 teaspoon cumin seeds

1 teaspoon fennel seeds

1 medium fennel bulb, trimmed and thinly shaved

1 small red onion, halved through the root and thinly sliced into half-moons

¾ cup chopped, toasted pecans

2 tablespoons fresh lemon juice

½ teaspoon salt

½ teaspoon red pepper flakes

1. Soak the beans overnight in a large bowl filled with water.

2. Drain the beans in a colander set in the sink, then pour them into a large saucepan and fill the pan about two-thirds with water. Bring to a boil over high heat, then reduce the heat and simmer until tender, 1½ to 2 hours. Drain again and refresh in the colander with cool tap water.

3. Set a large skillet over medium-high heat for a couple of minutes. Swirl in the oil, then add the cumin and fennel seeds. Cook until the seeds start to pop, about 1 minute, stirring often. Pour in the beans, increase the heat to high, and stir-fry until the beans are starting to blister and brown, about 5 minutes.

4. Move the skillet off the heat. Use a slotted spoon to remove the beans and seeds from the skillet, leaving as much of the oil behind as possible. Return the skillet to medium heat and add the fennel and onion. Cook, stirring often, until softened, about 5 minutes.

5. Stir in the pecans, then return the beans and seeds to the skillet. Stir-fry for 1 minute to heat through. Stir in the lemon juice, salt, and red pepper flakes. Mound the mixture onto small serving plates.

▷ AHEAD

● Complete the recipe through step 2 up to 6 hours in advance. Place the cooled beans in a large bowl, cover with plastic wrap, and store in the fridge.

▷ LESS

Substitute 5 cups drained and rinsed canned butter beans. They'll be more fragile—and starchier. Increase the oil to ½ cup to keep them from sticking. Stir-fry for only a couple of minutes, tossing the skillet more than stirring the beans, just until they begin to blister.

▷ GARNISH

Sprinkle the plates with a fine dusting of bright yellow fennel pollen—or even bee pollen.

▷ A MENU

SMALL PLATE: Blistered Butter Beans, Pecans, Fennel

SOUP: White Gazpacho, Fried Fennel Seeds (page 125)

LARGE PLATE: Cauliflower Strudel, Cranberry Chutney (page 226)

DESSERT: Orange/Coconut Bundt (page 268)

▷ POUR

A dry German Riesling (not the more standard sweet bottling) to wipe the palate clean after each bite and keep the flavors fresh throughout the course

Wilted Chard, Pistachios, Lovage

6 SERVINGS

Soft, wilted greens can be a problem for a first course. Yep, they're too squishy. But the flavors are certainly right: simple, sweet, and a little herbal. The trick to maintaining any appeal is to work quickly in a very hot skillet and cook the leaves less than you might expect, just until they begin to droop, not break down. Then pack distinct, even disparate flavors among the greens so you can fend off taste and texture exhaustion—and so you'll return greens like chard to their rightful place as a culinary (not just health) staple. We like to offer a prickly, hot chow-chow (a fiery cabbage condiment favored in the South) and crunchy little crackers as a cocktail nibble before we proceed to this plate, a tangy zip before the varied levels of earthiness on display here.

1¾ pounds rainbow chard, rinsed well to remove grit

3 tablespoons olive oil

6 tablespoons shelled unsalted pistachios

6 tablespoons dried currants

4 garlic cloves, slivered

3 tablespoons packed fresh lovage leaves, shredded

½ teaspoon salt, preferably flaked sea salt

½ teaspoon freshly ground black pepper

1. Remove the large stems from the chard leaves, cutting up into the leaves to get rid of any veins over ½ inch wide, but don't discard. Slice the stems and veins into thin bits and cut the leaves into 3-inch pieces.

2. Set a large skillet over medium heat for a couple of minutes, then swirl in the oil. Add the pistachios, currants, and garlic and cook, stirring often, until the garlic begins to brown, about 1 minute.

3. Stir in the chard stems and cook for no more than 3 minutes until somewhat softened, stirring often. Increase the heat to medium-high, add the rest of the chard, and toss for at most 2 minutes, just until wilted. Take the skillet off the heat and stir in the lovage, salt, and pepper. Serve without delay: Use tongs to gather up small bundles of the greens and other ingredients and transfer these to small plates.

AHEAD

- Chop and prep all the ingredients up to 2 hours in advance.

GARNISH

Sprinkle fresh blackberries around the servings.

NOTES

- Lovage is a leafy herb, common to European kitchens. It has a slightly bitter flavor, prized for the way it balances sweeter notes in salads.

- If you can't find lovage, substitute the shredded leaves from celery stalks, a much milder alternative.

A MENU

FIRST SMALL PLATE: Wilted Chard, Pistachios, Lovage

SECOND SMALL PLATE: Shredded Beets, Capers, Avocados (page 50)

THIRD SMALL PLATE: Cauliflower Grains, Cucumber, Parsley (page 53)

FOURTH SMALL PLATE: Pulled Vegetable Sliders (page 76)

DESSERT: Lemon Cream Donuts (page 277)

POUR

A red Côtes du Rhône with its dry, plummy acidity to pick out the fruit and nuts hidden in the leaves

Stir-Fried Parsnips, Black Pepper, Caramel

8 SERVINGS

Sort of Vietnamese, sort of French, this first course is a pop in the mouth, best in small portions to set everyone's palate buzzing. We remove the tough, inner core from the parsnips so they're as creamy as they can be. Thus, that slightly musky, very herbal sweetness can show through in glorious simplicity. Surprisingly, the parsnips stand up to all the black pepper as well as the slightly bitter caramel—but those root vegetables *just* stand up to them, a strangely comforting alignment of flavors.

1 cup sugar

⅔ cup boiling water

4 pounds parsnips

6 tablespoons peanut oil

10 garlic cloves, slivered

2 tablespoons cracked black peppercorns

½ cup vegetable broth

¼ cup soy sauce

1. Pour the sugar into a medium saucepan over medium-high heat. Cook until it melts at the edges. Stir, then continue cooking until melted and dark brown, stirring occasionally. Pour in the boiling water and stir over the heat until the sugar dissolves again. The mixture will bubble and froth like mad—work diligently and efficiently. Set the caramel syrup aside to cool to room temperature, about 2 hours.

2. Peel the parsnips, then cut them crosswise into 1½-inch-long sections. Slice thinner sections in half, fatter sections into quarters. Slice out and discard the tough, white core.

3. Bring a large saucepan of water to a boil over high heat. Add the parsnip pieces and cook until crisp-tender, even al dente, about 3 minutes from the time they hit the water. Drain in a colander set in the sink and rinse with cool water to stop the cooking.

4. Set a large wok over medium-high heat for a couple of minutes, then swirl in the oil. Add the garlic and stir-fry until lightly browned and a bit blistered, about 2 minutes. Add the cracked pepper and stir-fry about 10 seconds.

5. Stir in the broth, soy sauce, and 5 tablespoons of the caramel syrup and cook until bubbling. Add the blanched parsnips and stir-fry about 1 minute, to coat thoroughly.

6. Divide among small plates or bowls and serve with chopsticks or big spoons.

AHEAD

• Make the caramel syrup up to 1 month in advance. Store, covered, in the fridge.

• Blanch the cut-up parsnips up to 6 hours in advance. Store, covered, at room temperature.

MORE

Serve over cooked medium-grain brown rice or over wilted spinach or chard leaves.

NOTES

• You'll make more caramel syrup than you need. Save what you don't use in a small glass container, covered, in the fridge for up to 1 month. This will give you the chance to make this recipe again or to use the syrup in all sorts of drinks and cocktails.

• Crack the peppercorns on a cutting board under a heavy saucepan. Otherwise, use coarsely ground black pepper.

• Because canned vegetable broth can be salty, we advise using a reduced-sodium broth, particularly since the soy sauce adds plenty of sodium.

A MENU

SOUP: Pear Soup, Ginger, Buttery Leeks (page 129)

SMALL PLATE: Stir-Fried Parsnips, Black Pepper, Caramel

LARGE PLATE: Braised Kabocha Squash, Scallions, Miso (page 179)

DESSERT: Pineapple chunks tossed with lemon juice and toasted sesame seeds

POUR

A sweet, smooth Spätlese to calm the fire in the black pepper and bring the parsnips a little more to the fore

Shredded Beets, Capers, Avocados

8 SERVINGS

Shredded beets can actually recraft an age-old bistro favorite, tartare, into a vegan first course. We've nixed the egg, of course, but added capers for brightness in this layered starter. By using raw beets, rather than cooking them, we've kept their abundant sugars in check, not letting them overwhelm the natural rootiness of the vegetable. And when we set the raw beet tartare on creamy avocados, we let the sweetness lie elsewhere in the dish to keep the focus on the surprisingly savory flavors in raw beets. The finished plate only needs salty, wheaty crackers on the side—and a set of napkins that can be easily washed to remove the inevitable stains.

- 8 medium beets, any greens removed (about 2¼ pounds without the greens)
- ¼ cup minced shallots
- 2 tablespoons fresh lemon juice
- 1 tablespoon jarred prepared red horseradish
- 1 tablespoon capers, rinsed and chopped
- 1 tablespoon minced fresh chives
- ½ teaspoon salt
- ½ teaspoon freshly ground black pepper
- 3 Hass avocados
- 1 tablespoon fresh lime juice

1. Peel the beets, then cut them into 1-inch cubes. Place these in a large food processor and pulse until finely ground but not yet pureed. Stop the machine at least once and scrape down the inside while rearranging the beet pieces so they become evenly ground.

2. Scrape the ground beets into a fine-mesh sieve in the sink. Press gently with a rubber spatula to remove excess liquid. Transfer the beet puree to a large bowl. Stir in the shallots, lemon juice, horseradish, capers, chives, salt, and pepper. Cover and chill for at least 4 hours.

3. Halve, pit, peel, and dice the avocados. Toss them with the lime juice in a medium bowl.

4. Fill a 4-inch ring mold halfway with avocado bits, pressing lightly to compact with the back of a spoon. Keeping the mold in place, fill with the ground beet mixture again compressing lightly. Remove the mold and repeat to make 7 more servings.

▶ **AHEAD**

- The beet mixture can be made up to 1 day in advance. Cover and refrigerate.

▶ **LESS**

- Skip the mold. Smooth an even layer of the diced avocado on each of 8 small plates, and top each with a rounded mound of ground beets.

▶ **GARNISH**

Sprinkle with toasted pine nuts.

▶ **A MENU**

SMALL PLATE: Shredded Beets, Capers, Avocados

SOUP: Miso Soup, Celery Root, Rye Berries (page 131)

PASTA: Leek/Gorgonzola Lasagna (page 147)

LARGE PLATE: Zucchini Pancakes, Yellow Pepper Relish (page 192)

DESSERT: Fennel/Cardamom Pears, Ginger Mascarpone (page 247)

▶ **POUR**

A fruit-forward Pinot Noir with peppery raspberry notes to serve as a reminder of the beets' sweetness that cooking would have brought out

Walnuts, Peas, Daikon, Butter, Tomatoes

8 SERVINGS

Take a raw mix of nuts and vegetables, add a lemony cooked dressing from clarified butter, and you've got this fantastic starter that mixes bold flavors with both soft and firm levels of crunch. Those contrasts are gently underlined by the relaxed, firm pepperiness of the daikon bits. There's not much better. But if there's an Achilles heel in this dish, it's those tomatoes, a bed for the buttery mélange. Don't even think about serving this starter until tomatoes are at their peak in your area. The sweet, soft slices with their gentle acidity will be the sturdy fulcrum on which all the rest balances. As you'll see, they're necessary and yet strangely not primary.

1 cup walnut pieces

2 cups shelled fresh peas or thawed frozen peas

½ medium daikon radish, peeled and diced (about 2 cups)

8 tablespoons (1 stick) unsalted butter

2 tablespoons fresh lemon juice

2 teaspoons fresh thyme leaves

1 teaspoon sugar

½ teaspoon freshly grated nutmeg

½ teaspoon salt

½ teaspoon freshly ground black pepper

4 globe or beefsteak tomatoes

1. Toast the walnuts in a large skillet over medium-low heat until aromatic and lightly browned, stirring often, about 5 minutes. Spread the nuts on a cutting board, cool a few minutes, then chop into fairly small bits (nothing bigger than a pea). Scrape these into a big bowl. Stir in the peas and daikon.

2. Melt the butter in a small saucepan over medium-low heat. Remove the pan from the heat and cool for 10 minutes. Pour the clear, yellow fat into a large bowl and discard the remaining milky solids and liquid. Cool the clarified butter to room temperature, about 45 minutes. Stir in the lemon juice, thyme, sugar, nutmeg, salt, and pepper.

3. Pour the butter dressing over the nut mixture and toss well.

4. Thinly slice the tomatoes and fan onto small serving plates. Top with the dressed salad, scraping any extra dressing in the bowl over the servings.

▌ AHEAD

● Make the recipe through step 2 up to 2 hours in advance. Store the components separately but covered at room temperature. If the clarified butter dressing begins to solidify, warm over very low heat just to loosen it up.

▌ NOTE

● For a great presentation, overlap the tomato slices around the perimeter of the plate, leaving a little gap at the center. Spoon the salad right into the center of the plate, drizzling dressing over the tomato slices as well.

▌ A MENU

SOUP: Miso Soup, Celery Root, Rye Berries (page 13)

SECOND SMALL PLATE: Walnuts, Peas, Daikon, Butter, Tomatoes

PASTA: Kamut Pappardelle, Mushroom Ragù (page 140)

DESSERT: Sliced plums macerated in a little sugar, then set on top of store-bought orange sorbet

▌ POUR

A mellow, not too sweet Gewürztraminer that doesn't compete with the butter or mute the tomatoes' acidity, yet actually brings the (surprising) nutmeg forward

Cauliflower Grains, Cucumber, Parsley

6 SERVINGS

Call this one a cauliflower take on tabbouleh. The raw vegetable is pulsed and processed until it's about the size and consistency of coarse bulgur; it's then mixed with crunchy, summery vegetables to create a moist, refreshing range of raw textures. It all may seem like a side dish, but you'll find a small serving opens up a meal (and everyone's palate) to the more pronounced sour, bitter, and sweet notes that plants afford—and sets the stage for more complication to come. Originally, we blanched the cauliflower momentarily to heighten its natural sweetness, but we then lost the slightly bitter rawness in the dish and ended up with a more standard sweet/sour palette. So we went fully raw for a more rustic but oddly sophisticated starter.

- 1 medium cauliflower head, cut into small florets (about 5 cups)
- 8 yellow cherry tomatoes, quartered
- 1 cup finely chopped, seeded, and peeled cucumber (about ½ large)
- ½ cup finely chopped red onion (about 1 small)
- ½ cup minced fresh parsley leaves
- 5 tablespoons fresh lemon juice
- ¼ cup olive oil
- 1 teaspoon salt
- 1 teaspoon freshly ground black pepper

1. Put the florets in a large food processor. Pulse repeatedly, rearranging the florets as necessary, to create a coarse, grainlike, even seedlike mixture, like very coarse bulgur.

2. Scrape the cauliflower bits into a large bowl. Stir in everything else: the cherry tomatoes, cucumber, onion, parsley, lemon juice, olive oil, salt, and pepper. Spoon onto small plates to serve.

AHEAD

- Make the salad up to 4 hours in advance but omit the lemon juice, olive oil, and salt until just before you serve it. Store it covered at room temperature.

LESS

Look for already separated cauliflower florets in the refrigerated section of your supermarket's produce department. Slice these into smaller florets so they process evenly and efficiently.

MORE

Hollow out large yellow tomatoes, then stuff the cauliflower mixture into them to serve.

A MENU

SMALL PLATE: Cauliflower Grains, Cucumber, Parsley

LARGE PLATE: Vegetable/Lentil Balls, Brown Rice Pilaf (page 206)

SOUP: Pear Soup, Ginger, Buttery Leeks (page 129)

DESSERT: Maple/Oat Blondies (page 239)

POUR

An aromatic, almost floral, grapey Pinot Gris to counterbalance the dish's savory acidity

Roasted Brussels Sprouts, Farro, Dried Apricots

8 SERVINGS

When you first work with highly flavored vegetables and grains, there's little need to get too fussy. (That'll come.) It's important to let them first stand on their own. By combining whole-grain farro with crunchy nuts and tart dried apricots, we're letting these ingredients speak for themselves, as it were. That said, you also have to think about balance. So the surprise here that lets all three take equal billing is the bitterness in the two green vegetables: the Brussels sprouts and the arugula. Think of it this way: A bitter aperitif like Campari is said to set the stage for sweeter flavors to come in the dinner ahead. That's happening here, all on one plate.

⅓ cup whole-grain farro	½ cup chopped dried apricots
1½ pounds small Brussels sprouts, halved	¼ cup white wine vinegar
	1 tablespoon honey
⅓ cup olive oil	2 teaspoons Dijon mustard
½ cup chopped toasted walnuts	8 cups baby arugula

1. Soak the farro in a big bowl of cool water for at least 8 hours or up to 16 hours.

2. Drain the farro in a small-holed colander set in the sink, then pour it into a large saucepan. Fill the saucepan about two-thirds with water and bring to a boil over high heat. Stir well, reduce the heat to low, and simmer until tender, stirring occasionally, about 50 minutes.

3. Drain the farro again in that colander, then rinse the grains with cool tap water to stop the cooking. Drain thoroughly.

4. Position the rack in the center of the oven and heat to 400°F.

5. Toss the Brussels sprouts in a large roasting pan with the oil. Roast until lightly browned and crisp-tender, tossing occasionally, about 15 minutes.

6. Transfer the roasting pan to a wire rack. Stir in the walnuts, apricots, and cooked farro. Whisk the vinegar, honey, and mustard in a small bowl. Scrape the mixture into the warm roasting pan and toss well.

7. Pile the arugula on small serving plates. Spoon the warm Brussels sprouts mixture and any pan juices over the greens to serve.

AHEAD

- Cook the farro up to 24 hours in advance. Once cooled, store, covered, in the refrigerator but let the grain come back to room temperature before using.

- Get the arugula on the plates up to 2 hours in advance. Store at room temperature.

LESS

Although soaking the grains will give them a better texture when boiled, there's no strict need to do so. Simply boil longer, about 1 hour 10 minutes.

NOTE

- Farro is a strain of wheat, favored in Mediterranean cooking. For the best texture, look for whole-grain farro, not *perlato* (that is, pearled), which has had the germ and bran stripped away.

A MENU

SMALL PLATE: Roasted Brussels Sprouts, Farro, Dried Apricots

PASTA: Curried Spaetzle, Ginger Broth (page 155)

LARGE PLATE: Stewed Butternut Squash, Coconut Milk, Warm Spices (page 184)

DESSERT: Apricot No-Cheese Cake (page 262)

POUR

Hard cider to offer an effervescent sweet/tart mix that holds the bitter notes down to the floor of the dish's flavors

Roasted Cipollini Onions, Fava Beans Two Ways

6 SERVINGS

We have a decided preference for crunchy first courses. Still, it's sometimes delightful to go soft and luxurious. This dish fits that bill, riding the divide between winter and spring, using both dried and fresh fava beans. The former are used in the puree; the latter, for a bright garnish (and our vaunted crunch). Super-sweet, roasted cipollini are set down in that slightly sour and even musky puree—which is then studded with those crunchy favas, a green pop against winter white. You'll need to set big spoons for this one as well as some bread to scrape up every drop.

12 ounces dried fava beans (about 2 cups)

½ pound fresh fava beans in their pods

18 medium (1½ to 2 inches in diameter) cipollini onions, peeled

2 sprigs (4-inch) fresh rosemary

4 tablespoons olive oil, divided

1 teaspoon salt

1½ tablespoons aged, syrupy balsamic vinegar

1. Soak the *dried* favas in a big bowl of cool water for at least 8 hours or up to 16 hours.

2. The next day, bring a large saucepan of water to a boil over high heat. Remove the *fresh* fava beans from their pods, then add the beans to the boiling water and boil until tender, about 1 minute. Drain in a colander set in the sink. Run cool water over them to stop the cooking, then peel each bean from its tough, plasticlike hull. Discard those hulls.

3. Drain the soaked dried beans in a colander set in the sink and peel the hulls off those favas. Add the beans to a large pot, fill with water to cover them by about at least 3 inches, and bring to a boil over high heat. Reduce the heat to medium and simmer, uncovered, until beyond tender, even soft, about 45 minutes.

▶ **AHEAD**

● Boil and peel the fresh fava beans, make the puree, and roast the onions up to 4 hours in advance. Keep them separate, covered, and at room temperature.

▶ **MORE**

Drizzle a very fruity olive oil over each serving along with the aged balsamic.

▶ **GARNISH**

Sprinkle more syrupy balsamic vinegar over each plating.

▶ **NOTES**

● To hull fresh favas after blanching, slice off one tiny end of the hull with a clean fingernail, then gently squeeze out the bright green bean. If the bean splits in half when peeled, simply reserve both halves. You'll have more for garnishing.

● Dried green fava beans indeed need to be peeled after soaking. White or beige ones are most likely already peeled—and so are easier to work with. However, these latter types have a mushier flavor so we prefer the greener ones, often found at high-end supermarkets or speciality Italian food stores.

● You don't want tiny cipollini onions for this dish—but you also don't want large ones. Figure on onions about 2 inches in diameter.

4. Meanwhile, position the rack in the center of the oven and heat to 325°F. Toss the cipollini onions and rosemary with 2 tablespoons of the oil in a large roasting pan. Bake until the onions are soft and tender, stirring occasionally, about 45 minutes.

5. When the dried favas are soft, drain them in a colander set in the sink. Pour them into a large food processor and add the salt and remaining 2 tablespoons oil. Puree until smooth, stopping the machine and scraping down the inside of the bowl two or three times.

6. When the onions are soft, add the balsamic vinegar to the pan and toss gently. Discard the rosemary.

7. To serve, spoon the fava puree into 6 shallow soup bowls or small plates with some depth to hold that puree. Place the cipollini on top of the puree, 3 per bowl. Sprinkle the fresh fava beans over and around the onions.

A MENU

SMALL PLATE: Roasted Cipollini Onions, Fava Beans Two Ways

LARGE PLATE: Vegetable Kebabs, Saffron Oil, Quinoa Pilaf (page 190)

SALAD: Grapefruit/Avocado Salad, Pistachios (page 100)

DESSERT: Espresso/Chocolate Bundt, Ginger/Whisky Sauce (page 266)

POUR

A highball made of a little Cynar (an artichoke and herb amaro from Italy), lots of soda, ice, and a lemon twist to match the puree's strangely sweet bitterness and the balsamic vinegar's tangy redolence

Kohlrabi, Enoki, Peanuts, Grilled Scallions

8 SERVINGS

A global favorite yet barely known in this country, kohlrabi is a rather sweet vegetable with a mild, broccoli-like flavor. When it's quickly cooked and then pureed, it can become a creamy (if cream-free) canvas for delicate, sweet enoki mushrooms and crunchy, salty peanuts. Talk about juxtapositions and contrasts! That said, the best things in this dish may well be the grilled scallions. Their smoky sweetness ties these other, earthier ingredients together—especially once they're spiked with sambal oelek, a fiery condiment.

6 medium kohlrabi (each just slightly smaller than a baseball)

½ teaspoon salt

24 scallions

5 ounces enoki mushrooms, cleaned

½ cup salted, roasted peanuts, chopped

½ cup olive oil

Up to 2 tablespoons sambal oelek

1. Trim the stems off the kohlrabi, peel them, and cut them into quarters. Bring a large saucepan of water to a boil over high heat. Add the kohlrabi and boil until tender, about 15 minutes.

2. Use a slotted spoon to transfer the kohlrabi to a food processor (reserve the cooking water). Add the salt to the kohlrabi and cool for a few minutes. Then puree the kohlrabi, adding just enough of the cooking water through the tube to make a silky puree—not so thin that it runs, but about like a minimally grainy sauce, a puree that holds its shape like a soft, slightly runny whipped cream. Less liquid is better.

3. Heat a grill pan over medium-high heat. Grill the scallions until marked and soft, turning occasionally, about 4 minutes. Transfer to a platter; maintain the heat under the grill pan.

4. Grill the mushrooms just until barely softened, less than 1 minute, without turning. Transfer to the platter with the scallions.

5. To serve, divide the kohlrabi puree among 8 small serving plates. Top with scallions and mushrooms, all grill-marked sides up. Sprinkle with the peanuts. Whisk the oil and sambal in a small bowl. Drizzle on top.

AHEAD
- Make the puree up to 4 hours in advance. Store, covered, at room temperature.
- Make the rest of the recipe through step 4 up to 1 hour in advance. Store the scallions and mushrooms at room temperature.

NOTES
- To make that kohlrabi puree, start out with no cooking water in the food processor, then add it in very small amounts, no more than 1 tablespoon for the first splash, then in smaller increments after that.
- The best tool for turning and eventually retrieving those softened scallions are cooking tongs.
- Enoki mushrooms are sometimes sold attached in a clump. Clean them but keep them together for easier grilling. You can break them apart right before serving.
- Sambal oelek is one of dozens of sambals, which are hot sauces from Southeast Asia and the Philippines. Sambal oelek is a wet mix of chiles, vinegar, and salt; other sambals will be too complicated for this dish.

A MENU
FIRST LARGE PLATE: Braised Kabocha Squash, Scallions, Miso (page 179)

SMALL PLATE: Kohlrabi, Enoki, Peanuts, Grilled Scallions

SECOND LARGE PLATE: Coconut Tofu, Sour Beans (page 202)

DESSERT: Fresh mango slices drizzled with aged, syrupy balsamic vinegar

POUR
A light Sancerre to offer a mild acidity that further highlights the mushrooms' and kohlrabi's sweetness without muting the fire of the sambal

Stewed Giant Lima Beans, Dandelion Greens, Feta

8 SERVINGS

Giant lima beans are sometimes cooked with tomatoes and red pepper flakes for a meze plate at a Mediterranean meal. We've tweaked that homey preparation to make even heartier bowlfuls, spiked with peppery dandelion greens, summery comfort in a dish fit for a chilly evening. If it all sounds complex, we've still got you covered: The sour feta will provide the necessary counterweight to those flavors.

1 pound dried giant lima beans

2 tablespoons olive oil

1 large yellow onion, chopped

2 medium garlic cloves, minced

1 quart vegetable broth

1 can (15 ounces) diced tomatoes

¼ cup dry white wine, such as Chardonnay

2 teaspoons dried oregano

½ teaspoon red pepper flakes

8 ounces small dandelion greens, washed and cut into 2-inch pieces

¼ cup white wine vinegar

2 tablespoons chopped fresh dill fronds

¼ teaspoon salt

8 ounces feta cheese, crumbled

1. Soak the beans in a large bowl of cool water for at least 12 hours but not more than 16 hours. Drain the beans in a colander set in the sink.

2. Set a large saucepan over medium heat for a few minutes, then swirl in the oil. Add the onion and cook, stirring often, until translucent and soft, about 4 minutes. Add the garlic and cook, stirring all the while, for 30 seconds.

3. Add the broth, tomatoes, wine, oregano, and red pepper flakes. Stir in the drained beans, increase the heat to high, and bring to a simmer, stirring occasionally. Cover the pan, reduce the heat to low, and simmer slowly for 1 hour. Uncover and cook, stirring occasionally, until the beans are tender and much of the liquid has been absorbed, about 1 hour longer.

4. Meanwhile, bring a medium saucepan of water to a boil over high heat. Add the greens and blanch for 1 minute from the moment they hit the water. Drain the greens in a colander set in the sink and shake dry.

5. Stir the greens into the saucepan with the beans, along with the vinegar, dill, and salt. Simmer slowly, covered, for 10 minutes over low heat, stirring occasionally but gently. Ladle into small, shallow soup bowls and crumble the feta on top.

AHEAD
● Blanch the greens up to 6 hours in advance. Store, covered, at room temperature.

NOTES
● The desired consistency in step 3 is not soup but stew, thick but not at all dried out. If the mixture dries too quickly, add more broth and reduce the heat further.

● If the greens won't fit in the saucepan all at once, stir in a third or half, wait for them to wilt, then stir in more, until you can get them all in the water.

A MENU
SMALL PLATE: Stewed Giant Lima Beans, Dandelion Greens, Feta

LARGE PLATE: Grilled Cauliflower, Thai Chili Sauce, Sweet Potato Puree (page 180)

PASTA: Fig/Olive Ravioli, Cardamom/Orange Flower Cream (page 154)

DESSERT: Pecan/Coconut Cake, Orange Marmalade (page 269)

POUR
A delicate but perfumed cava to give sweet, light bubbles to an otherwise dense and satisfying stew

Baked Artichokes, Dulse Flakes, Pine Nuts

6 SERVINGS

This Roman casserole is traditionally made with anchovies, but we've replaced them with dulse flakes for a briny, more subtle flavor that better foregrounds the nosy essence of the pine nuts. Although we most often plate our courses, we make exceptions for dishes like this one. Everyone loves to dig in! But remember this tip: If you start family-style service at a dinner party, continue on with it through the courses. Otherwise, during some of the meal your table will have a hole at its center where a platter is supposed to go.

- 8 cups frozen artichoke heart quarters, thawed (about four 9-ounce packages)
- ¼ cup plus 3 tablespoons olive oil, divided
- 3 medium garlic cloves, minced
- 2 tablespoons fresh lemon juice
- 1½ tablespoons minced fresh rosemary
- 1 tablespoon dulse flakes
- ½ teaspoon red pepper flakes
- 1 teaspoon salt, divided
- ⅔ cup panko breadcrumbs
- ½ cup finely grated Parmigiano-Reggiano cheese
- ¼ cup pine nuts
- 2 teaspoons finely grated lemon zest
- ½ teaspoon freshly ground black pepper

1. Position the rack in the center of the oven and heat to 375°F. Gently squeeze the artichoke quarters by the handfuls over the sink to remove excess moisture. Dump them in a big bowl as you finish. Stir in ¼ cup of the oil along with the garlic, lemon juice, rosemary, dulse flakes, red pepper flakes, and ½ teaspoon of the salt. Scrape this mixture into a 6-cup oval baking or gratin dish.

2. Pulse the panko, Parmesan, pine nuts, lemon zest, black pepper, remaining 3 tablespoons olive oil, and remaining ½ teaspoon salt in a food processor until the mixture resembles coarse sand. Sprinkle and spread this mixture over the artichoke quarters.

3. Bake until bubbling and browned, about 25 minutes. Cool for 5 to 10 minutes before scooping it up onto serving plates.

MORE

A little dollop of sour cream or crème fraîche on top of each serving would be welcome. Or offer warm, grilled lemon wedges.

NOTE

- Dulse flakes are bits of a large, red sea algae, dried and eaten across the world as a briny snack. Look for them in large supermarkets, particularly in the health food aisle, or in almost all health food stores.

A MENU

FIRST SMALL PLATE: Baked Artichokes, Dulse Flakes, Pine Nuts

SECOND SMALL PLATE: Squash Noodles, Almond Chimichurri (page 45)

THIRD SMALL PLATE: Blue Cheese Cheesecake, Walnuts, Dill (page 86)

DESSERT: Pecan Baklava, Fennel Syrup (page 245)

POUR

A sharp, somewhat acidic, and fairly young Grüner Veltliner to refresh the palate between bites

Cauliflower/Green Olive Gratin

8 SERVINGS

Don't wait for a winter dinner party to make this pure-comfort dish. It's a rich, briny take on a traditional gratin: a creamy Mornay sauce for the cauliflower with a crunchy breadcrumb topping. It'll be a wonderful addition to a summer meal, particularly if it's served at room temperature. In fact, it's probably hearty enough to be a "large plate" if you pair it with a generous selection of hot and sweet pickles. (In which case, it'll probably make just 6 servings.)

3 tablespoons olive oil

1 large cauliflower head (about 3 pounds), cored and cut into small florets

½ cup thinly sliced pitted green olives

1 large shallot, sliced into thin rings

2 tablespoons unsalted butter

2 tablespoons all-purpose flour

1½ cups whole or low-fat milk

½ cup finely grated Gruyère cheese (about 2 ounces)

½ teaspoon freshly grated nutmeg

½ teaspoon salt

½ teaspoon freshly ground black pepper

¼ cup panko breadcrumbs

¼ cup finely grated Parmigiano-Reggiano cheese (about 1 ounce)

1. Position the rack in the center of the oven and heat to 375°F.

2. Pour the oil into a 14-inch oval gratin dish or into a 9 x 13-inch broilerproof baking dish. Add the cauliflower, olives, and shallot. Toss well so everything's coated. Bake until tender and lightly browned, stirring occasionally, about 20 minutes. Transfer to a wire rack.

3. Use oven mitts to move the oven rack 4 to 6 inches from the broiler. Heat that broiler.

4. Melt the butter in a large skillet over medium heat. Whisk in the flour to make a smooth paste, then whisk in the milk in a slow, steady, thin stream. Continue whisking over the heat until the mixture thickens slightly. Stir in the Gruyère, nutmeg, salt, and pepper. Pour the sauce over the cauliflower mixture in the baking dish.

5. Mix the panko and Parmesan in a small bowl. Sprinkle the panko mixture over the casserole, coating it completely. Broil until browned and bubbling, 1 to 2 minutes, taking care not to burn the breadcrumbs. Cool for 10 minutes before dishing up with a large spoon.

AHEAD

• Serve the dish at room temperature. Make it up to 2 hours in advance, then store it, uncovered, at room temperature.

NOTES

• As you pour the hot sauce over the vegetables, try not to disturb them so they rest in a fairly even layer in the pan.

• Plain breadcrumbs will not get crunchy enough under the broiler before they burn. Thus, panko are the best option.

A MENU

FIRST SMALL PLATE: Blistered Butter Beans, Pecans, Fennel (page 46)

SOUP: White Gazpacho, Fried Fennel Seeds (page 125)

SECOND SMALL PLATE: Cauliflower/Green Olive Gratin

SALAD: Roasted Pears, Fig Caponata (page 110)

DESSERT: Olive Oil/Vin Santo Cake, Pine Nuts, Dried Apples (page 265)

POUR

A sturdy, full Cabernet Franc with a long, blueberry-jam finish that can cut through but also connect the bites of this rich casserole

Parsnip Flans

6 SERVINGS

Chilly evenings call out for a creamy starter like these flans, savory baked custards that are comfort food deluxe. We can't wait for the abundance of parsnips from our CSA in the autumn, mostly because we're such fans of that herbal sweetness the root affords. Believe it or not, this recipe started out as a sweet parsnip dessert flan; it slowly morphed into this more savory preparation for dinner parties because we felt it better highlighted the vegetable's unique perfume.

1 pound parsnips

1½ tablespoons unsalted butter, plus more for greasing the ramekins

1 small white onion, chopped (about ¾ cup)

1 cup vegetable broth

½ cup heavy or whipping cream

4 large egg yolks

1 teaspoon salt

½ teaspoon ground white pepper

1. Peel the parsnips, then cut them into 2-inch chunks. Cut these in half or in quarters; slice out and discard the tough, white cores. Bring a large saucepan of water to a boil over high heat. Add the parsnip bits and boil until soft, about 10 minutes. Drain completely in a colander set in the sink.

2. Melt the butter in a large skillet over medium-low heat. Add the onion, reduce the heat to low, and cook, stirring often, until softened and golden, about 10 minutes.

3. Scrape the contents of the skillet into a blender. Add the boiled parsnips and cool for 15 minutes. Add the broth, cream, egg yolks, salt, and white pepper. Blend until smooth, stopping the machine and scraping down the inside of the canister at least once.

AHEAD

● Make the puree through step 3 up to 1 day in advance. Store it, covered, in the fridge, but allow the puree to come back to room temperature before continuing.

● Bake the flans up to 2 hours in advance, holding them at room temperature on the wire rack.

MORE

Blend 2 cups packed watercress leaves, 2 to 3 tablespoons olive oil, and a pinch of salt in a blender. Smear some of this puree on the plates before setting the flan on top for a peppery contrast to the creamy flan.

GARNISH

Snip chives to sprinkle on the flans. Or sprinkle them with fresh thyme leaves, finely grated lemon zest, or even finely chopped toasted pecans.

4. Position the rack in the center of the oven and heat to 350°F.

5. Meanwhile, butter the insides of six ¾- to 1-cup ovenproof ramekins. Set them in a large, high-sided roasting pan. Bring a kettle of water to a boil over high heat.

6. Set the roasting pan on the pulled-out oven rack, and pour ½ cup parsnip mixture into each ramekin. Fill the roasting pan with boiling water so that it comes between one-third and halfway up the sides of the ramekins. Gently slide the rack into the oven.

7. Bake until set when jiggled, about 35 minutes. Remove the ramekins from the water bath and transfer to a wire rack to cool for at least 15 minutes.

8. Serve in their ramekins or invert each onto a plate. (If any stick, run a very thin knife around the inside edge of the dish, set a plate over the dish, and invert the whole kit and caboodle before removing the ramekin.)

A MENU

FIRST SMALL PLATE: Roasted Grapes/ Olives (page 37)

SECOND SMALL PLATE: Shredded Beets, Capers, Avocados (page 50)

THIRD SMALL PLATE: Parsnip Flans

FOURTH SMALL PLATE: Crunchy Runner Beans, Pickled Shallots (page 43)

DESSERT: Banana Shortbreads, Peanut Cream, Grape Granita (page 251)

POUR

A light Viognier so it won't compete with the cream but merely accent it with a soft sweetness amid the pear and apricot notes

Portobello Confit, Pickled Ramps

8 SERVINGS

Poaching portobello caps in olive oil yields a sumptuous first course. But maybe one too rich on its own? So we spike those mushrooms with vinegar-laced, vibrant ramps for a contrast that lifts the plate into something ethereal—a new take, as it were, on "oil and vinegar." (We've also been known to confit these mushrooms with no dinner party in the offing and chop them up as condiment for bean burgers.)

1 pound ramps, washed, roots and any greens removed

1 cinnamon stick (4-inch)

4 fresh sprigs thyme

1½ cups red wine vinegar

1½ cups sugar

8 large portobello mushroom caps

1 medium leek (white and pale green parts only), halved lengthwise, carefully washed, and thinly sliced

2 (4-inch) fresh rosemary sprigs

4 medium garlic cloves

4 cups olive oil, or more as needed

1. To pickle the ramps, place them in a 1-quart canning jar along with the cinnamon stick and thyme sprigs. Bring the vinegar and sugar to a boil in a large saucepan over high heat, stirring until the sugar dissolves. Pour the boiling mixture over the ingredients in the jar. Cool at room temperature for 1 hour, then seal with the lid or foil (see Note) secured with a rubber band and refrigerate for at least 24 hours.

2. Position the rack in the center of the oven and heat to 225°F.

3. Lay the mushrooms gill side down in a large roasting pan. Sprinkle the leek, rosemary, and garlic around them (but not on them). Pour the oil over the mushrooms until they could be submerged. (They won't actually be, because they float.) Set an ovenproof plate or plates on top of them to keep them in the oil.

4. Cover with foil and bake until the mushrooms are very tender, about 3 hours 30 minutes. Serve warm or remove them from the oil and cool to room temperature.

5. To serve, place a portobello cap on each serving plate. Drain the ramps and lay them across the mushrooms.

AHEAD

• The ramps can be pickled up to 5 days in advance. Store in the refrigerator.

• The portobello caps can be poached up to 4 hours in advance. Once cooled, store, covered, at room temperature.

LESS

Skip the pickled ramps and top the portobello confit with a store-bought, vinegary chow-chow or coleslaw.

GARNISH

Lay an edible nasturtium on each serving.

NOTES

• Make ramp pesto out of the removed greens, substituting ramp greens for half the basil in your recipe. Or sauté the greens in butter and use them to top a pizza with a spicy tomato sauce.

• Make sure that no foil touches the vinegar marinade in the jar with the ramps. The acid can corrode the foil. A canning lid is the safest bet.

A MENU

FIRST SMALL PLATE: Portobello Confit, Pickled Ramps

SECOND SMALL PLATE: Warm Buffalo Mozzarella, Yellow Tomato Sauce (page 39)

THIRD SMALL PLATE: Roasted Grapes/ Olives (page 37)

FOURTH SMALL PLATE: Masa Tarts, Caramelized Garlic Custard, Radish Slaw (page 79)

DESSERT: Chocolate Pots de Crème (page 253) and Chocolate Chip Cookies, Maple, Tahini, Dates (page 236)

POUR

A refreshing, slightly effervescent pilsner to offer a necessary, lemony sweetness to the oil and vinegar combo

Tomato Gelée, Pistachio Shortbread

8 SERVINGS

Here, the first-course flavor juxtaposition is found between the preparation of two ingredients, not just the ingredients themselves. The two halves of this elegant starter may seem far apart: the old-fashioned tomato gelée (sort of like an aspic but without the consommé) and the crunchy, short crust. The smooth gelée is set off by the crisp crumb below because we used shortening in the shortbread dough rather than butter, thereby giving us less moisture in the final product (and turning the dish vegan). We also used plenty of black pepper for essential pop.

- 1 cup all-purpose flour
- ½ cup solid vegetable shortening (see Note), plus more for greasing
- ½ cup shelled, unsalted pistachios
- ⅓ cup confectioners' sugar
- 1 teaspoon salt, divided
- 2 to 3 tablespoons ice water
- 1¾ pounds plum or Roma tomatoes
- 1 teaspoon freshly ground black pepper
- 2 teaspoons agar-agar

1. Position the rack in the center of the oven and heat to 375°F.

2. Combine the flour, shortening, pistachios, confectioners' sugar, and ½ teaspoon of the salt in a large food processor. Process until finely ground, about like coarse sand. Add 2 tablespoons ice water and pulse to form a dough; add a little more water until the mixture begins to clump.

3. Use a little shortening on a paper towel to grease the inside of an 8-inch square baking pan. Plop the dough into the pan and press it to the sides, coating the bottom evenly and smoothly. Poke the dough all over with a fork to keep it from puffing up.

4. Bake the shortbread until set and firm to the touch, about 15 minutes. Transfer to a wire rack and cool completely in the pan, at least 4 hours.

5. Put a cutting board over the pan, turn it upside down, and release the shortbread inside. Remove the pan (keep the shortbread in place on the cutting board) and line the inside of the baking pan with plastic wrap so that the wrap laps over the edges. Invert the pan over the shortbread and turn the cutting board upside down to drop the shortbread back into the pan.

(continued)

AHEAD
- Make the dish through step 9 up to 2 days in advance. Store, covered, in the refrigerator. Set it out at room temperature for 20 minutes before serving.

LESS
Skip the crust and just make the gelée in a plastic-lined, 8-inch square baking pan. Remove the gelée from the pan, peel off the plastic wrap, and slice into squares. Crumble shortbread cookies, preferably savory shortbreads, over each serving.

MORE
For a vegetarian version, mash 2 tablespoons blue cheese into ¼ cup crème fraîche until fairly smooth and dollop a tiny bit on each square.

NOTES
- Search out expeller-pressed, non-hydrogenated shortening, a better tasting and more healthful alternative to the more standard stuff.

- Agar-agar is a setting agent—that is, a vegetable gelatin—made by boiling down red sea algae. It's used in place of animal-based gelatins throughout much of Asia to create jellylike desserts. Agar-agar (also called just agar or sometimes *kanten*, its Japanese name) is sold in dried strips or a powder. We call for the latter here because it's easier to work with.

6. Chop the tomatoes and transfer them to a food processor. Process until pureed. Put a large colander over a bowl and line the colander with two sheets of cheesecloth or set up a jelly bag over a big bowl. Pour the tomatoes into the colander or bag and drain thoroughly, about 1 hour.

7. Fold up the sides of the cheesecloth or the jelly bag and squeeze gently to release more juice without any pulp. You should end up with 2 cups tomato juice. Stir in the remaining ½ teaspoon salt and the pepper.

8. Mix the agar-agar with 2 tablespoons water in a small saucepan until softened. Set it over medium heat and whisk in 1 cup of the tomato juice. Whisk until dissolved and bubbling, then simmer for 1 minute.

9. Pour this tomato mixture into the bowl with the remaining tomato juice. Whisk well and cool for 15 minutes. Pour over the shortbread crust in the pan. Refrigerate until set, about 2 hours.

10. Use the overlapping plastic wrap like handles and lift the shortbread and its gelée out of the baking pan. Transfer to a cutting board, slip the plastic wrap out from under the shortbread, and slice into 16 squares (2 per serving).

A MENU

SMALL PLATE: Tomato Gelée, Pistachio Shortbread

SALAD: Beet/Orange Salad, Spicy Gingerbread Croutons (page 104)

LARGE PLATE: Goat Cheese Fondue, Grilled Bread, Pears (page 173)

DESSERT: Dark chocolate bars and bourbon

POUR

Ice-cold vodka shots for liquefied clarity against the complex pairing of preparations

Fiddlehead Tacos, Almond Romesco

8 SERVINGS

Who said tacos don't make a sophisticated first course? Especially when we're talking about this crazy combo of ingredients! Here, the corn tortillas, sweet and aromatic, set off the bright but dense mélange of fiddlehead ferns and hominy. Skip the pico de gallo. Instead, top these tacos with our thick, rich, yeasty romesco sauce, sort of like an almond and tomato pesto. Have forks and knives on hand.

1 garlic head (do not peel)

3 cups small fiddlehead ferns, trimmed and washed

10 tablespoons olive oil, divided

1 cup canned hominy, drained and rinsed

1 teaspoon cumin seeds

1 slice (½-inch-thick) stale baguette

1 plum tomato, quartered

1 jarred roasted red pepper

¼ cup blanched almonds

1½ tablespoons fresh lemon juice

8 corn tortillas

1. Position the rack in the center of the oven and heat to 350°F. Cut the top third off the garlic head, exposing most of the cloves below. Wrap the garlic head in foil.

2. Bake the garlic until soft and aromatic, about 1 hour. Set aside to cool at room temperature while you proceed with the recipe.

3. Meanwhile, bring a large saucepan of water to a boil over high heat. Add the fiddleheads and blanch for 3 minutes from the moment they hit the water. Drain in a colander set in the sink.

4. Set a large skillet over medium heat for a couple of minutes, then swirl in 2 tablespoons of the oil. Add the blanched fiddleheads and cook, stirring all the while, for 1 minute. Add the hominy and cumin seeds and cook, stirring often, until the fiddleheads are tender, about 5 minutes. Pour the mixture into a large bowl.

> AHEAD

- Roast the garlic up to 2 days in advance. Store in its foil packet in the fridge.

- Make the almond romesco sauce up to 6 hours in advance. Store, covered, at room temperature.

- Prepare the fiddleheads up to 2 hours in advance. Store, uncovered, at room temperature.

> NOTES

- Fiddlehead ferns are a springtime delicacy in New England and the Canadian Maritimes, around for a couple of weeks before they're gone for another year. Because of quick distribution networks, you can now find this regional ingredient in early May throughout North American supermarkets—if your timing is just right. Otherwise, look for frozen fiddleheads at very high-end markets; thaw according to the package instructions. Look for small, tight heads, barely unrolled. Any yellow or brown discoloration should be removed before cooking. Prepare them on the day of purchase.

- Fiddleheads contain a toxin that can cause stomach distress in many people. The bad chemical is destroyed through proper cooking. Although you lose some of the crunch in the vegetable, it's important to blanch the fiddleheads even before they hit the hot oil in the skillet.

- Romesco sauce is a traditional Iberian condiment of nuts, garlic, and red peppers, thickened with stale bread, often served with fish or grilled spring onions. We've tamed the heat and dropped the spices in this version so the sauce won't overshadow the fiddleheads.

5. Add ½ tablespoon of the oil to the skillet, still over medium heat. Slip in the bread and toast on both sides until browned, about 3 minutes, turning once. Tear the bread into quarters and transfer to a large food processor.

6. Put the tomato quarters in the skillet, still over the heat. Cook, turning often, until somewhat softened, about 3 minutes. Transfer the tomato to the food processor, along with the red pepper, almonds, and lemon juice. Squeeze the roasted garlic cloves into the food processor. Process, drizzling in the remaining 7½ tablespoons olive oil through the tube, until it forms a thick puree, like a pesto.

7. Warm the tortillas on the grate over a low gas flame until lightly marked and softened, about 20 seconds, turning once. If you don't have a gas stove, wrap the tortillas in foil and heat in a 400°F oven until soft, about 20 minutes. Set the warm tortillas on serving plates.

8. Divide the fiddlehead mixture among the tortillas. Drizzle each open taco with 2 to 3 tablespoons of the romesco sauce from the food processor.

▶ **A MENU**

SMALL PLATE: Fiddlehead Tacos, Almond Romesco

SOUP: Gazpacho Shooters (page 126)

LARGE PLATE: Tortilla Casserole, Eggplant, Cheddar (page 214)

DESSERT: Pumpkin Pie Tamales (page 256)

▶ **POUR**

A Tinta Pinheira from Portugal for both its incredibly pronounced plumminess that'll smooth out both the bitterness and the dank earthiness in the fiddleheads

Jerusalem Artichoke Fritters, Cranberries, Almonds

6 SERVINGS

Although preparing a fried first course can be nerve-racking at a dinner party, you just might want to throw caution to the wind for these little bits of crunchy bliss, made with savory Jerusalem artichokes and peppery scallions to contrast with the sour fresh cranberries. It's all spiked with caraway seeds for a beery, aromatic push that actually keeps the others flavors more distinct. (These fritters would also be a great Thanksgiving starter!)

1 pound Jerusalem artichokes, scrubbed but not peeled

3 large eggs, at room temperature and lightly beaten in a small bowl

4 scallions, thinly sliced

½ cup fresh cranberries, chopped

½ cup sliced almonds, toasted

¼ cup all-purpose flour

2 tablespoons yellow cornmeal

1 teaspoon caraway seeds

1 teaspoon salt

½ teaspoon freshly ground black pepper

Olive oil, for deep-frying (2 to 3 cups)

1. Shred the Jerusalem artichokes through the large holes of a box grater and into a large bowl. Stir in the eggs, scallions, cranberries, almonds, flour, cornmeal, caraway seeds, salt, and pepper to form a thick but even batter.

2. Pour about 1 inch of oil into a large, high-sided sauté pan. Clip a deep-frying thermometer to the inside of the pan and heat the oil over medium heat to 350°F.

3. Scoop up ¼ cup of the batter, plop it into the hot oil, and flatten it into a ½-inch-thick patty. Drop the patty in the oil and make a couple more. (No crowding!) Cook until browned and crisp, about 6 minutes, turning once. Adjust the burner heat to keep the oil's temperature constant. Use a slotted spatula to transfer the patties to a wire rack set over paper towels. Continue frying the rest of the patties.

> ### AHEAD
> • The batter can be stirred together up to 30 minutes in advance; cover and let stand at room temperature.
>
> ### MORE
> Serve on a bed of applesauce.
>
> ### NOTES
> • Jerusalem artichokes, sometimes called "sunchokes," are the tuber of a common form of North American sun-flower. The vegetable is mild and starchy, more earthy than a potato, and sweeter, too. We'd be remiss if we didn't tell you they can cause gastric upset in some people. You might poll your guests the week before the party, just to be sure.
> • Flatten the batter in the skillet with the bottom of the measuring cup.
>
> ### A MENU
> FIRST SMALL PLATE: Squash Noodles, Almond Chimichurri (page 45)
>
> PASTA: Polenta, Chestnuts, Balsamic Vinegar, Roasted Radicchio (page 163)
>
> SECOND SMALL PLATE: Jerusalem Artichoke Fritters, Cranberries, Almonds
>
> DESSERT: Summer Pudding, Black Currants, Blackberries (page 263)
>
> ### POUR
> An oaky California Chardonnay to give woody/leathery accents to the sweet/sour flavors in the dish without the complication of red-wine tannins

Chickpea Blini,
Curried Sweet Potatoes

8 SERVINGS

Although we certainly prefer dinner party dishes that can be made ahead and assembled at the last moment, here's one of our notable exceptions. These savory pancakes are topped with a creamy spread made from white sweet potatoes and laced with a tongue-spanking Thai curry paste. Believe it or not, those white sweet potatoes will give the dish a less-sweet finish, a little more earthy than the standard, orange sweet potatoes. If you want a more sugary topping for the blini, substitute Asian purple sweet potatoes, a garish bash of sweet.

- 2 medium white sweet potatoes (about 10 ounces each)
- 1 tablespoon Thai yellow curry paste
- 1 cup chickpea flour
- ⅔ cup regular or low-fat buttermilk
- 1 large egg, at room temperature
- ½ teaspoon ground ginger
- ½ teaspoon salt
- ½ teaspoon freshly ground black pepper
- 1 to 2 tablespoons olive oil, divided
- 6 tablespoons regular or low-fat sour cream

1. Position the rack in the center of the oven and heat to 375°F. Place the sweet potatoes on a large baking sheet and roast until soft, about 45 minutes. Transfer the baking sheet to a wire rack and cool for 15 minutes.

2. Peel the sweet potatoes, transfer them to a large bowl, and mash them with the curry paste.

3. Puree the chickpea flour, buttermilk, egg, ginger, salt, and pepper in a blender until smooth, stopping the machine and scraping down the inside of the canister occasionally.

4. Coat the inside of a 10- or 12-inch nonstick skillet with about 1 teaspoon olive oil, then set it over medium heat for 1 minute. Pour in 2 tablespoons of the batter, like a pancake. Make two or three at a time, depending on the size of your skillet. Cook until small bubbles pop around the batter, 1 to 2 minutes. Flip and continue cooking for 1 minute. Transfer to a large plate or serving platter and continue making more blini, adding more oil for each batch.

5. To serve, lay 2 blini on each plate and top each with 2 tablespoons sweet potato mixture and 2 teaspoons sour cream.

▶ AHEAD

- Bake the sweet potatoes and mix them with the curry paste up to 4 hours in advance. Store, covered, at room temperature.

- Make the blini up to 30 minutes in advance. Store, uncovered, at room temperature.

▶ MORE

Make your own Thai curry paste. Check out the lemongrass paste recipe on page 184.

▶ GARNISH

Snip chives over the blini on the serving plates. Or sprinkle with minced hard-boiled egg.

▶ NOTES

- Chickpea flour is sometimes called garbanzo bean flour or gram flour (not to be confused with "graham flour")—or as *besan* in East Indian markets or *farina di ceci* in Italian ones. Store, tightly covered, in a cool dark pantry for up to 6 months.

- Yellow curry paste shouldn't be confused with yellow curry powder. The former is a Thai or Southeast Asian ingredient, often found in tubs in the international aisle.

▶ A MENU

SMALL PLATE: Chickpea Blini, Curried Sweet Potatoes

LARGE PLATE: Stuffed Pears, Wild Rice, Mushrooms (page 228)

PASTA: Curried Spaetzle, Ginger Broth (page 155)

DESSERT: Dried figs and aged goat cheese

▶ POUR

A chilled Monbazillac to offer copious amounts of honey tones and floral sweetness against the hot curry

Chestnut/Cashew/Porcini Pâté

6 TO 8 SERVINGS

A velvety pâté is a perfect way to start a family-style dinner party, a wonderful first course in the center of the table. Porcinis do most of the heavy lifting here, aided by the creaminess in the cashews and then rounded out by the more economical cremini mushrooms. All in all, this vegan pâté is quite intense and so a great start for a chilly evening. You'll need a main course that's big on sour or spicy flavors to make a good contrast. (And pray for leftovers because you really want a pâté sandwich with romaine lettuce, sliced tomatoes, and deli mustard the next day.)

5 tablespoons olive oil, divided

½ cup thinly sliced shallot (about 1 large)

2 cups thinly sliced cremini mushrooms (about 5 ounces)

2 tablespoons brandy

¾ cup roasted, unsalted cashews

⅓ cup jarred roasted chestnuts

1 tablespoon finely ground dried porcini mushrooms

1 teaspoon dried sage

1 teaspoon dried thyme

½ teaspoon salt

½ teaspoon freshly ground black pepper

¼ teaspoon ground turmeric

1. Set a large, lidded skillet over medium heat for a couple of minutes, then swirl in 2 tablespoons of the oil. Add the shallot and cook, stirring often, until softened, about 4 minutes. Add the mushrooms and cook just until softened and damp, about 2 minutes, stirring almost all the time.

2. Have the skillet's lid nearby. If the exhaust fan is on, turn it off. Add the brandy—be careful, it can ignite—pouring it deliberately and slowly from the side of the pan, not from a great height. If the alcohol flames, cover the skillet immediately, then remove it from the heat for a minute or so. Uncover, put it back over the heat, and continue on. Stir quickly to scrape up any browned bits in the skillet, then scrape the contents of the skillet into a food processor. Cool for 5 minutes.

3. Add the cashews, chestnuts, dried porcini powder, sage, thyme, salt, pepper, turmeric, and the remaining 3 tablespoons oil. Process until smooth, scraping down the bowl a few times to make sure you get every speck of nuts or spices. Scrape and smooth the pâté into a serving bowl, such as a soufflé dish. Cover and refrigerate for at least 4 hours.

AHEAD

● Make the recipe up to 2 days in advance. Store in the refrigerator, but let the pâté come back to room temperature for 1 hour before serving.

MORE

Cut a crunchy loaf of bread into thin slices, then smear one side with a little olive oil. Grill until marked, then serve as a vehicle for the pâté.

GARNISH

Set up everyone's plate with cornichons, sliced radishes, and Dijon mustard, placed around the rim in little piles or dollops. And make sure there's crunchy bread or crackers at the ready.

NOTES

● Don't be tempted to use fresh herbs. The dried ones give the pâté a slightly musky headiness.

● Grind dried porcini in a spice grinder or a scrupulously cleaned and dried electric coffee grinder. If you make more than you need, save it in a small, sealed bag in the freezer to add to soups and stews for a seriously intense flavor pop.

A MENU

SMALL PLATE: Chestnut/Cashew/Porcini Pâté

SALAD: Frisée Salad, Smoked Bread Cubes, Poached Egg (page 120)

LARGE PLATE: Bolita Bean Stew, Fall Vegetables, Lemon Breadcrumbs (page 220)

DESSERT: Fleur de Sel Caramels (page 279)

POUR

An intense, velvety red from Gigondas or Sablet to offer tobacco and leathery notes with jammy fullness

Pulled Vegetable Sliders

8 SERVINGS

By cooking shredded vegetables in an all-American, sweet-and-sour sauce of tomatoes, beer, vinegar, and brown sugar, we can morph them into a dinner-party version of the classic summer sandwich. Admittedly, the vegetables aren't "pulled," but they've got enough of the flavors of the classic pulled dishes from America's barbecue stands that we thought we'd be forgiven a little leeway in the recipe title. These sliders are pretty messy, so be ready with napkins. They're also quite filling, so plan on slowing down. Don't rush off to the next course. If you've got kids playing video games in the next room during dinner, double this recipe and offer it to them, too.

1 can (15 ounces) crushed tomatoes (about 1¾ cups)

½ cup cider vinegar

¼ cup packed dark brown sugar

2 tablespoons tomato paste

1 tablespoon mustard powder

1 tablespoon sweet smoked paprika

1 teaspoon dried oregano

½ teaspoon celery seeds

½ teaspoon ground cloves

½ teaspoon hot red pepper sauce

1½ cups shredded carrots

1½ cups shredded yellow potatoes (no need to peel)

4 cups shredded Savoy cabbage

1 bottle (12 ounces) dark beer, preferably a porter, divided

8 small challah rolls

1. Combine the crushed tomatoes, vinegar, brown sugar, tomato paste, mustard powder, smoked paprika, oregano, celery seeds, cloves, and hot sauce in a large pot or Dutch oven over medium heat, stirring until the brown sugar dissolves. Stir in the carrots and potatoes, then bring to a simmer. Cover, reduce the heat to low, and simmer slowly for 10 minutes, stirring occasionally.

2. Stir in the cabbage and ¼ cup of the beer. Cover and continue cooking, stirring occasionally, until the vegetables are tender, about 20 minutes, adding more beer as necessary to keep the vegetables from scorching. If you end up adding too much beer, simply cook uncovered for a couple of minutes, stirring almost all the while, until the mixture is fairly dry, not soupy at all.

3. Mound the vegetable mixture onto the bottom of the challah roll set on each of 8 serving plates. Top each with the bun's other half.

AHEAD

● Make the slider filling up to 24 hours in advance. Store, covered, in the refrigerator. Reheat for 15 minutes over medium heat, stirring often, before serving.

LESS

Look for shredded vegetables on the salad bar at your supermarket.

GARNISH

Top the "pulled" vegetables with pickled jalapeño rings, pickle relish, chow-chow, or even a dab of creamy coleslaw.

NOTES

● The carrots and potatoes should be shredded through the large holes of a box grater or with the shredding blade of a food processor. The cabbage can be shredded with a knife after coring; lay the vegetable on its side and slice it widthwise into very thin strips, less than ¼ inch each.

● Unfortunately, vegetables lose essential moisture in transport and on the shelf. Your vegetables may take longer to get tender than we suggest. If so, add a little more beer and keep the pan tightly covered as they continue to soften.

A MENU

SMALL PLATE: Pulled Vegetable Sliders

SALAD: Peanut Chaat, Cardamom Yogurt (page 107)

LARGE PLATE: Stir-Fried Bok Choy, Dried Mushrooms, Preserved Black Beans (page 183)

DESSERT: Maple/Oat Blondies (page 239) and Vanilla Gelato (page 270)

POUR

A dark porter that offers subtle bitter notes to the sweet/sour palette

Raclette/Potato/Pickle Focaccia

8 SERVINGS

Sometimes, the best dishes for dinner parties are based on old-fashioned ones, morphed with modern flare. Here's the old '60s standby: raclette, a mélange of melted cheese, pickles, potatoes, and bread. We've turned it into a focaccia—the chewy, homemade bread—to balance the slightly sour, rich cheese. You may just want to try this recipe some time over beer or cocktails with no dinner party in sight.

⅔ cup lukewarm water (105° to 115°F)

1½ teaspoons active dry yeast

½ teaspoon sugar

½ teaspoon salt

1 cup all-purpose flour, plus more for dusting

1 cup bread flour

Olive oil, for greasing

8 small red potatoes

3 tablespoons Dijon mustard

8 ounces raclette cheese, shredded

12 cornichon pickles, thinly sliced

1. Mix the water, yeast, sugar, and salt in a large bowl. Set aside until foamy and bubbling, about 5 minutes.

2. Add both flours and mix until a soft dough forms. Turn the dough out onto a lightly floured, clean, dry surface and knead until smooth, up to 15 minutes.

3. Lightly coat the inside of a large bowl with olive oil. Shape the dough into a compact lump and dump it into the bowl. Turn the dough over so it's lightly coated with oil. Cover and set aside to rise in a warm, draft-free place until doubled in bulk, about 2 hours.

4. Meanwhile, boil or steam the potatoes until tender. Place them in a strainer and rinse with cool water to stop the cooking. Drain thoroughly, then slice them into thin rounds.

5. Position the rack in the center of the oven and heat to 400°F. Lightly grease a large rimmed baking sheet with olive oil. Turn the dough onto the baking sheet and use your fingertips to dimple it into about a 9 x 15-inch rectangle. (Rustic is good!)

6. Smear the mustard over the dough, leaving a ½-inch border all around. Top with the cheese, thinly sliced potatoes, and sliced cornichons. Bake until the cheese has melted and is bubbling, about 20 minutes. Cool on a rack for 10 minutes before slicing into squares.

AHEAD

● Make the entire, topped focaccia up to 2 hours in advance. Serve at room temperature.

LESS

Use store-bought pizza dough.

NOTES

● Raclette is a semifirm, mild, cow's milk cheese, renowned for its fantastic meltability.

● You can also knead the dough with a dough hook in a stand mixer at medium speed for 10 minutes.

A MENU

FIRST SMALL PLATE: Blistered Butter Beans, Pecans, Fennel (page 46)

SALAD: Apple Slaw, Fried Chickpeas (page 108)

SECOND SMALL PLATE: Raclette/Potato/Pickle Focaccia

SOUP: Plum Soup, Cinnamon, Cloves (page 121)

DESSERT: Almond/Cardamom Biscotti (page 238)

POUR

A chilled Chasselas from Switzerland, considered the perfect pairing with raclette because of its dry, mineraly finish

Masa Tarts, Caramelized Garlic Custard, Radish Slaw

6 TARTS

This substantial starter is a mash-up of three preparations: a hearty crust, a creamy filling, and a bracing, peppery, raw-vegetable slaw. Given that complication, you might actually want to start off with another small plate that leads into this one, something lighter and brighter. Then follow this up with a third small plate, again fairly light. As to the tarts themselves, by combining masa harina with flour, we can make a crust that replicates the dough in tamales. We then fill those tarts with a flanlike cream and add the slaw on top. In a word, heaven.

1 garlic head (do not peel)

2 cups all-purpose flour, plus more for dusting

2 cups masa harina

1¾ teaspoons salt, divided

16 tablespoons (2 sticks) cold unsalted butter, cut into small bits

½ cup solid vegetable shortening, preferably expeller-pressed

⅓ to ⅔ cup ice-cold water

1½ cups whole or low-fat milk

4 large egg yolks

1 cup shredded red radishes

1 tablespoon fresh lime juice

½ teaspoon ground cumin

1. Position the rack in the center of the oven and heat to 350°F.

2. Slice about a quarter off the top of the garlic head, cutting through and/or exposing most of the cloves below. Wrap the garlic head tightly in a small foil packet, set it on a baking sheet, and roast for 1 hour, or until the cloves inside are soft and sweet. Open the packet and cool on a plate for at least 1 hour. Leave the oven on.

3. Meanwhile, combine the all-purpose flour, masa harina, and 1 teaspoon of the salt in a large bowl. Use a pastry cutter or a fork to cut the butter and the shortening into the flour mixture until the whole thing resembles coarse sand. Stir in just enough cold water to form a coherent dough, at least ⅓ cup but perhaps up to ⅔ cup. It's best to work in small increments so you can tell when the dough comes together. It shouldn't be sticky but should cohere into a soft mass.

4. Lightly flour a clean, dry work surface. Roll the dough into a sheet about ¼ inch thick and cut this sheet into six 6-inch rounds, gathering fragments together and rerolling them as necessary. Lay these rounds

(continued)

AHEAD

● Roast the garlic up to 1 day in advance. Store in its packet at room temperature.

● Rather than serving warm flans, make them up to 6 hours ahead and store at room temperature without the topping, covered with a clean kitchen towel when cooled.

● Shred the radishes up to 4 hours in advance. Store, covered, at room temperature in a small bowl.

LESS

Instead of roasting garlic, substitute ¼ cup roasted garlic cloves purchased from the salad bar at your supermarket.

GARNISH

Sprinkle pomegranate seeds around the plates.

NOTE

● Look for the necessary small tart pans at specialty kitchen stores or online.

in six 4½-inch individual tart pans with removable bottoms, pressing the dough against the sides and bottom to make an even crust. Set the tart pans on a large rimmed baking sheet.

5. Squeeze the soft garlic pulp from the skins into a large blender. Add the milk, egg yolks, and ½ teaspoon of the salt. Cover and blend until smooth, stopping the machine and scraping down the inside of the canister occasionally to make sure all the garlic gets pureed.

6. Pour this garlic mixture evenly into the tart shells. Bake until set when jiggled, about 25 minutes. Transfer the warm tarts to a wire rack to cool a bit, at least 20 minutes.

7. As the tarts cool, toss the shredded radishes with the lime juice, cumin, and remaining ¼ teaspoon salt in a large bowl.

8. To serve, first unmold the tarts: Slip off the outer rings of the tart pans, then run a long, thin knife between the tart and the pan's bottom to remove the latter. Transfer the tarts to serving plates and top each with a small mound of the radish slaw.

A MENU

SMALL PLATE: Masa Tarts, Caramelized Garlic Custard, Radish Slaw

SOUP: Pear Soup, Ginger, Buttery Leeks (page 129)

LARGE PLATE: Stuffed Escarole, Agrodolce Sauce (page 223)

DESSERT: Dark chocolate bars and grappa

POUR

A highball of Bonal (an herbal, gentian-and-quinine aperitif from France), soda, ice, and a lemon twist for a dark, slightly bitter taste against the more complex flavor palette in the dish

Butternut Squash Tart, Toasted Almonds, Roquefort

8 SERVINGS

Because roasted butternut squash is so sweet, we controlled its natural sugariness in this creamy, even savory tart with slightly sour Parmigiano-Reggiano and lots of ground nuts—and then a rich Roquefort sauce! That'll knock the sugariness right off the plate and let you experience the butternut squash without incessant caramelization, a little more earthy and mellower than you might expect. You'll need to watch the tart carefully during the last 10 minutes or so of its baking: There's a fine line between set and dry. Keep tapping the pan to see just when the tart firms up at its center. Once it's out of the oven, cool it to room temperature before you attempt to slice it into servings.

▶ **AHEAD**

● Keep the baked tart on the wire rack for up to 4 hours—or make it the day before and store, covered, in the refrigerator once cooled. If refrigerated, allow the tart to come back to room temperature before unmolding and slicing into wedges.

● Make the sauce up to 2 hours in advance. Store, covered, on the back of the stove. Warm over very low heat, stirring often, just before serving.

▶ **LESS**

Look for cubed butternut squash in the produce section of your supermarket.

TART

- 8 cups peeled, seeded, and cubed butternut squash
- 1 medium yellow onion, chopped
- 3 tablespoons olive oil
- 4 tablespoons (½ stick) unsalted butter, plus more for greasing the pan
- ¼ cup all-purpose flour
- 2 cups whole or low-fat milk
- 2 ounces Parmigiano-Reggiano cheese, finely grated (about ½ cup)
- 3 large egg yolks
- 1 teaspoon salt
- ½ teaspoon freshly grated nutmeg
- ½ teaspoon freshly ground black pepper
- ½ cup finely ground toasted almonds

SAUCE

- 1 tablespoon unsalted butter
- 3 tablespoons finely chopped shallot
- 1 tablespoon white wine vinegar
- 6 ounces Roquefort cheese

1. To make the tart: Position the rack in the center of the oven and heat to 350°F.

2. Mix the squash, onion, and olive oil in a large roasting pan. Roast until the squash is tender, about 1 hour, tossing at least twice. Transfer the roasting pan to a rack and cool for at least 30 minutes. Leave the oven on.

3. Meanwhile, melt the butter in a large saucepan over medium-low heat. Whisk in the flour until a paste forms, then whisk in the milk in a slow, steady stream until the flour dissolves. Continue whisking until the mixture bubbles and thickens a bit, about 2 minutes. Set the pan aside off the heat to cool for 30 minutes.

4. Scrape the contents of the roasting pan into a large food processor and process until smooth, scraping down the inside of the bowl at least once. Add the thickened milk mixture and process until smooth. Add the Parmesan, egg yolks, salt, nutmeg, and pepper; process again until smooth.

5. Grease the inside walls and bottom of a 9-inch springform pan with some butter, then add the ground nuts and turn the pan to coat the sides and bottom thoroughly. Pour in the batter from the food processor. Bake until the custard is browned and set when the pan is tapped, about 1 hour, maybe a little more. Cool on a wire rack for at least 1 hour.

6. To make the sauce: Melt the butter in a medium saucepan over medium heat. Add the shallot and cook, stirring often, until softened, about 3 minutes. Stir in the vinegar and keep stirring until it's almost evaporated. Crumble in the cheese, reduce the heat to low, and stir until it melts.

7. To serve, unlatch the springform pan and unmold the tart. Spoon a small pool of the warm sauce onto small serving plates. Slice the tart into wedges and set one piece on each plate, preferably standing up on its bottom like a tall slice of cake.

A MENU

FIRST SMALL PLATE: Steamed Artichokes, Red Peppers, Basil (page 42)

SECOND SMALL PLATE: Butternut Squash Tart, Toasted Almonds, Roquefort

THIRD SMALL PLATE: Asparagus Spears, Pickled Radicchio (page 40)

PASTA: Orecchiette, Cauliflower, Raisins, Olives (page 156)

DESSERT: Sliced, cold, ripe peaches and an aged, firm goat Gouda.

POUR

A crisp, light, cold Sauvignon Blanc with plenty of grapey notes to bring a floral balance to the dish

Potato/Cucumber Mille-Feuille

6 SERVINGS

A mille-feuille (*meel-FUH-ee*, "thousand leaves") is a French concoction, and usually an afternoon sweet—lots of flaky layers held together by pastry cream. Here, we've transformed that idea into first-course fare. The creaminess of potatoes and the firm bite of cucumber "noodles" are complemented by the savory, dill-loaded sour cream. The final preparation is the odd paradox of crunchy velvetiness, all bound up in a summery blast. You'll definitely need to put out knives for this course. In fact, we often break out the steak knives, so that we don't risk a mille-feuille sliding off a plate and into someone's lap.

2 large russet (baking) potatoes
About ½ cup olive oil

1 large cucumber

½ cup regular or reduced-fat sour cream

1 tablespoon minced dill fronds

1 tablespoon white balsamic vinegar

½ teaspoon salt

1. Position the rack in the center of the oven and heat to 375°F. Generously oil a large rimmed baking sheet.

2. Peel the potatoes, then cut them lengthwise into ⅛-inch-thick slices, using either a mandoline or a *very* sharp, thin knife. Lay them in a single layer on the baking sheet and lightly oil their tops.

3. Bake the potatoes until lightly browned, about 20 minutes. Transfer the baking sheet to a wire rack. Cool for 10 minutes, then carefully transfer the slices to the rack itself so they continue to cool off the baking sheet.

4. Meanwhile, peel the cucumber and cut it lengthwise into ⅛-inch-thick slices, working down to the core on all sides before discarding the core.

5. Cut the cucumber slices so they are approximately the length of the potato slices. Whisk together the sour cream, dill, vinegar, and salt in a small bowl.

6. Now build the mille-feuilles on serving plates: 1 potato slice, 1 cucumber slice, 1 teaspoon sour cream mixture—then repeat two more times with a potato slice added to the top of each stack.

▶ AHEAD

● Prepare the sour cream mixture up to 8 hours in advance. Cover and refrigerate until 1 hour before you're ready to serve it.

● Prepare the potato and cucumber slices up to 3 hours before dinner. Store at room temperature.

▶ GARNISH

Lay a pickled baby carrot or pickled green bean on each plate.

▶ NOTE

● To make a vegan version of this dish, substitute a cashew cream for the sour cream. To make cashew cream: Soak 1 cup raw cashews in a bowl of water overnight. Drain in a colander set in the sink. Add the nuts to a blender along with the juice of a medium lemon and 1 teaspoon salt. Cover and blend until a smooth cream, scraping down the inside of the canister occasionally and adding dribs and drabs of cool tap water if the mixture refuses to blend well. Store in a covered bowl in the fridge for up to 1 week.

▶ A MENU

FIRST LARGE PLATE: Asparagus/Morel Sauté, Poached Eggs (page 177)

SMALL PLATE: Potato/Cucumber Mille-Feuille

SECOND LARGE PLATE: Ratatouille Crudo (page 171)

DESSERT: Walnut/Honey Semifreddo, Pomegranate Molasses (page 257)

▶ POUR

A chilled Bourgogne Mousseux (that is, a red crémant) to provide some bubbles that will keep the dish light, while also offering more pronounced tannins to cut through the cream filling

Blue Cheese Cheesecake, Walnuts, Dill

8 SERVINGS

We're unabashed fans of savory cheesecakes, a festive start to a meal that should be followed up with less pungent, sweeter fare in another small plate or the main course. With nuts and aromatic herbs in the mix, plus some spinach to add necessary moisture as well as a slightly bitter back taste among the more distinct flavors, this tart will prove irresistible. And we know this from experience. We once made this first course for a dinner party and made the mistake of leaving it out in the kitchen while we busied ourselves making cocktails and such. Before we knew it, our guests had cut into the cheesecake and polished half of it off. Ah, well. So went the first course at that dinner party.

Unsalted butter, for greasing the pan

¼ cup finely ground walnuts

¼ cup unseasoned dried breadcrumbs

1 teaspoon dried thyme

1 pound regular or reduced-fat cream cheese

2 ounces blue cheese, crumbled

½ cup sliced almonds, toasted

5 ounces frozen chopped spinach, thawed and squeezed dry

2 large eggs, at room temperature

¼ cup heavy cream

2 tablespoons all-purpose flour

1 teaspoon dried dill

¾ teaspoon freshly ground black pepper

> **AHEAD**
>
> ● Make the cheesecake up to 2 hours in advance and store it in the soufflé dish, covered, at room temperature. Or make it up to 3 days in advance and store it, covered, in the fridge. If refrigerated, allow it to come back to room temperature before unmolding and serving.

> **GARNISH**
>
> Pile a little mâche or baby arugula leaves, dressed with a light lemony vinaigrette, next to each slice.

> **NOTES**
>
> ● Make sure the spinach is squeezed dry. Work by the handful over the sink. The amount required is half a standard 10-ounce carton.
>
> ● For a lighter version, use cream cheese that is labeled ⅓-less-fat, not the "light" cream cheese that is about half the fat of standard cream cheese. (And do not use fat-free cream cheese under any circumstances.)

1. Position the rack in the center of the oven and heat to 325°F. Lightly butter the inside of a high-sided, round, 1-quart soufflé dish.

2. Combine the walnuts, breadcrumbs, and thyme in a small bowl. Pour the mixture into the prepared soufflé dish and turn the dish so the sides and bottom are coated in an even film of the breadcrumb mixture. Leave any excess mixture in an even layer across the bottom.

3. Place the cream cheese, blue cheese, sliced almonds, and spinach in a large food processor and process until smooth. Scrape down the inside of the bowl, add the eggs and cream, and process until smooth. Add the flour, dill, and pepper and process until well combined.

4. Spoon and spread this mixture carefully into the soufflé dish, taking care to keep the bottom crumb layer intact. Set the soufflé dish in a large roasting pan. Set the roasting pan on the pulled-out oven rack and fill the pan about halfway with hot tap water.

5. Bake until somewhat browned and set when tapped, about 45 minutes. Cool on a wire rack for 1 hour. Set a cutting board over the soufflé dish, invert both together, let the cheesecake fall free, and remove the soufflé dish. Slice into 8 wedges, then invert these crust side down as you set them on serving plates.

◗ A MENU

FIRST SMALL PLATE: Blue Cheese Cheesecake, Walnuts, Dill

SECOND SMALL PLATE: Stir-Fried Parsnips, Black Pepper, Caramel (page 49)

LARGE PLATE: Buttery Black-Eyed Pea Stew, Fried Corn Cakes (page 196)

DESSERT: Porter Pie, Graham Cracker Crust, Meringue (page 260)

◗ POUR

A chilled, dry, sparkling rosé to add sweet floral notes to the dish while those bubbles keep the palate fresh

Asiago Cookies, Tahini/Lentil Cream

16 COOKIES

Who doesn't love presents? And when they're given at a dinner party? Even better! We often serve these little cookies in gift boxes, wrapped with raffia, one at each place at the table. Guests unwrap theirs to find savory, crunchy, cheese-laced cookies inside. In fact, they're sandwich creams, although the filling isn't really a cream at all. It's a smooth but earthy lentil spread, rather Middle Eastern in its flavor palette. In other words, the whole megillah is ridiculously over the top. If you don't have a dinner party in the near future, try these cookies at a cocktail party soon.

AHEAD

- Make, wrap, and store the dough log in the refrigerator for up to 3 days.

- Prepare the lentil filling up to 1 day in advance. Store, covered, in the fridge but allow to come back to room temperature for 1 hour before using.

- Bake the cookies up to 4 hours in advance and store at room temperature, uncovered, on a wire rack.

NOTE

- The cookies won't stay crisp if you fill them early. Plan on sandwiching them no more than 30 minutes before serving.

COOKIES

- 12 tablespoons (1½ sticks) cool unsalted butter, cut into little bits
- 8 ounces aged Asiago cheese, finely grated
- 1½ cups all-purpose flour
- 2 teaspoons finely grated lemon zest
- 1 teaspoon freshly ground black pepper
- ½ teaspoon salt
- 6 tablespoons cold whole or low-fat milk

FILLING

- 6 ounces brown lentils
- 1 scallion, thinly sliced
- 2 tablespoons chopped fresh parsley leaves
- 2 tablespoons fresh lemon juice
- 1 tablespoon tahini
- ½ teaspoon salt

1. To make the cookies: Process the butter and Asiago in a large food processor until the mixture resembles coarse sand. Add the flour, lemon zest, pepper, and salt and process until dry and crumbly. Add the milk and pulse repeatedly to form a dough, scraping down the inside of the bowl with a rubber spatula at least once.

2. Gather the dough together and dump it out onto a clean, dry counter or cutting board. Form the dough into an 8-inch log, wrap it in plastic wrap, and refrigerate for at least 24 hours.

3. Position the rack in the center of the oven and heat to 350°F.

(continued)

4. Slice the log into thirty-two ¼-inch-thick rounds. Space the rounds evenly over a large rimmed baking sheet. Bake until lightly browned and set, about 18 minutes. Cool on the baking sheet on a wire rack for 5 minutes, then transfer the cookies to the rack to cool completely.

5. To make the filling: Fill a large saucepan about two-thirds full of water and bring to a boil over high heat. Add the lentils, reduce the heat to medium, and boil until the lentils are tender, about 20 minutes. Drain in a colander set in the sink and rinse with cool water to stop the cooking. Drain well.

6. Pour the lentils into a clean, dry food processor. Add the scallion, parsley, lemon juice, tahini, and salt. Process until a paste, scraping down the inside of the bowl once.

7. To assemble the cookies, use about 2 tablespoons lentil mixture as the filling between 2 cookies, thereby making 16 sandwich cookies.

◗ A MENU

FIRST SMALL PLATE: Asiago Cookies, Tahini/Lentil Cream

SECOND SMALL PLATE: Butternut Squash Tart, Toasted Almonds, Roquefort (page 82)

PASTA: Drunken Spaghetti, Pine Nuts, Parsley (page 137)

DESSERT: Chocolate Chip Cookies, Maple, Tahini, Dates (page 236) and aged Armagnac

◗ POUR

A red, semisweet Banyuls, often served with dessert, but to match the cheese *and* bring out the lemony notes

VEGAN

Red Cabbage Pot Stickers, Raisin Chipotle Dip

32 POT STICKERS

Pot stickers may be our quintessential dinner-party food. Yes, they take a lot of work, but they're make-aheads, finished off while our guests are sitting down at the table. Although we've developed lots of vegetarian and vegan recipes over the years, these are our clear favorite, a flight of fancy: savory red cabbage and scallions, laced with five-spice powder, then dunked in an East-West mash-up of raisins, ginger, soy sauce, and chipotle. The flavors offer an unforgettable set of side-by-side flavor contrasts, a new experience for probably everyone at the table.

- 2 tablespoons toasted sesame oil
- 4 cups finely chopped red cabbage (about a 1-pound head)
- ¼ cup minced scallions
- 2 tablespoons rice vinegar
- 2 tablespoons packed light brown sugar
- ½ teaspoon five-spice powder
- 1 cup raisins
- 6 tablespoons soy sauce
- 2 tablespoons fresh lime juice
- 1 tablespoon minced fresh ginger
- 1 canned chipotle in adobo sauce, seeded
- 32 Chinese dumpling wrappers
- 2 tablespoons peanut oil
- 1 to 2 cups water

1. Set a large sauté pan or wok over medium-high heat for a couple of minutes. Add the sesame oil, then the cabbage and scallions. Stir-fry until wilted, about 3 minutes. Stir in the vinegar, brown sugar, and five-spice powder. Cover, reduce the heat to low, and simmer until the liquid has been fully absorbed, about 15 minutes, stirring occasionally. Set aside, covered, to cool and soften, about 1 hour.

2. Meanwhile, bring a small saucepan of water to a boil over high heat. Add the raisins, reduce the heat to low, and simmer for 10 minutes. Reserving 2 tablespoons of the liquid, drain the raisins in a colander set in the sink. Put the raisins and reserved cooking liquid in a blender along with the soy sauce, lime juice, ginger, and chipotle. Cover and blend until pureed, stopping the machine and scraping down the inside of the canister at least once.

AHEAD

- Fill the dumplings up to 6 hours ahead. Seal them on the baking sheet under plastic wrap and store in the fridge.
- Make the dipping sauce up to 4 hours ahead. Store, covered, at room temperature.

MORE

Make your own five-spice powder. Toast 1 tablespoon black peppercorns, 1 tablespoon fennel seeds, 4 whole cloves, 2 whole star anise pods, and a 2-inch cinnamon stick broken into several pieces in a dry skillet over medium heat, stirring constantly until aromatic and lightly browned, 3 to 4 minutes. Cool, then grind in a spice grinder until powdery. Seal in a jar and store at room temperature for up to 6 months.

NOTE

- Some dumpling wrappers are made with eggs. Read the labels carefully to make sure you have a vegan product, if this distinction matters to you.

3. Fill the dumplings. Line a large baking sheet with parchment paper or a silicone baking mat. Set a dumpling wrapper on a clean, dry work surface. Set a rounded teaspoon of the cabbage mixture in the center of the wrapper. Wet your finger, then run it around the perimeter of the wrapper. Fold the wrapper over, creating a stuffed half-moon, and seal the edges. Wet your finger again and run it around the rounded edge. Crimp that edge, starting at one end and folding little bits of it over onto itself. Set aside on the prepared baking sheet. Continue making more dumplings.

4. Pour the peanut oil into a large nonstick skillet and set it over high heat for 1 minute. Add the dumplings, crimped edge up and flatter bottoms down. Cook until the bottoms are well browned, about 2 minutes.

5. Pour water into the skillet until it comes halfway up the dumplings. Cover and cook over high heat until the water has been absorbed, about 4 minutes. Uncover and continue cooking until the bottoms are crisp again, about 1 minute. Serve at once with the dipping sauce on the side.

A MENU

SMALL PLATE: Red Cabbage Pot Stickers, Raisin Chipotle Dip

SALAD: Peanut Chaat, Cardamom Yogurt (page 107)

LARGE PLATE: Stir-Fried Bok Choy, Dried Mushrooms, Preserved Black Beans (page 183)

DESSERT: Coconut Cheesecake Flan (page 273)

POUR

A cold, sparkling Riesling to calm the chipotle heat and offer dried apricot notes, a complement to the raisins in the sauce

Mushroom Bao

6 BUNS

Our last starter is a no-holds-barred affair, complicated but elegant, despite its street cred. The dough is quite tender with two leaveners (yeast and baking powder, for extra rise) and yet has a decidedly firm texture. The filling is less complex than some Chinatown offerings because we omit any preserved vegetables for a more earthy flavor overall, a laser focus on the mushrooms. We really want their dank flavors to stand on their own, with the soft buns as merely the wheaty base.

▶ AHEAD

● Make the filling up to 2 days in advance. Store, covered, in the refrigerator.

● Once stuffed, freeze the unsteamed buns on a large baking sheet until firm, then dump them all in a zip-closed plastic bag and freeze for up to 3 months. Cook them right out of the freezer, adding 7 minutes to the steaming time.

▶ NOTE

● Bamboo steamers will impart a distinct, woody flavor to the buns. Yes, you can use a metal steamer, but the final taste will be flatter, far less interesting.

FILLING

- 16 whole dried shiitake mushrooms or other dried Chinese black mushrooms
- 6 scallions, thinly sliced
- 1½ tablespoons hoisin sauce
- 1 tablespoon rice vinegar
- 1 tablespoon soy sauce
- 1 tablespoon honey
- 1 teaspoon ginger juice

DOUGH

- ½ cup warm water (105° to 115°F)
- 1½ tablespoons sugar
- 1 teaspoon active dry yeast
- 1½ tablespoons canola or safflower oil, plus more for greasing
- 1½ cups plus 2 tablespoons all-purpose flour, plus more for dusting
- 1 teaspoon baking powder

DIPPING SAUCE

- ⅓ cup soy sauce
- ⅓ cup rice vinegar
- 2 tablespoons mirin
- 2 teaspoons toasted sesame oil

1. To make the filling: Set the mushrooms in a large bowl and cover with boiling water. Soak for 30 minutes.

2. Drain the mushrooms in a colander set in the sink. Remove and discard the stems. Squeeze the caps dry over the sink. Quarter them, then transfer to a food processor and process until about like ground beef. Add the scallions, hoisin sauce, vinegar, soy sauce, honey, and ginger juice and pulse a few times to combine. Scrape the mixture into a large bowl and set aside.

3. To make the dough: Mix the warm water, sugar, and yeast in a large bowl and set aside for about 5 minutes, until bubbling and frothy. Stir in the canola or safflower oil and the flour. Dump the dough out onto a lightly floured, clean, dry work surface and knead until smooth and supple, about 10 minutes. Oil a large, clean, dry bowl. Drop the dough in it, turn the dough over, and cover the bowl with plastic wrap. Set aside in a warm, dry place until doubled in bulk, 1 to 2 hours.

4. Punch the dough down and turn it out onto a clean, dry work surface. Knead in the baking powder, only adding any additional flour if the dough is sticking. Let the dough rest for 5 minutes.

5. Divide the dough into 6 balls (about ¼ cup each). Roll each into a 4½-inch round on a dry surface. Only use extra flour if the dough is sticking.

6. Place ¼ cup filling in the center of each round. Fold closed by gathering the perimeter of the dough toward the center and giving it a slight twist at the top to seal closed.

7. Oil a large bamboo steamer (see Note) and set it over a pot of simmering water. Add the buns, cover, and steam for 15 minutes, until set but soft.

8. Meanwhile, to make the dipping sauce: Whisk together the soy sauce, rice vinegar, mirin, and sesame oil in a small bowl.

9. Serve the buns with little bowls of the dipping sauce near each place setting.

▶ **A MENU**

FIRST SMALL PLATE: Mushroom Bao

SECOND SMALL PLATE: Stir-Fried Parsnips, Black Pepper, Caramel (page 49)

PASTA: Soba Noodles, Edamame, Kumquats (page 143)

DESSERT: Fennel/Cardamom Pears, Ginger Mascarpone (page 247)

▶ **POUR**

An IPA or a lager to foreground the yeasty flavors—or perhaps (surprisingly) a California Cabernet Sauvignon with blackberry and fig notes against the earthy mushrooms

4

SALADS AND SOUPS

If the flavors of a first course should be elemental but juxtaposed, it's often good to follow them with something not more sophisticated but in fact a tad more rustic, less city and more country. Simple as they are, those pairings in the first course can be intense and surprising: kohlrabi and enoki mushrooms, radishes and caramelized garlic. It's important to build in a breather.

With the second course, we also want to begin to change the dinner narrative in favor of melding basic flavors—that is, not merely juxtaposition but not yet a full marriage either. Salad dressings accomplish that task without a stove in sight. A whisk brings a better cohesion among basic flavors that will then lightly coat the rustic textures of the raw, leafy greens or other vegetables on the plates. And soups are a step further down that road, much closer to the full marriage of flavors in a main course, although not yet as mature or complex. Indeed, a soup can make a fine main course at a lighter dinner party of mostly small plates.

Although salads and soups are great second acts, we find that

they're less successful as starters. Yes, salads are tart and bright without fussiness. In fact, they're *too* tart and bright. A first plate should balance sweet, sour, savory, and other notes to get the meal (and the appetites) rolling. We sometimes put a simple salad *last* among the savory courses. Sure, it's old-fashioned, but a cold tangle of vinegary, crisp greens puts a definite full stop to the meal before dessert.

More frequently, however, we offer salads and soups like these recipes as a bridge between the small and large plates. These help us shift the tonality, like that fast scherzo in a symphony right before the brassy fourth movement. And of course salads and soups are also a great chance for further exploration of the culinary

possibilities of vegetarian fare—despite sometimes losing face with bland incarnations that are nothing more than bagged lettuce and bottled dressing, or canned broth gussied up with chopped vegetables. Instead, when salads and soups offer that big range of flavors and textures that only plants afford, they become one of the best arguments for what the herbivore palate can do for the dinner table. Thus, you'll find that many of the combos here—like pears and ginger, Brussels sprouts and kumquats, rye berries and miso—are quite bold, constructed from disparate elements that build to a consistent and balanced whole.

If this all sounds complicated, don't worry. Most of these recipes are make-aheads. We certainly don't want to be caught fussing with an intermediary course between more complicated ones. Palates may need breathing space, but we do, too.

In fact, not all of these recipes are strictly second- or third-course offerings. Some like Watermelon Panzanella, Capers, Basil (page 118) or Frisée Salad, Smoked Bread Cubes, Poached Egg (page 120) can be main courses on their own. To do so, choose a couple of preceding small plates that will highlight distinct flavor combinations, moving from light to more substantial. Then move to one of these two as the main event, a more rustic way to focus your guest's attention on the myriad flavors and tastes of vegetables and fruits.

After the salads, we turn to seven soups. Four are cold; some can be served in shot glasses, a chaser between courses. The three hot soups are mellow, none a main course in itself unless a menu is constructed to make them an end stop. They seem to call out for something next, something to round out the meal before dessert.

Or, okay, you might want to throw all our theorizing to the wind and start your dinner party off with one of these salad or soup recipes. They'll definitely give you a big splash. Or forgo the dinner party and make that rye berry and miso soup or that panzanella on an average weeknight when there are no guests in sight. If so, cue up something on the DVR from your must-watch list and make a meal of some pretty tasty fare. We can hardly blame you. We've done it often enough.

THE BETWEEN-COURSE HITCH

Clearing the plates and glassware from the table is often a hiccup at a dinner party, especially when you're offering multiple plated courses. In our house, we've got two to man the stations. He who prepares dinner does not clear. But no guests clear. We always say, "I won't lift a finger at your house, so please don't lift a finger at mine." That usually lets the clearer get on with his job—which is to take the plates and any unneeded silverware and glassware away, put them in the dishwasher, maybe start said dishwasher for an entre-meal quickie, and lay out the plates for the next course on the kitchen counter. It's backstage work that always pays off with better production values. If you have an open-concept kitchen, drop the lights over the counters when you return to the table. Nobody wants to stare at those dirty bowls and skillets.

If you're not part of a twosome, consider appointing a good friend to help. Make sure the duties are well understood. *Can you help me get the plates and glassware off the table, then pour some more wine?* Most of the time, your friend will be flattered you asked. But we don't advise making new boyfriends or girlfriends the evening's clearer. *You're asking me to do what?* will be quickly followed up by *Can you just hurry up?* Best leave that sequence to us married pros.

Grapefruit/Avocado Salad, Pistachios

8 SERVINGS

Spiky and sour notes need special care in a balanced dish. They should be controlled without being muted. Surprisingly, the answer sometimes comes down to greater *textural* contrasts rather than more layers of flavors. Thus, we've calmed down the natural pucker of the grapefruit by adding a sweet but earthy crunch to this flavorful vinaigrette: minced pistachios. Make sure you indeed mince the nuts, rocking a large heavy knife through them repeatedly on a cutting board, gathering them together, and going at them from a different direction. The dressing will be even more flavorful if allowed to stand for at least 1 hour before serving.

¼ cup fresh lemon juice	½ teaspoon salt
3 tablespoons olive oil	½ teaspoon freshly ground black pepper
3 tablespoons white balsamic vinegar	2 large ripe Hass avocados
2 tablespoons minced unsalted pistachios	2 large grapefruit, cut into supremes (see Note)
1 tablespoon honey	2 medium fennel bulbs (about 1 pound), trimmed and shaved into paper-thin strips
1 tablespoon minced shallot	
1 teaspoon mustard powder	

1. Whisk the lemon juice, oil, vinegar, pistachios, honey, shallot, mustard powder, salt, and pepper in a medium bowl until smooth and even a bit creamy.

2. Halve, pit, peel, and thinly sliced the avocados. Arrange the grapefruit supremes, shaved fennel, and avocado slices on serving plates. Drizzle the vinaigrette over the top.

> AHEAD

● Make the dressing up to 6 hours in advance. Store, covered, at room temperature.

> NOTES

● To supreme grapefruits, cut off a small slice of the fruit's top and bottom. Stand it up on a cutting board and use a paring knife to cut the peel off the flesh in long arcs, starting at the top and following down along the fruit's natural curve. Cut far enough into the flesh to remove the white pith and membrane layer but not so far as to damage too much of the pulp. Once peeled, hold the fruit in one hand over a serving bowl, then use the paring knife to cut between the flesh and the white membranes separating the individual segments and allowing these to fall into the bowl along with any juice. Discard any membranes and the peel. You won't use the juice for this recipe, but it can make a killer cocktail before dinner.

● Shave the fennel with a long, thin, sharp knife or on a mandoline with the slicing blade at its thinnest setting.

> A MENU

SMALL PLATE: Chickpea Blini, Curried Sweet Potatoes (page 74)

SALAD: Grapefruit/Avocado Salad, Pistachios

LARGE PLATE: Millet/Brown Rice Casserole, Antipasti (page 199)

DESSERT: Candied orange peels and Armagnac

> POUR

Iced seltzer with a drop or two of bitters to offer a sophisticated, woody, herbal back taste against the dish

Brussels Sprout/Fennel Salad, Kumquats

8 SERVINGS

We're not exactly sure what it is about raw ingredients that make them so perfect before a main course. Is it the crunch? The uncomplicated flavors? The no-guilt factor? Whatever it is, we're in. We've served this salad countless times, often after a slightly more complicated first course. It's always a welcome change, refreshing (*raw Brussels sprouts?*) and appealing (*Brussels sprouts!*). The fennel adds licorice notes that tame the sprouts' vaunted bitterness (which is much less pronounced when they're raw). The thinly shaved kumquats act as the true acid, the sour pop in the salad, so that the other flavors stay bright, never dulled. The prep's a little intense for a salad, but you can do it most of it in advance.

¾ cup pine nuts

5 cups small, trimmed Brussels sprouts (about 1¼ pounds)

2 small fennel bulbs (about 11 ounces each), trimmed

2 cups kumquats (about 1 pound)

¼ cup blood orange juice

¼ cup roasted hazelnut oil

1 tablespoon white wine vinegar

1 teaspoon salt

1 teaspoon freshly ground black pepper

1. Toast the pine nuts in a large skillet over medium-low heat, stirring occasionally, until lightly browned and aromatic, about 5 minutes. Scrape them into a big bowl and cool for 10 minutes.

2. Use a mandoline to shave the Brussels sprouts into that big bowl. Separate the tiny threads from each other. Then shave the fennel into the bowl as well.

3. Use a sharp paring knife to slice the kumquats into paper-thin rounds, seeding the slices as necessary. Add these kumquat slices to the salad and toss well.

4. Whisk the blood orange juice, oil, and vinegar in a small bowl until emulsified, almost creamy. Whisk in the salt and pepper. Pour the dressing over the salad and toss again, then serve it by stacking small mounds on each plate.

AHEAD

- Complete the salad through step 3. Cover the bowl with plastic wrap and refrigerate for up to 6 hours. For the best flavor, set the bowl on the counter for at least 1 hour before serving.

- Whisk the dressing in a bowl up to 2 hours in advance. Store, covered, at room temperature. Whisk once more before pouring over the salad.

GARNISH

Grate fresh nutmeg over the servings.

NOTES

- Working with a mandoline can be daunting. Always have the safety guard in hand—never run ingredients over the blade with unprotected fingers. We often use a hand-held mandoline for small jobs like this one. If you don't have a mandoline, the prep just got more intense. We find that a food processor tends to "juice" the vegetables, so we'd rather do it by hand on a cutting board with a sharp paring knife.

- If you can't find blood oranges, substitute tangerines.

A MENU

FIRST SMALL PLATE: Chestnut/Cashew/Porcini Pâté (page 75)

FIRST SALAD: Brussels Sprout/Fennel Salad, Kumquats

SECOND SMALL PLATE: Stewed Giant Lima Beans, Dandelion Greens, Feta (page 60)

SECOND SALAD: Fava Bean/Sugar Snap Salad, Warm Breadcrumbs (page 103)

DESSERT: Peppermints and lemon seltzer

POUR

A sweet Riesling with citrus notes to complement the kumquats while further controlling the fennel's edge

Fava Bean/Sugar Snap Salad, Warm Breadcrumbs

8 SERVINGS

Green vegetables are flavorful enough that they can stand up to a complex set of balancers: hot, sour, musky, and even wheaty. Here, we start by mixing earthy fava beans and super-sweet sugar snaps. Together, they'll stand up to lemon juice, garlic, and lots of grated cheese. The breadcrumb dressing keeps the dish pretty hearty, probably making it best on a chilly spring evening, when the vegetables are first fresh in the market but the weather still calls for comforting fare. The dressing's also best when it's still warm from the stove.

◗ AHEAD

● Complete steps 1 and 2 up to 3 hours in advance. Cover the bowl and set aside at room temperature.

◗ LESS

Substitute shelled, unsalted, frozen edamame, thawed, for the fava beans. No peeling necessary! (But you'll still need to blanch them.)

◗ A MENU

SMALL PLATE: Cauliflower/Green Olive Gratin (page 62)

PASTA: Ziti, Chard, Beans, Poached Eggs (page 138)

SALAD: Fava Bean/Sugar Snap Salad, Warm Breadcrumbs

DESSERT: Chocolate Pots de Crème (page 253)

◗ POUR

A smooth, buttery white Burgundy, like one from Meursault, to offer lots of velvety, vanilla sweetness against the cheese and breadcrumbs

- 4 pounds fresh fava beans in their pods
- 1½ pounds sugar snap peas, halved widthwise
- 3 tablespoons fresh lemon juice
- 6 tablespoons olive oil
- ¼ cup pine nuts, chopped
- 1 tablespoon minced garlic
- ⅔ cup unseasoned dried breadcrumbs
- 1 tablespoon finely grated lemon zest
- ½ teaspoon red pepper flakes
- ¼ teaspoon salt
- 1½ ounces Parmigiano-Reggiano cheese, finely grated (about 6 tablespoons)

1. Split the pods open and remove the fava beans inside; discard the pods. Bring a large saucepan of water to a boil over high heat. Meanwhile, set up a large bowl of ice water on the counter.

2. Blanch the fava beans and sugar snap peas for 1 minute. Drain in a large colander set in the sink, then use a slotted spoon to transfer the vegetables to the ice water bath. Drain again and blot dry with paper towels. Peel the fava beans, slipping each bean out of its fibrous shell. Discard those shells. Toss both the peeled favas and the sugar snaps in a bowl with the lemon juice.

3. Set a large skillet over medium heat for a couple of minutes. Add the oil, then the pine nuts and garlic. Cook for 1 minute, stirring all the while. Add the breadcrumbs, lemon zest, red pepper flakes, and salt. Toss until the breadcrumbs are lightly toasted, about 2 minutes. Scrape the contents of the skillet over the vegetables in the bowl, add the cheese, and toss well before mounding servings onto plates.

Beet/Orange Salad, Spicy Gingerbread Croutons

8 SERVINGS

You're going to have to exercise steel-strong willpower to keep from eating these croutons once they're out of the oven. Spicy and sweet, their crunch seems to call out for a cup of hot tea. So snitch a few, then turn away. Just keep telling yourself they'll be even better when mixed with the beets (steamed to bring out the sweetness) and juicy little orange bits. And then there's a little secret in the dish: It's set off with salty/briny ricotta salata, an assertive match for those croutons. All in all, it's an incredibly satisfying salad, as much a small plate as any salad we can imagine.

CROUTONS

- 1 ¼ cups all-purpose flour
- 1 teaspoon baking soda
- ½ teaspoon ground cinnamon
- ½ teaspoon ground ginger
- ½ teaspoon chipotle chile powder
- ¼ teaspoon ground cloves
- ¼ teaspoon salt
- ¼ cup roasted walnut oil, plus more for greasing the baking pan
- ¼ cup packed dark brown sugar
- 1 large egg, at room temperature
- ½ cup molasses (do not use blackstrap molasses)
- ½ cup strong coffee

SALAD

- 6 medium beets, any greens and root ends removed
- 6 large navel oranges
- ¼ cup raspberry vinegar
- 2 tablespoons roasted walnut oil
- ¾ teaspoon salt
- ¾ teaspoon freshly ground black pepper
- ¼ pound ricotta salata cheese

1. Position the rack in the center of the oven and heat to 375°F.

2. To make the croutons: Whisk the flour, baking soda, cinnamon, ginger, chipotle powder, cloves, and salt in a large bowl until the spices are mixed evenly throughout the flour.

3. Place the walnut oil and brown sugar in a large food processor and process until well combined, about 30 seconds. Add the egg and continue processing until smooth, scraping down the inside of the bowl once. Add the molasses and process until again smooth.

▶ AHEAD

● Make the croutons up to 1 day in advance. Store the cooled croutons in a sealed plastic bag. Before using, crisp them on a baking sheet in a 375°F oven for 5 to 10 minutes.

● Steam the beets and supreme the oranges up to 6 hours in advance. Store them in separate, covered bowls in the fridge, but let them come to room temperature before serving.

▶ LESS

Look for steamed and peeled beets in packages in the refrigerator case of your produce section. The market may even carry fresh orange supremes in that case.

▶ NOTES

● To get beet stains from your hands, pour a little kosher salt into your palms, then rub them together in warm water, abrading the stains before adding soap to wash off the salt grit. Use hand lotion afterwards because the salt will dry out your skin unmercifully.

●If you use a glass 9 x 13-inch baking dish, reduce the oven temperature to 350°F and grease it very generously.

4. Pour in the flour mixture and process until a smooth batter. Scrape down the inside of the bowl once again, add the coffee, and process until uniform.

5. Use some walnut oil on a paper towel to grease the inside of a 9 x 13-inch baking dish. Pour the batter into the baking dish and smooth it even with a rubber spatula. Bake until set but still soft, even spongy, about 13 minutes. Remove the baking pan from the oven but leave the oven on. Immediately turn the gingerbread cake out by setting a cutting board over the still hot baking dish, inverting them both, and then removing the baking dish.

6. Cut the cake into 1-inch squares while still warm and place on a large rimmed baking sheet. Bake until toasted and a little crisp, about 15 minutes, tossing once. Turn the squares out onto a wire rack and cool completely, about 2 hours.

7. To make the salad: Put about 2 inches of water in a pan underneath a vegetable steamer and bring to a boil over high heat. Peel the beets and cut them into quarters, leaving 2 inches of the root and about 1 inch of the stems attached. Set them in the steamer, cover, reduce the heat to medium, and steam until tender, about 15 minutes. Cool for a few minutes, then slice each quarter in half or even in thirds.

8. Make orange supremes from the oranges: Cut off a small slice of each fruit's top and bottom so the round fruit can stand steadily on the counter. Use a sharp paring knife to cut the peel off the flesh in long arcs, starting at the top and following down along the natural curve of the fruit. Cut far enough into the flesh to remove the white pith and membrane layer but not so far as to damage the pulp. Once peeled, hold the fruit in one hand over a serving bowl, then use the paring knife to cut between the flesh and the white membranes separating the individual segments, allowing these to fall into the bowl along with any juice. Discard any membranes and the peel; quaff the juice at will.

9. Whisk the vinegar, oil, salt, and pepper in a large bowl. Add the beet bits and orange supremes and toss well. Plate up the salads. Shave some ricotta salata over each serving and top with a handful of the croutons (or maybe more).

A MENU

FIRST SMALL PLATE: Roasted Grapes/Olives (page 37)

SECOND SMALL PLATE: Walnuts, Peas, Daikon, Butter, Tomatoes (page 52)

SALAD: Beet/Orange Salad, Spicy Gingerbread Croutons

THIRD SMALL PLATE: Blue Cheese Cheesecake, Walnuts, Dill (page 86)

DESSERT: A selection of dried fruit and champagne

POUR

A wheaty Hefeweizen to balance the hot and sweet croutons with its light, toasty, slightly sour notes

Peanut Chaat, Cardamom Yogurt

8 SERVINGS

A *chaat* is any one of a number of snacks sold at roadside carts and trucks across India: spicy pancakes, small bits of stew and yogurt, vegetable patties with cold condiments, and even light, highly spiced salads. The name is not so much about the ingredients as the gustatory pleasure; it comes from an old Prakrit word that means to *eat with a lot of noise and gusto.* You'll certainly understand that name with this textural mix: peanuts, cucumbers, tomatoes, and jalapeños, all seasoned with highly aromatic spices and then set on a yogurt sauce with even more aromatic spices. These are indeed *big* flavors with lots of contrasts. To that end, this recipe is a good way station between courses, something designed to perk up flagging palates and spur them on to even bigger tastes. Brace yourself for the slurping.

▶ AHEAD

• Make the yogurt mixture up to 24 hours in advance. Store, covered, in the refrigerator.

• Make the peanut salad up to 6 hours in advance. Store, covered, at room temperature.

▶ NOTES

• Amchur powder is a common East Indian spice, made from dried unripe mangos. It provides a sour pop to curries and chaats. Look for it at East Indian supermarkets or from their outlets online. If you can't find it, substitute finely grated lime zest.

• If you can't find cardamom seeds in the spice rack, buy green cardamom pods and remove the tiny seeds yourself.

▶ A MENU

SMALL PLATE: Masa Tarts, Caramelized Garlic Custard, Radish Slaw (page 79)

SALAD: Peanut Chaat, Cardamom Yogurt

LARGE PLATE: Red-Braised Tofu, Mushrooms, Scallions (page 212)

DESSERT: Fennel/Cardamom Pears (page 247), just in their own sauce, no Ginger Mascarpone on the side

▶ POUR

A Belgian blond ale like Duvel for its light, sweet citrus notes and pronounced malt overtones

4 cups water

1 cup raw, unsalted peanuts

½ teaspoon turmeric

2 large beefsteak or globe tomatoes, seeded (page 118) and diced

1 medium English cucumber, diced

1 small fresh jalapeño chile, stemmed, seeded, and minced

2 tablespoons fresh lime juice

1 teaspoon amchur powder (ground dried mango)

1 teaspoon ground cumin

1 teaspoon sugar

½ teaspoon salt

½ teaspoon freshly ground black pepper

2 cups whole-milk or fat-free plain Greek yogurt

¼ cup finely minced candied (or crystallized) ginger

½ teaspoon cardamom seeds

1. Combine the water, peanuts, and turmeric in a large saucepan and bring to a boil over high heat. Reduce the heat to medium and boil, uncovered, until the peanuts are tender and have almost doubled in size, about 25 minutes. Drain in a colander set in the sink (do not rinse).

2. Transfer the peanuts to a large bowl. Stir in the tomatoes, cucumber, jalapeño, lime juice, amchur powder, cumin, sugar, salt, and pepper.

3. Whisk the yogurt, ginger, and cardamom in a small bowl. Smooth or mound about ¼ cup of this mixture on each of 8 serving plates. Top with the peanut mixture.

Apple Slaw, Fried Chickpeas

6 SERVINGS

A slaw may seem too downscale for dinner-party fare, but think about what you get with a plate of it: raw vegetables, lots of textural contrasts, and a decidedly tart pop in the flavors. Suddenly, a slaw seems exactly like the kind of salad course we think fits best in a run of plates. This one's not creamy, so the spiky bite of the daikon radish and the tart sweetness of the apple aren't obliterated by mayonnaise or sour cream. With the pomegranate seeds and crunchy chickpeas, it adds up to an abundance of flavors and bites, bound together by a walnut oil/sherry vinegar dressing that serves to bring the dish to a better marriage of its disparate flavors.

½ cup dried chickpeas

1 teaspoon salt, divided

½ teaspoon ground coriander

½ teaspoon ground cumin

¼ teaspoon ground cinnamon

¼ teaspoon ground ginger

¼ teaspoon cayenne pepper

Safflower or peanut oil, for deep-frying

2 cups julienned daikon (about 1 medium)

2 cups julienned tart, crisp apple, such as Pippin or Braeburn (about 1 large)

½ cup pomegranate seeds (about 1 small pomegranate)

2 tablespoons roasted walnut oil

1½ tablespoons sherry vinegar

1 tablespoon olive oil

½ teaspoon freshly ground black pepper

1. Fill a large bowl about three-quarters full with cool tap water, add the chickpeas, and set aside on the counter at room temperature for 24 hours. Drain well in a colander set in the sink.

2. Mix ½ teaspoon of the salt, the coriander, cumin, cinnamon, ginger, and cayenne in a large bowl. Set aside.

3. Pour about 3 inches deep-frying oil into a large saucepan. Clip a deep-frying thermometer to the inside of the pan and heat the oil over medium heat to 350°F. Adjust the heat so the oil's temperature remains stable.

> AHEAD

● Unfortunately, the slaw will not keep long: The vegetables will darken if left undressed but they'll begin to break down and "juice" once dressed. You can julienne the daikon and apple about 30 minutes before dinner if you put them into a big bowl of water laced with some lemon juice—and of course, you can separate the pomegranate seeds from the pith several hours before dinner. The chickpeas will stay crisp at room temperature for about 6 hours, provided the weather is dry, not humid.

> NOTE

● Julienned vegetables are those cut into tiny, long matchsticks. The easiest way to get the job done is with a hand-held julienne slicer, running the daikon and apple sections over the teethlike blade. Failing that tool, you can do the task by hand, although it involves slicing the vegetables into paper-thin sheets before slicing these into long, thin matchsticks.

> A MENU

FIRST SMALL PLATE: Red Cabbage Pot Stickers, Raisin Chipotle Dip (page 92)

SALAD: Peanut Chaat, Cardamom Yogurt

SOUP: Garlic Soup, Gruyère, Cognac (page 130)

PASTA: Soba Noodles, Edamame, Kumquats (page 142)

DESSERT: Coconut Cheesecake Flan (page 273)

4. Spoon some of the chickpeas into the oil and fry until crisp, turning occasionally, about 5 minutes. Use a slotted spoon to lift them out of the hot oil, draining them a bit by gently shaking the spoon—then dump them into the bowl with the spices. Repeat with more chickpeas without ever overloading the pan. Once all are fried, toss well to coat thoroughly.

5. Mix the daikon, apple, pomegranate seeds, walnut oil, vinegar, olive oil, black pepper, and the remaining ½ teaspoon salt in a large bowl. Toss well, then spoon the salad onto serving plates. Top with the coated chickpeas, leaving any excess spice powder behind in their bowl.

> **POUR**
>
> Homemade ginger ale, a combination of a little ginger syrup and chilled sparkling water, to refresh the palates even more and keep the focus on those spicy flavors

Roasted Pears, Fig Caponata

8 SERVINGS

You might think of roasted pears as solely a dessert. This elegant and flavorful preparation will convince you of their somewhat savory qualities, even with all those natural sugars in the mix. Rather than bread, offer peppery crackers on the side.

- 4 ripe but still firm Comice or Anjou pears
- 2 tablespoons roasted walnut oil
- 1 small eggplant (about 10 ounces)
- 5 small fresh figs, preferably Black Mission, stemmed and halved (about 6 ounces)
- 1 tablespoon pine nuts
- 2 tablespoons olive oil, plus more for oiling the grill or grill pan
- 3 tablespoons minced shallot
- 3 tablespoons minced celery
- 2 tablespoons white balsamic vinegar
- 2 tablespoons minced fresh parsley leaves
- 1½ tablespoons packed light brown sugar
- 1 teaspoon capers, rinsed and minced
- ½ teaspoon dried oregano
- ½ teaspoon salt
- ¼ teaspoon red pepper flakes
- ¼ teaspoon fennel seeds

1. Position the rack in the center of the oven and heat to 450°F.

2. Peel the pears, then halve them through the stem ends. Remove the stems as well as any seeds and seed pockets in the flesh. (A serrated grapefruit spoon or melon baller are the best tools for that latter task.) Rub the pears with the walnut oil.

3. Heat a large cast iron skillet or a flameproof roasting pan over medium-high heat until smoking. Set the pears cut side down in the skillet or pan. Cook for 2 minutes, then put the hot skillet or pan in the oven and roast for 15 minutes. Turn the pears over, cover, and continue roasting until brown and tender if still a bit al dente, about 20 minutes.

▶ AHEAD

● Roast the pears up to 3 hours in advance. Store at room temperature.

● Make the caponata up to 3 hours in advance. Store, covered, in its skillet at room temperature. Warm over low heat for a couple of minutes before serving.

▶ NOTES

● Look for ripe but firm pears that can hold their shape after roasting. But use your nose: The fruit should smell sweet while exhibiting a distinct tautness to the skin.

● For a vegetarian version, lay thin strips of shaved aged Asiago or Pecorino Romano cheese over the pears and caponata.

4. Meanwhile, remove the stem and slice the eggplant lengthwise into ½-inch-thick slabs. Oil the grill grates with olive oil and prepare the grill for medium-high, direct-heat cooking (or oil a grill pan with olive oil and set over medium-high heat until smoking).

5. Grill the eggplant slices until browned and soft, about 4 minutes per side. Transfer to a cutting board. Grill the figs until soft and lightly browned, about 2 minutes per side. Transfer to the same cutting board, then chop the eggplant and figs into small bits, no bigger than ½ inch.

6. Set a large skillet over medium heat for a couple of minutes, then pour in the pine nuts. Cook, stirring often, until toasted—that is, lightly browned and fragrant—about 3 minutes. Pour the pine nuts among the eggplant and fig bits.

7. Return the skillet to medium heat. Swirl in the 2 tablespoons olive oil, then add the shallot and celery. Cook, stirring often, until softened, about 2 minutes. Scrape everything from the cutting board into the skillet. Stir in everything else: the vinegar, parsley, brown sugar, capers, oregano, salt, red pepper flakes, and fennel seeds. Stir over medium heat until bubbling, about 1 minute. Set aside off the heat until the pears are ready.

8. Cool the pears in their skillet or roasting pan on a wire rack for 5 to 10 minutes, then set each half on a serving plate. Top with the fig caponata to serve.

▶ A MENU

FIRST SALAD: Roasted Pears, Fig Caponata

PASTA: Leek/Gorgonzola Lasagna (page 147)

SECOND SALAD: Brussels Sprout/ Fennel Salad, Kumquats (page 102)

DESSERT: Olive Oil/Vin Santo Cake, Pine Nuts, Dried Apples (page 265)

▶ POUR

A crisp, moderately sweet Riesling, especially a full-bodied Alsatian variety with apple and peach notes to complement the pears and figs

Bulgur Salad, Roasted Cherry Tomatoes, Basil Confetti

8 SERVINGS

Back in the first heyday of vegetarianism, tabbouleh was too often just a lackluster, overparsleyed mound. But no more! We can give it a nip-and-tuck for new times. We start by modifying the amount of parsley to make sure that wheaty aroma from the bulgur comes riding up over the vinegar. And we add roasted, almost-candied tomatoes for a sweet ping against the chopped pecans, an American twist, justifiably world-renowned for their subtle, sweet flavor. We top it all off with fried basil strips, bits of herby crunch that further pull the salad out of its hippy roots. This is no ordinary tabbouleh! (It also doesn't hurt if there are leftovers for lunch the next day.)

4 cups small cherry tomatoes (about 1½ pounds)

¾ cup olive oil, divided

2 cups boiling water

1½ cups coarse, whole-grain bulgur

1 cup pecan pieces

1½ cups packed fresh basil leaves, divided

Safflower oil, for deep-frying

¼ cup white wine vinegar

1 garlic clove, minced

½ teaspoon salt

½ teaspoon freshly ground black pepper

1. Position the rack in the center of the oven and heat to 225°F.

2. Line a large rimmed baking sheet with parchment paper or a silicone baking mat. Halve the tomatoes and lay them cut sides up on the prepared baking sheet. Drizzle them with ¼ cup of the olive oil.

3. Bake until condensed, even shriveled, and very sweet, 2 to 3 hours, depending on how moist they were.

4. Meanwhile, pour the boiling water over the bulgur in a large heatproof bowl. Cover and set aside until the water has been fully absorbed, about 45 minutes. Uncover, break up the grains with a fork, and cool to room temperature.

5. As the cherry tomatoes continue to roast, pour the pecans into a large skillet and toast over medium heat until lightly browned and ridiculously fragrant, about 4 minutes, stirring often. Pour the nuts onto a cutting board, cool for a bit, then chop into very small pieces, rocking a large, heavy knife back and forth through them.

(continued)

AHEAD

• Prepare the dressed bulgur up to 2 days in advance. Store, covered, in the fridge but allow it to come back to room temperature for 1 hour before serving.

• Prepare the tomatoes and basil confetti up to 3 hours in advance. Store, uncovered, at room temperature.

LESS

Skip making the timbales and simply mound the grain salad on the plates. Ring the mounds with the roasted cherry tomatoes and sprinkle the basil confetti over everything.

NOTES

• Although rarely so labeled, almost all bulgur sold in this country is "instant"—that is, it can be rehydrated with boiling water. Whole-grain bulgur—or the even more fantastic Kamut bulgur—will take longer than standard bulgur to plump, but even these grains are parboiled and don't need the complicated steaming and drying of traditional Middle Eastern bulgur. If you're at all in doubt, read the package instructions before proceeding with the recipe.

• Cherry tomatoes have been getting bigger and bigger. Some of them are almost the size of Romas! Look for small ones, no more than 1 inch in diameter. Or search out grape tomatoes, often smaller (and sweeter, to boot).

6. And one last thing to do: Fry the basil. Cut ½ cup of the basil leaves into long, thin strips, no wider than ¼ inch. Pour about 2 inches deep-frying oil into a large, high-sided sauté pan or skillet. Clip a deep-frying thermometer to the inside of the pan and heat the oil over medium heat to 350°F. Add the basil strips and fry until crisp, about 30 seconds. Use a slotted spoon to transfer them to a plate lined with paper towels.

7. Once the cherry tomatoes are ready, set the baking sheet on a wire rack and cool for at least 10 minutes. Mince the remaining 1 cup basil leaves and stir them into the bulgur. Also stir in the remaining ½ cup olive oil, the vinegar, garlic, salt, and pepper.

8. Set a 4-inch ring mold on a serving plate and pack in the bulgur salad, pressing down gently to form a fairly compact disk. Remove the mold and continue making more of these timbales on other serving plates. Top each timbale with an even, overlapping layer of the roasted cherry tomato halves. Then sprinkle the fried basil confetti around the plates before serving.

▶ A MENU

FIRST SALAD: Frisée Salad, Smoked Bread Cubes, Poached Egg (page 120)

SMALL PLATE: Jerusalem Artichoke Fritters, Cranberries, Almonds (page 73)

SECOND SALAD: Bulgur Salad, Roasted Cherry Tomatoes, Basil Confetti

LARGE PLATE: Kale/Apple Stew, Kidney Bean Puree (page 194)

DESSERT: Dark chocolate bars and espresso

▶ POUR

A mildly acidic German Grüner Silvaner, which has no oak at all and so lets its refined, citrusy fruitiness burst to the fore of each sip

Wedge, Ginger, Miso

6 SERVINGS

Instead of the standard blue cheese dressing for an iceberg wedge, here's our take on that carrot and ginger dressing beloved in Japanese restaurants. If you haven't had iceberg lettuce in a while, you're missing the best crunch in the salad bin. We've added a little almond oil to the dressing for a sweet richness. And we include a touch of sesame oil to darken the flavor palette a tad, all to give this rather rustic starter a bit of panache.

4 medium carrots, diced (about 2 cups)

¼ cup minced fresh ginger

¼ cup minced shallot

¼ cup water

¼ cup almond oil

¼ cup rice vinegar

1 tablespoon white miso paste

1 tablespoon toasted sesame oil

½ tablespoon mirin

1 teaspoon sugar

1 large iceberg lettuce head, cut through the stem into 6 wedges

1. Process the carrots, ginger, shallot, water, almond oil, vinegar, miso paste, sesame oil, mirin, and sugar in a food processor until a somewhat pasty dressing forms, scraping down the inside of the bowl once or twice to make sure everything takes a dive on the blades. Scrape the dressing into a large bowl.

2. To serve, set the iceberg wedges on 6 serving plates. Pour and drizzle about ⅓ cup dressing over each.

⬗ AHEAD

• The dressing can be made up to 1 day in advance. Store, covered, in the refrigerator.

⬗ GARNISH

Sprinkle the dressed wedges with purchased wasabi peas; strips of pink, pickled, sushi ginger; and/or little nests of daikon radish shredded through a Benriner spiral vegetable slicer to make long threads. (You can also find these daikon threads for sale at sushi counters in supermarkets or on the salad bar of larger, gourmet markets.)

⬗ NOTES

• Rice vinegar comes in two varieties: with or without sugar, the former often called "seasoned" rice vinegar. In this book, we always call for the latter, sometimes called "unseasoned rice vinegar." Read the label to make sure you have the right one in hand.

• White miso paste is the most common form of fermented sesame paste sold in the United States, the basis of almost all the miso soup made in our sushi restaurants. It's not toasted, wheaty, or earthy but rather bracingly salty and savory.

⬗ A MENU

SMALL PLATE: Blistered Butter Beans, Pecans, Fennel (page 46)

SALAD: Wedge, Ginger, Miso

LARGE PLATE: Stuffed Pears, Wild Rice, Mushrooms (page 228)

DESSERT: Espresso/Chocolate Bundt, Ginger/Whisky Sauce (page 266)

⬗ POUR

Sparkling water to add fizz without fuss so that the ginger cuts through unimpeded

Watercress/Celery Root Salad, Za'atar

8 SERVINGS

In this rather straightforward salad, we let the celery root and watercress work with this renowned Middle Eastern spice blend, known for its murky, savory flavors. There are probably as many versions of za'atar (*zah-ah-tar*) as there are cooks in North Africa and the Arabian Peninsula. Some blends have sesame seeds, some are quite salty, and some rely primarily on fresh herbs. Our recipe—the essential marriage in the dish underneath the flavor contrasts—twists the blend back to the north side of the Mediterranean with dried thyme and marjoram, which maintains that Europe-to-Asia "spice route" savoriness. You'll make more za'atar than you need. Save the remainder in a zip-closed plastic bag or small glass bottle. Store at room temperature in a cool, dark place for up to 1 year. Sprinkle it on hummus to extend the range of its flavors immeasurably.

2 tablespoons ground sumac

2 tablespoons dried thyme

1 tablespoon toasted white sesame seeds

1 tablespoon dried marjoram

2 teaspoons dried oregano

1 teaspoon salt

1½ cups whole-milk or low-fat plain yogurt

¼ cup fresh lemon juice

2 tablespoons tahini

1 teaspoon minced garlic

2 pounds celery root (aka celeriac), trimmed, peeled, and julienned

2 cups lightly packed, lightly shredded watercress, the leaves washed well for grit and any thick stems already removed

AHEAD

● Make the za'atar up to 3 months in advance. Store in a sealed jar in your spice drawer or pantry.

● Blanch the celery root and toss it with the yogurt dressing up to 4 hours in advance. Store, covered, in the refrigerator, but let sit at room temperature for 30 minutes before serving.

LESS

Use a purchased za'atar blend. If there's no salt in the mix, you'll need to sprinkle some over the salads.

MORE

Add up to ½ cup dried currants, fresh pomegranate seeds, or toasted pecan pieces to the salad.

GARNISH

Stand a few grilled pita quarters in the salad on the plates.

NOTES

● Za'atar is a Middle Eastern spice blend, made from ground sumac, sesame seeds, and other herbs, often added to breads, used to spice meats, or sprinkled onto hummus. It's quite aromatic, thanks largely to the sumac, the ground, dried fruit from a variety of tree native to southern Europe.

● For a quick starter, sprinkle 1 tablespoon za'atar into ½ cup olive oil, set aside for 30 minutes, then use as a dip for bread.

● To julienne celery root, cut the vegetable in half, then cut each side into half-moons no more than ¼ inch thick, preferably ⅛ inch thick. Stack a few of these half-moons on top of each other and slice them into thin matchsticks. Or use a handheld julienne cutter on sections of the root.

1. Make the za'atar by mixing the sumac, thyme, sesame seeds, marjoram, oregano, and salt in a small bowl.

2. Whisk the yogurt, lemon juice, tahini, and garlic in a large bowl.

3. Set up a second, large bowl of ice water. Bring a large saucepan of water to a boil over high heat. Add the celery root pieces to the boiling water and blanch for 1 minute from the time the vegetable hits the water. Use a slotted spoon to transfer the celery root to the ice water. Cool to room temperature, then drain into a colander set in the sink.

4. Squeeze the celery root bits dry by the handful and transfer them to the bowl with the yogurt dressing. Stir to coat and add the watercress. Stir well, then divide among 8 serving plates. Sprinkle ¼ teaspoon za'atar over each serving.

▶ A MENU

FIRST SMALL PLATE: Squash Noodles, Almond Chimichurri (page 45)

PASTA: Curried Spaetzle, Ginger Broth (page 155)

SALAD: Watercress/Celery Root Salad, Za'atar

LARGE PLATE: Tomatoes, Mushrooms, Phyllo Nests (page 208)

DESSERT: Pecan Baklava, Fennel Syrup (page 245)

▶ POUR

Some well-chilled, barrel-aged bourbon to cut through the spicy creaminess with caramel overtones

Watermelon Panzanella, Capers, Basil

8 SERVINGS

A traditional bread salad, usually rich in tomatoes, panzanella is one of those dishes that can cross the line into a main course, depending on what comes before it at a dinner party. For this version, we paired those tomatoes with watermelon, a summery treat that makes the flavors refreshing but still fairly elemental. All in all, it's a good palate cleanser before a heavier main course or a fine way to end a lighter meal. Of course, no one would complain if you made it for dinner on an average Wednesday night either.

8 slices (1-inch-thick) hearty country-style bread

½ cup olive oil

4 large yellow beefsteak or globe tomatoes

4 cups cubed, seedless watermelon, preferably red

2 cups seeded, diced cucumber

½ cup finely chopped red onion

20 fresh basil leaves

2 tablespoons capers, rinsed and minced

¾ teaspoon salt

¾ teaspoon freshly ground black pepper

¼ cup white balsamic vinegar

1. Prepare the grill for high-heat, direct cooking (or heat a large grill pan over medium-high heat until smoking).

2. Brush the bread slices on both sides with the olive oil and grill, working in batches as necessary, until well-marked and crisp, about 3 minutes, turning once. Transfer to a wire rack and cool a bit, then slice into 1-inch cubes.

3. Quarter the tomatoes through their stem ends. Use a paring knife to slice along the inner edge, removing the seeds, their pulp, and any connective tissue. Discard these bits, then chop the tomatoes into 1-inch pieces.

4. Toss these in a large bowl with the watermelon, cucumber, and onion. Tear the basil leaves into the bowl, then add the capers, salt, and pepper. Toss gently.

5. Drizzle with the vinegar, add the bread cubes, and toss one more time before serving immediately (before the bread gets soggy) by simply mounding it on the plates—or bringing the large bowl to the table.

▶ AHEAD

● Grill the bread slices up to 2 hours in advance, but do not cut them into cubes until you're ready to prepare the salad. Store, uncovered, on the wire rack at room temperature.

▶ NOTES

● There's a heavy douse of oil on that bread—partly to get it crunchy and partly to provide the oil for the salad. The more fragrant the oil, the better.

● Although the bread cubes are often stale for panzanella, we've shifted the standard by using grilled bread for a slightly smoky flavor in the salad. As such, fresh bread works much better, its crumb still tender when grilled.

● You want the vegetables in a descending order of size: 1-inch tomato and watermelon cubes, ½-inch diced cucumber pieces, and ¼-inch (or less) onion bits.

▶ A MENU

FIRST SMALL PLATE: Cauliflower/Green Olive Gratin (page 62)

SECOND SMALL PLATE: Tomato Gelée, Pistachio Shortbread (page 67)

THIRD SMALL PLATE: Grilled Leeks, Hazelnuts, Lemon (page 38)

SALAD: Watermelon Panzanella, Capers, Basil

DESSERT: Pecan Baklava, Fennel Syrup (page 245)

▶ POUR

A bright, light, sparkling Spumante for a refreshing hit of lemony accents and lots of bubbles

Frisée Salad, Smoked Bread Cubes, Poached Egg

6 SERVINGS

The secret to this (mostly) main-course salad of tender, slightly bitter lettuce and lots of vegetables is the smoked olive oil, a specialty product found at high-end kitchen stores and from specialty suppliers online like the Smoked Olive. By coating the bread in it, you can achieve a very smoky flavor with very little work. If you're serving this dish as a second or later course at a dinner party, bring the pot of water to a very low simmer back in the kitchen and leave it bubbling slowly during the preceding course. The water will already be close to the correct temperature to poach the eggs.

2 cups baguette cubes (about 1½ inches each)

2 tablespoons smoked olive oil

2 large frisée heads, stemmed and chopped (about 6 cups)

1 large red bell pepper, diced

1 medium shallot, peeled and sliced into very thin rings

⅓ cup roasted walnut oil

3 tablespoons sherry vinegar

2 teaspoons Dijon mustard

1 teaspoon minced garlic

½ teaspoon salt

6 large eggs, at room temperature

3 ounces Parmigiano-Reggiano cheese, finely grated (about ¾ cup)

1. Position the rack in the center of the oven and heat to 350°F.

2. Toss the bread cubes and smoked olive oil on a large rimmed baking sheet until the cubes are evenly coated. Bake until browned and crisp, about 15 minutes, tossing once. Cool on a wire rack.

3. Mix the frisée, bell pepper, shallot, and croutons in a large bowl.

4. Whisk the walnut oil, vinegar, mustard, garlic, and salt in a medium bowl until creamy.

5. Bring a Dutch oven or large pot of water to a boil over high heat. Reduce the heat to low so that there are no bubbles in the pot. Crack an egg into a custard cup or ramekin and slip the egg into the water. Repeat with 2 more eggs and poach until the whites are set but the yolks are soft, about 3 minutes. Use a slotted spoon to transfer the eggs to a plate lined with paper towels. Poach the remaining 3 eggs.

6. Toss the dressing with the salad, then mound the salad on serving plates. Set the eggs over the salads. Sprinkle with the cheese.

AHEAD

• The croutons, salad, and dressing can be made up to 4 hours in advance. Store separately at room temperature.

GARNISH

Grind lots of black pepper over each salad before serving. For even more flavor, try a smoked black pepper.

NOTES

• Frisée, sometimes called "baby curly endive," is a chicory with a mild taste and a feathery texture. Choose compact leaves without any wilted or squishy bits—and with a distinctly white or yellow center.

• The poached eggs can be quite watery. Drain each, shaking the slotted spoon gently over the pot.

• The yolks will be runny. For those at your table who prefer eggs with more hard-cooked yolks, choose the later ones out of the pot—or let the whole batch steep for 2 extra minutes.

A MENU

FIRST SMALL PLATE: Asiago Cookies, Tahini/Lentil Cream (page 89)

SECOND SMALL PLATE: Roasted Radishes, Their Greens, Browned Butter (page 35)

SALAD: Frisée Salad, Smoked Bread Cubes, Poached Eggs

DESSERT: Summer Pudding, Black Currants, Blackberries (page 263)

POUR

A spicy, blackberry-jam Grenache for more complex sweet-sour notes that will cut through the smoky flavor without negating it

Plum Soup, Cinnamon, Cloves

8 SERVINGS

A chilled fruit soup is a perfect second or third course—or maybe even a starter on its own, particularly in the summer when hot things may be too heavy to spur anyone's appetite. Although we've been known to serve this dish in shot glasses, or even white wine glasses, it also works well the old-fashioned way: with a bowl and spoon. In that case, have a baguette at the table, too. And if you're feeling adventurous and have some buttery shortbread on hand, sweeten some plain yogurt with maple syrup and use it to garnish this tasty soup for a different twist on dessert.

4 cups water

2 pounds red or black plums, halved

¼ teaspoon freshly grated nutmeg

¼ teaspoon salt

One 4-inch cinnamon stick

4 whole cloves

½ cup sugar

½ cup medium-dry red wine, such as a Pinot Noir or red Friuli

½ cup sour cream

1. Combine the water, plums, nutmeg, salt, cinnamon stick, and cloves in a large saucepan. Bring to a simmer over medium-high heat, stirring occasionally.

2. Cover, reduce the heat to low, and simmer slowly until the fruit is quite soft, about 20 minutes.

3. Use a slotted spoon to transfer the plums to a large blender. Crank the heat to high under the saucepan and boil the remaining liquid until reduced by half. Fish out and discard the cinnamon stick and cloves. Pour the reduced liquid into the blender. Add the sugar and wine.

4. Cover the blender, remove the lid's center knob, place a clean kitchen towel over the opening, and blend until smooth, turning off the machine to scrape down the inside of the canister at least once. Pour the puree into a large bowl, cover, and refrigerate for at least 4 hours—or simply set the blender canister in the fridge, covered, for 4 hours.

5. Whisk in the sour cream—or add the sour cream to the blender canister and blend until smooth. Cover and chill again for at least 3 hours before serving.

AHEAD

- Make the soup through step 4 up to 2 days in advance.
- Chill the prepared soup with the sour cream up to 6 hours in advance.

LESS

Use frozen sliced plums, thawed.

GARNISH

Snip chives over the servings. Or drip bottled hot red pepper sauce on top.

NOTES

- If you don't have a large blender, you'll need to puree the soup in batches. Divide the plums and other ingredients in half so that each batch is fairly even.
- The plums should be ripe but not too soft. Otherwise they can develop a slightly fermented taste when cooked.

A MENU

FIRST SMALL PLATE: Grilled Leeks, Hazelnuts, Lemon (page 38)

SECOND SMALL PLATE: Chickpea Blini, Curried Sweet Potatoes (page 74)

SOUP: Plum Soup, Cinnamon, Cloves

THIRD SMALL PLATE: Potato/Cucumber Mille-Feuille (page 84)

DESSERT: Maple/Oat Blondies (page 239)

POUR

Iced green tea with floral and herbaceous notes to enrich the creamy sweetness in the soup

Cucumber Soup, Basil, Buttermilk

6 SERVINGS

Cold buttermilk soups are an old-fashioned tradition, a tangy zip for fresh, summer vegetables that need little else. Here, the sweet, grassy mellowness of cucumbers is paired with that summery perfume of basil, distilled into a finishing oil you can keep on hand to drizzle on future soups and salads. It's an irresistible, bright, almost ethereal combination that may well sum up the season. But we didn't stop there. We gave the pairing a tangy jolt with the buttermilk and sour cream so that the flavors can't turn listless. If you've got weekend guests for a dinner party this evening, skip this one as a second or third course and consider serving it in shot glasses as a midday pick-me-up on the deck.

> AHEAD

● Prepare the basil oil up to 1 week in advance. Store, covered, in the fridge. If it hardens, run warm water over the container to loosen the oil.

● Prepare the soup through step 3 up to 1 day in advance.

> LESS

Use purchased basil oil.

> NOTES

● Look for real buttermilk, not the more common cultured substitute in our supermarkets. Real buttermilk—the liquid after making butter—will have a less sour, more savory finish, better to match the cucumbers and basil.

● For proper body and mouth feel, do not use "lite" or fat-free sour cream.

SOUP

- 2 pounds cucumbers (about 4 medium)
- 3 medium celery stalks, thinly sliced
- 3 medium scallions, thinly sliced
- ¼ cup olive oil
- ¼ cup loosely packed fresh basil leaves
- 1 teaspoon salt
- ½ teaspoon ground white pepper
- ¾ cup regular or low-fat buttermilk
- ¼ cup regular or reduced-fat sour cream

BASIL OIL

- 2 cups packed fresh basil leaves
- 1 cup olive oil

1. To make the soup: Peel the cucumbers, halve them lengthwise, and use a small spoon to scrape out (and discard) the seeds. Chop the cucumbers into small bits and add them to a large blender.

2. Add the celery, scallions, olive oil, basil, salt, and white pepper. Cover and blend until fairly smooth (there will be bits of celery string in the mix).

3. Strain the puree into a large bowl through a fine-mesh sieve or a colander lined with cheesecloth. Whisk in the buttermilk and sour cream. Cover and refrigerate for at least 4 hours.

(continued)

4. Meanwhile, to make the basil oil: Fill a large bowl with ice water. Bring a medium saucepan of water to a boil over high heat. Add the basil leaves and blanch for 10 seconds from the first bubble after they hit the water. Use a slotted spoon to transfer the leaves from the saucepan to the bowl with the ice water. Add more ice, chill for a few minutes, then skim the leaves out of the bowl with a slotted spoon and dry the leaves on paper towels.

5. Puree the basil with the olive oil in a blender. Let stand at room temperature for 1 hour to settle. Strain into a small bowl through a colander lined with cheesecloth.

6. To serve, ladle the soup into bowls. Drizzle each serving with basil oil.

▌ A MENU

SMALL PLATE: Baked Artichokes, Dulse Flakes, Pine Nuts (page 61)

SOUP: Cucumber Soup, Basil, Buttermilk

SALAD: Brussels Sprout/Fennel Salad, Kumquats (page 102)

PASTA: Drunken Spaghetti, Pine Nuts, Parsley (page 137)

DESSERT: Candied almonds and iced vodka shots

▌ POUR

Chilled sparkling water, preferably one with a very pure, clean taste

White Gazpacho, Fried Fennel Seeds

6 SERVINGS

This gazpacho is less American summery tradition and more European fancifulness. Versions of it have long been a favorite in Spain where the acidic sweetness of white grapes has been put to great culinary use. Light, flavorful, and best served at room temperature, this soup can mark an aromatic beginning to a meal or a shift between courses, maybe from something heavy back to something lighter. Although it's thickened with bread and stocked with vermouth, it's perhaps best in the summer when the bright flavors fit the weather—although surely welcome in the winter as a blues-dasher. It's so rich that you might consider serving slightly smaller portions, then having extra on hand for anyone who wants seconds.

- 3 cups stale baguette cubes
- 2 cups dry vermouth
- 3 cups salted, roasted Marcona almonds
- 3 cups seedless green grapes
- 3 tablespoons sherry vinegar
- 1 garlic clove, peeled
- 1½ cups ice-cold water
- 1 cup olive oil, divided
- 2 teaspoons fennel seeds

1. Pile the bread cubes in a large bowl, then souse them with the vermouth. Set aside until soft, about 20 minutes, stirring once to make sure they're all moist.

2. Gently squeeze the bread dry by the handful over the sink and put them in a large food processor. Add the almonds, grapes, vinegar, and garlic. Process to a thick puree, scraping down the inside of the bowl at least once.

3. With the machine running, drizzle in the cold water, then all but 1 tablespoon of the oil (that is, 15 tablespoons oil). If the soup remains too thick, drizzle in a little extra water, just to get it to the consistency of a thin porridge.

4. Warm the remaining 1 tablespoon oil in a medium skillet over medium heat for a couple of minutes. Add the fennel seeds and fry until crisp, less than 1 minute.

5. To serve, fill serving bowls with the soup and spoon the fried fennel seeds and even a little of their oil from the skillet over the bowlfuls.

▷ **AHEAD**

● Make the soup up to 6 hours in advance. Store it, covered, in the refrigerator. Since it may continue to thicken as it sits, you'll need to process in a little extra water to get it to the right consistency before serving. If you store it right in the food processor bowl, there'll be no trouble rehomogenizing it.

▷ **NOTES**

● If you've got a small food processor, smaller than a 6-cup model, you'll need to divide the ingredients in half and work in batches.

● Marcona almonds are a Spanish cultivar, most often fried in oil and served lightly salted. You can find them so prepared at most large supermarkets and from a bevy of online suppliers. They make great snacks before dinner, too, especially when paired with a glass of cava or even a fine sherry.

● Don't let the fennel seeds burn. The moment they turn fragrant or start to pop, remove them from the oil.

▷ **A MENU**

FIRST SMALL PLATE: Asiago Cookies, Tahini/Lentil Cream (page 89)

SECOND SMALL PLATE: Stewed Giant Lima Beans, Dandelion Greens, Feta (page 60)

SOUP: White Gazpacho, Fried Fennel Seeds

LARGE PLATE: Ratatouille Crudo (page 171)

DESSERT: Walnut/Honey Semifreddo, Pomegranate Molasses (page 257)

▷ **POUR**

Sparkling water, one that's quite minerally, with complexity and lots of sophistication

Gazpacho Shooters

8 SERVINGS

Years ago, we were at the Castine Inn on the coast of Maine and the chef served what he called "clear gazpacho." What came at us was a bowl of what looked like water but tasted exactly like cold, spicy, aromatic tomato soup. We instantly named him the "Master of the Cheesecloth." Since then, we've played with countless versions but have finally landed on this pale pink version, sweetened with watermelon but still laced with plenty of vegetables. You'll clarify it until it's nothing but the liquid essence of summer. You might even feel called upon to serve this in the winter when you're hankering for sunnier times. You won't need much else for this course, other than a piece of toasty bread.

8 cups peeled, cubed, seedless watermelon

1 large red bell pepper, diced

3 medium scallions, white and pale green parts only, thinly sliced

¼ cup white balsamic vinegar

Up to 3 small serrano chiles, seeded and thinly sliced

1 teaspoon salt

1. Puree the watermelon chunks in a large food processor until juicy and thick. Pour into a large bowl.

2. Add the bell pepper and scallions to the processor and pulse-chop until finely minced and somewhat juicy. Scrape and pour this mixture into the watermelon puree.

3. Stir the vinegar, serranos, and salt into the puree. Cover and chill for at least 8 hours or up to 24 hours.

4. Set up a jelly bag over a large bowl or line a fine-mesh sieve with a double layer of cheesecloth and set it over a large bowl. Ladle the watermelon gazpacho into the bag or sieve, working in batches to make sure nothing overflows. When all the gazpacho is in the bag or sieve, set aside for 1 hour to drain.

5. Discard the solids. Pour the strained liquid into a tall glass bottle or jar. Set aside in the fridge for at least 24 hours, allowing the remaining solids to fall to the bottom, leaving the "clear" pink liquid on top. Pour off this top liquid to serve cold in shot glasses.

AHEAD

The clarified gazpacho can be made up to 3 days in advance. Store, covered, in the refrigerator.

LESS

Look for cut-up watermelon in containers in the produce section of your supermarket. These chunks may not be seedless chunks, so you may have to spend your time seeding each. Which saves you zilch time. But at least you don't have to cut up a watermelon. Pureed seeds, even though they're strained out, will put an unappetizing bitterness in the soup.

GARNISH

Drip Basil Oil (page 123) or smoked olive oil over the shots.

A MENU

FIRST LARGE PLATE: Goat Cheese Fondue, Grilled Bread, Pears (page 173)

SOUP: Gazpacho Shooters

SECOND LARGE PLATE: Eggplant Wontons, Tomato Sauce, Gooey Fontina (page 230)

DESSERT: Olive Oil/Vin Santo Cake, Pine Nuts, Dried Apples (page 265)

POUR

Nothing. Let this surprising soup stand on its own.

Pear Soup, Ginger, Buttery Leeks

6 SERVINGS

This hot soup is sweet and rich, mostly thanks to creamy pears, which are balanced by earthy leeks and brightened with a spicy hit of ginger. Although it's pretty simple, you can see that we're leaving juxtaposition behind and moving into a more profound melding of flavors in the dishes. So you'll want a more acidic palette of flavors in the dishes surrounding this one. When you're at the store, remember the rule for fruit: If pears don't smell like anything, they won't taste like anything.

2 tablespoons unsalted butter

1 large leek (white and pale green part only), halved lengthwise, carefully washed, and thinly sliced

3 pounds very ripe Bartlett pears, peeled, cored, and sliced

¾ cup dry white wine, such as Chardonnay

5 cups vegetable broth

One 2-inch piece fresh ginger, peeled and cut into thin matchsticks

1 teaspoon salt

1. Melt the butter in a large pot or Dutch oven over low heat. Add the leek and cook, stirring frequently, for 5 minutes. Add the pears and cook until quite soft, about 15 minutes, stirring very often.

2. Use the back of a wooden spoon to mash the pears against the side of the pan. Stir in the wine. Cook, stirring often, until the wine is reduced by half, about 3 minutes.

3. Stir in the broth and ginger. Increase the heat to medium-high and bring to a simmer. Cover, reduce the heat to low, and simmer slowly until thickened and creamy, about 30 minutes. Stir in the salt before serving.

AHEAD

● Make the soup up to 2 days in advance. Store, covered, in the refrigerator. Add a little extra broth to thin it out and warm over medium heat before serving.

GARNISH

Grind black pepper and sprinkle minced parsley leaves over each bowl.

NOTES

● The pears should be so ripe that if you bite into one, the juice will run down your chin. If they're firmer, you'll need to cook them longer in step 1, up to 30 minutes. Test repeatedly to see when you can mash them into a pulp.

● To ripen pears, place them in a brown paper bag, seal, and set on the counter for 1 to 2 days.

● Mash the pears but don't puree them. You want some texture in the final dish.

A MENU

FIRST SMALL PLATE: Steamed Artichokes, Red Peppers, Basil (page 42)

SOUP: Pear Soup, Ginger, Buttery Leeks

LARGE PLATE: Stuffed Escarole, Agrodolce Sauce (page 223)

SECOND SMALL PLATE: Blue Cheese Cheescake, Walnuts, Dill (page 86)

DESSERT: Nothing but strong coffee

POUR

A floral but balanced New Zealand Sauvignon Blanc to foreground the pears with its peach undertones

Garlic Soup, Gruyère, Cognac

8 SERVINGS

Here's a twisted version of French onion soup, all the onions replaced by garlic and shallots. We roast the garlic to sweeten its flavors—but there's still a lot of that nose-spanking punch left. The cheesy bread rounds in the soup help calm down those pugilistic tendencies, but you'll want to have even more bread on hand—or else melt additional Gruyère over more baguette rounds under the broiler to ensure you've got extra on hand for those who want more. Make sure the soup is quite hot when you ladle it into the bowls so the cheese melts properly.

6 garlic heads

6 tablespoons olive oil, divided, plus more for the bread

12 medium shallots, peeled

10 cups (2½ quarts) vegetable broth

¼ cup Cognac

1 tablespoon fresh thyme leaves

1 teaspoon salt

½ teaspoon freshly ground black pepper

8 slices (1-inch-thick) baguette

8 ounces Gruyère cheese, finely grated

1. Position the rack in the center of the oven and heat to 400°F.

2. Slice the top third off the garlic heads so that most of the cloves are exposed. Place them on a large sheet of foil, drizzle with 3 tablespoons of the oil, and seal closed. Roast on a baking rack in the oven until the cloves are as soft as room-temperature butter, about 40 minutes.

3. At the same time, place the shallots in a small, shallow baking dish and drizzle with the remaining 3 tablespoons oil. Roast until browned, caramelized, and even a little crispy, stirring occasionally, about 30 minutes.

4. Remove both the garlic and shallots from the oven and cool at room temperature for 15 minutes.

5. Squeeze the soft pulp out of the garlic heads and into a large saucepan. Roughly chop the shallots and add them to the pan. Stir in the broth, Cognac, thyme, salt, and pepper. Set the pan over medium heat and bring to a simmer. Cover, reduce the heat to low, and simmer slowly for 45 minutes to blend and soften the flavors.

6. Rub both sides of the baguette slices with olive oil. Toast the slices on a baking sheet 4 to 6 inches from a heated broiler.

7. To serve, place a baguette toast in each of 8 serving bowls. Top each toast with ¼ cup cheese. Ladle the hot soup into the bowls.

AHEAD

● Prepare the recipe through step 5 up to 6 hours in advance. Store, covered, in the refrigerator. When ready to serve, bring back to a simmer, covered, over medium heat, while you make the toast rounds.

NOTE

● Ladle the soup around the bread, not on it, to keep more of the cheese in place.

A MENU

FIRST SMALL PLATE: Walnuts, Peas, Daikon, Butter, Tomatoes (page 52)

SOUP: Garlic Soup, Gruyère, Cognac

SALAD: Apple Slaw, Fried Chickpeas (page 108)

SECOND SMALL PLATE: Butternut Squash Tart, Toasted Almonds, Roquefort (page 82)

DESSERT: Almond/Cardamom Biscotti (page 238) and champagne

POUR

An aromatic Spanish Albariño with its food-friendly acidity and mild herbal notes

Miso Soup, Celery Root, Rye Berries

8 SERVINGS

This is the heartiest soup in this book, a new take on traditional miso soup, pumped up a bit with the heft of whole grains and skewed more to the earth with the root vegetable. Yes, there's still a little seaweed in the mix, but it serves only to bring forward the dank sweetness of those rye berries, perhaps a surprise ingredient. Since a yeasty bread may prove too confusing as an accompaniment, we'd suggest some warmed lavash or lefse; a simpler taste to match the simpler flavors in this winter warmer.

¾ cup dried rye berries

1 ounce kombu (six 2-inch squares)

1½ pounds celery root (aka celeriac), trimmed, peeled, and cut into ½-inch cubes

¼ cup white miso paste

3 scallions, thinly sliced

1. Place the rye berries and kombu in a large pot or Dutch oven and fill the pot two-thirds full of water. Bring to a boil over high heat, stirring occasionally. Reduce the heat to low and simmer uncovered for 20 minutes. Use kitchen tongs to transfer the kombu from the pot to a small bowl. Keep simmering the rye berries until tender, about 40 more minutes.

2. Set a colander over a large bowl. Drain the rye berries, catching the liquid in the bowl below. Remove the bowl and rinse the grains in the colander with cool tap water to stop the cooking. Drain thoroughly.

3. Add enough water to the liquid in the bowl so that it measures 6 cups. Pour this mixture back into the pot. Stir in the celery root and miso paste. Bring to a simmer over medium-high heat, stirring often. Cover, reduce the heat to low, and simmer until the celery root is tender, about 20 minutes.

4. Shred the kombu into little strips. Stir these and the rye berries into the pot. Cover and simmer for 5 minutes to heat through.

5. To serve, ladle the soup into bowls and top each with sliced scallion.

AHEAD

• Prepare the soup through step 3 up to 2 hours in advance. Store the soup in the fridge; store the kombu and rye berries at room temperature. Bring the soup back to a simmer before proceeding with step 4.

NOTE

• Rye berries are not berries but instead the rye grains themselves, which can be ground to make rye flour. They're chewy and sweet, a firm contrast to the salty miso paste. Look for them at most health food stores, at high-end supermarkets, and (of course) from online whole-grain suppliers. If you can't find them, substitute hard red wheat berries, cooked in the same manner.

A MENU

SMALL PLATE: Red Cabbage Pot Stickers, Raisin Chipotle Dip (page 92)

SOUP: Miso Soup, Celery Root, Rye Berries

PASTA: Soba Noodles, Edamame, Kumquats (page 143)

DESSERT: Fresh peach halves, sprinkled with warm, toasted sliced almonds and drizzled with aged balsamic vinegar

POUR

A chilled Japanese beer like Kirin Ichiban, notably sweet

5

PASTAS

Pasta has a split personality. Sure, a box of spaghetti and a quick sauce make an easy Wednesday night dinner. But rolling out pasta signals a dinner party like nothing else. Carefully crafted noodles and a long-simmered sauce are the hallmarks of a celebration. Yes, there's flour everywhere. And the counter's a mess. But there's also something peaceful about the process: the repetitive and steady progress toward a great meal. All that hard work will pay off.

We don't expect everyone to pull out a pasta roller. Such tasks will come when you're more comfortable with your skills at throwing one of these multicourse affairs. While some of the following recipes do indeed include hand-rolled pasta, they all have a *Less* option that lets you know how to use purchased pasta to great effect. In fact, some of the recipes *must* be made with dried pasta. You need its extra chew to stand up to some of the sauces. And some of these dishes are made with large pasta sheets, available at high-end supermarkets and many Italian specialty stores.

As befitting pasta's split personality, these dishes ride the line between small and large plates. Some can be a first course, part of a larger meal; others can be a final course after a couple of small plates. Ending with pasta may not be an authentic Italian adventure, but we'll bet you're not interested in standing on ceremony where great food and good company are concerned. A plate of pasta is often a satisfying and substantial end in and of itself.

With a vegetarian dinner party, we're in luck. Vegetables readily take to pasta. The fresh, herbaceous flavors blend naturally with the wheaty or starchy noodles. But it's not just simple alignment: some vegetables, some fettuccine. Throughout these recipes, we're consistently building a better meld than in the small plates and salads. The sauces are more

complex, reduced or baked to harmonize the flavors; any fillings, married for a deeper palette.

But there are a few caveats. As we've said, the basic flavors of vegetarian fare make up a bigger range than those found in meatish dishes. So pasta sauces have to balance musky, sour, and/ or spicy notes that a pan sauce for, say, a chicken sauté would never have to deal with. We have to give the sauce extra oomph with herbs, vinegar, wine, or even unusual flavorings so it'll stand up to its varied vegetable ingredients.

For example, when we first started making our fig and olive ravioli baked in a cardamom cream sauce, we loved the North African flavors, the briny stuffing for the ravioli, and the overall luxurious texture in the casserole. But the pasta itself seemed rather forlorn, almost an afterthought, its bready creaminess lost in translation. How to bring it back into the dish? After a couple of tries, we added a drop or two of floral orange flower water to the sauce. The flavors instantly came back to a better balance, the pasta now equal with other ingredients and the fig/olive combo in the filling a tad tamed in the overall effect of the dish.

Beyond pasta, there are also two versions of gnocchi (little potato dumplings), a well-stocked polenta, and two risottos. None of these latter recipes seem fit for a main course. They all look forward to an even more complex blend of flavors in a large plate.

Once you've done the kitchen work, it's just a matter of plating. Pasta, gnocchi, and risotto don't take to fussy presentations. A few herbs sprinkled on top might be nice, but it's about as far as you'll want to go. Tell your inner art director to have a seat. Offer the dishes with a clean, straightforward look. The flavors on the plate

are moderately complex; there's no need to complicate them visually. Or just have a family-style Italian meal: Pile the pasta or risotto in a big bowl and put it in the middle of

the table. Even the fussiest guest won't blink when they taste the fabulous balance of vegetables and noodles you're created.

KEEPING IT TOGETHER

Although most of the recipes in this book include lots of pieces or parts that can be made in advance (including the whole dish for some of them), you do often lash yourself to a few last-minute tasks when you're pulling together a pasta dish for the table. Here are some good strategies to get you through the crush:

1. Don't leave your guests unattended. Make sure someone keeps the conversation flowing.
2. Use downtime while a sauce is simmering or a pasta is cooking to do simple tasks. Get the dishes out of the sink and into the dishwasher. Or check on the kids. Or take the dog out for a quick break.
3. Don't create a menu that includes pasta if this is your first dinner party. Keep things within your skill set. You've got to enjoy this celebration, too.
4. Be honest. You can always say, *This next course is going to take me about 10 minutes.* As a guest, there's nothing worse than hearing pots rattling and kettles whistling in the kitchen, all the while wondering what in the world is going on. If you let your friends know the full story, they can relax.
5. Plan. Know how long you need for each task; cheat where you can. Start that water boiling for the pasta while you're eating the previous course.
6. Open that next bottle of wine before you leave the dining room.

Saturday night

- Masa tarts, caramelized garlic custard, radish slaw?

- Walnuts, Peas, Daikon

- Fettucine, Curried Chickpeas, Dried Apricots

- Fleur de Sel Caramels + Amontill...

Did you get the apples?

Firewood?

Jim — is some

Wine
 — White?
 — Cab Franc

Drunken Spaghetti, Pine Nuts, Parsley

8 SERVINGS

Sometimes, even more modernist vegetarian dinner-party fare has to go with the classics, particularly if the preceding course (or courses) included innovative flavor combinations. And there's not much more classic than this dish! Cooking spaghetti in red wine has long been an Italian extravagance. In our version, we use a full bottle of hearty wine for the pasta (and thus get it "drunk"), then we go on to add lots of garlic along with lemon zest, red pepper flakes, and (yes) more red wine (although of a different variety) for a fairly simple dish that's quite elegant, despite its rustic roots. Tuck your napkin under your chin and dig in!

4 quarts water

1 bottle (750ml) sturdy, dry red wine, preferably an Italian Chianti

1½ pounds dried spaghetti

½ cup olive oil

3 garlic cloves, minced

6 tablespoons pine nuts

1 tablespoon finely grated lemon zest

1 teaspoon red pepper flakes

1 cup dry but fairly fruit-forward red wine, preferably a California Syrah

¾ cup minced fresh parsley leaves

1. Combine the water and the bottle of wine in a Dutch oven or stock-pot and bring to a boil over high heat. Add the pasta and cook until tender but still firm, 6 to 9 minutes. (Fish out a noodle and check. If you break open a noodle, there should still be a white center running through it.) Drain the spaghetti in a colander set in the sink.

2. Put a large skillet over medium heat for a few minutes, then pour in the oil. Add the garlic and fry just until browning at the edges, about 1 minute.

3. Add the pine nuts and cook about another minute, stirring often, just until they begin to brown. Stir in the lemon zest and red pepper flakes, then pour in the 1 cup red wine. Increase the heat to high and boil hard for 2 minutes.

4. Add the pasta and toss in the sauce for 2 to 3 minutes, until the liquid has been absorbed. Stir in the parsley and serve.

AHEAD

● Boil the spaghetti in the wine and water, then drain it up to 30 minutes in advance. Rinse with cool water and drain again before adding it to the skillet in step 4.

NOTES

● Don't even think about using fresh pasta here—it'll be too fragile, particularly for the second cooking in more wine. In fact, remove the spaghetti from the pot of boiling water before you think it's ready. It'll cook another few minutes in the skillet.

● If you use a dried pasta other than spaghetti, make sure there's no egg in the mix to keep the dish vegan.

A MENU

FIRST SMALL PLATE: Roasted Cipollini Onions, Fava Beans Two Ways (page 56)

SECOND SMALL PLATE: Parsnip Flans (page 64)

PASTA: Drunken Spaghetti, Pine Nuts, Parsley

DESSERT: Walnut/Honey Semifreddo, Pomegranate Molasses (page 257)

POUR

More of the same full-bodied, plum-and-blueberry-laced Syrah from the recipe

Ziti, Chard, Beans, Poached Eggs

8 SERVINGS

For us, standing at the counter in the afternoon while forming these little ziti around the wooden handle of a spoon and listening to good music in the background just spells *stay-at-home comfort*: a challenging if doable task, friends on their way later, a wonderful meal ahead in the evening. Then to toss that hand-made pasta with earthy chard and sweet beans? Does it get any better? Well, yes. We top each serving with a poached egg. Comfort becomes dinner-party bliss in generous portions.

◗ AHEAD

● Make the pasta dough up to 8 hours in advance. Dust a couple of large rimmed baking sheets with all-purpose flour, arrange the pasta in a single layer, cover tightly in plastic wrap, and refrigerate.

◗ LESS

Use 1½ pounds dried ziti, cooked and drained according to package instructions.

PASTA

- 4 cups all-purpose flour, plus more for kneading
- 2 teaspoons salt
- 6 large eggs, at room temperature
- 6 tablespoons olive oil

SAUCE

- ¼ cup olive oil
- 2 small yellow onions, chopped (about 1½ cups)
- 4 medium garlic cloves, minced
- 12 cups washed, stemmed, and chopped Swiss chard leaves
- 1 can (28 ounces) white beans, drained and rinsed (about 3½ cups)
- 1½ cups fruit-forward but dry white wine, such as Vouvray
- 1 cup finely grated aged Asiago cheese (about 4 ounces)
- 2 tablespoons minced fresh sage leaves
- 1 teaspoon salt
- 1 teaspoon freshly ground black pepper
- 8 large eggs
- 4 teaspoons finely grated lemon zest

1. To make the pasta: Mix the flour and salt in a large bowl. Make a well in the center, then crack the eggs into the hole. Add the oil and whisk with a fork until smooth without picking up much of the flour. Slowly whisk in the flour mixture, a little from the walls at a time, incorporating as you whisk until you've added about two-thirds. Collapse the walls into the center and stir with a fork—and then with your clean, dry hands—until a soft, smooth dough forms.

2. Dust a clean, dry work surface with flour, then turn the dough out onto it. Knead until smooth and elastic, folding the dough over and pressing those folds into the dough with the heel of your hand while pulling it gently, then continually turning the dough to new sides and repeating this process, about 10 minutes.

3. Divide the dough into 8 equal pieces, then run these one at a time through a pasta machine, flouring the dough to keep it from sticking at first and lowering the settings until the pasta sheet has been rolled out at #5 (the next to last setting on the machine).

4. Cut these strips into 1½-inch squares. Flour the handle of a wooden spoon, then roll each square around the handle. Remove the handle and press the edges to seal. Repeat, flouring the handle as necessary to prevent sticking.

5. Bring a large pot of water to a boil over high heat. Add the ziti and cook for 3 minutes from when they hit the water, just to set the pasta and offer it some chew. Drain in a colander set in the sink.

6. To make the sauce: Put a large skillet or sauté pan over medium heat for a few minutes, then pour in the oil. Add the onions and cook, stirring often, until soft, about 4 minutes. Stir in the garlic and cook until fragrant, about 1 minute.

7. Dump in the chard and use tongs to toss it over the heat until wilted, about 2 minutes. Stir in the beans and white wine. Bring to a simmer, toss well, cover, reduce the heat to low, and simmer until the sauce has reduced and the chard is tender, about 10 minutes, stirring occasionally. Stir in the cooked pasta, Asiago, sage, salt, and pepper. Set aside.

8. Bring a large Dutch oven or soup pot of water to a simmer over high heat. Reduce the heat to low and simmer slowly. Working in batches, crack an egg into a custard cup and slip the egg into the water. Repeat with 2 more eggs. Poach at the slowest simmer until the whites are set but the yolks are still runny, about 3 minutes. With a slotted spoon, scoop them out and onto a plate lined with paper towels. Continue poaching more eggs, cooking no more than 3 eggs at a time.

9. Divide the pasta and sauce among 8 serving bowls. Top each with a poached egg and sprinkle each serving with ½ teaspoon lemon zest.

A MENU

SMALL PLATE: Portobello Confit, Pickled Ramps (page 66)

PASTA: Ziti, Chard, Beans, Poached Eggs

LARGE PLATE: Grilled Cauliflower, Thai Chili Sauce, Sweet Potato Puree (page 180)

DESSERT: Coconut Crepes, Passion Fruit Cream (page 264)

POUR

A gorgeously golden Marsanne with its spicy apricot hints, like jam on toast to those eggs

Kamut Pappardelle, Mushroom Ragù

8 SERVINGS

If a pasta dish becomes a main course, it then has to live up to its billing. The good news is that no one will mistake this hearty dish for anything but a showstopping climax to the meal. We use Kamut flour for a more wheaty flavor and texture in the wide noodles. A great many Italian chefs believe it is the preferred flour for pasta. But it's high time we got in on the act with luxurious, full-flavored noodles like these! We mix them with an earthy ragù made from dried porcini and two kinds of fresh mushrooms, bound together by herbaceous Marsala wine, a Sicilian staple.

PASTA

- 2⅔ cups Kamut flour (see page 27)
- 1⅓ cups all-purpose flour, plus more for kneading and rolling
- 1 teaspoon salt
- 6 large eggs, at room temperature
- 6 tablespoons olive oil
- Water as needed

RAGÙ

- 2 ounces dried porcini mushrooms
- 4 cups boiling water
- ¼ cup olive oil
- 2 medium yellow onions, chopped (about 2 cups)
- 8 cups thinly sliced cremini or brown mushrooms
- 4 medium garlic cloves, minced
- 6 ounces fresh shiitake mushrooms, stems discarded, caps thinly sliced
- 2 tablespoons minced fresh rosemary leaves
- 4 teaspoons fresh thyme leaves
- 1 teaspoon salt
- Up to 1 teaspoon red pepper flakes
- 2 cups Marsala wine
- 12 ounces tomato paste

❱ AHEAD

● Make the ragù up to 24 hours in advance. Cool and store, covered, in the refrigerator. Rewarm over low heat before dinner.

● Make the pasta up to 8 hours in advance. Dust a large rimmed baking sheet with all-purpose flour, arrange the pasta in a single layer, cover tightly in plastic wrap, and refrigerate.

❱ LESS

Look for fresh pappardelle at large or high-end supermarkets. Cook and drain according to the package instructions.

❱ GARNISH

Sprinkle finely grated Pecorino Romano cheese and/or fresh thyme leaves over each serving.

1. To make the pasta: Mix both flours and salt in a large bowl. Make a well in the center, then crack the eggs into the hole. Add the oil and whisk with a fork until smooth without picking up much of the flour. Slowly whisk in the flour mixture, a little from the walls at a time, incorporating as you whisk until you've added about two-thirds. If the mixture at the center is already stiff, add water 1 teaspoon at a time to loosen it up. Collapse the flour walls into the center and stir with a fork, again adding a little more water if necessary to keep the mixture pliable but not sticky. Finally, use your clean, dry hands to knead the mixture until a soft, smooth dough forms.

2. Dust a clean, dry work surface with all-purpose flour, then turn the dough out onto it. Knead until smooth and elastic, folding the dough over and pressing those folds into the dough with the heel of your hand while pulling it gently, then continually turning the dough to new sides and repeating this process, about 10 minutes.

3. Pull off an egg-shaped piece of dough, dust it with flour, and roll it through a pasta machine repeatedly, working it through the machine time and again as you lower the settings to #5 (the next to lowest one). Cut these sheets of dough lengthwise into 1-inch-wide strips with a pizza roller, pasta roller, or very sharp paring knife. Dust with flour and set aside on a parchment-lined baking sheet while you continue making more.

4. To make the ragù: Cover the dried porcini with the boiling water in a large heatproof bowl and set aside. Set a large saucepan or high-sided sauté pan over medium heat, then add the oil. Toss in the onion and cook, stirring often, until softened, about 5 minutes.

5. Add the cremini mushrooms and cook, stirring occasionally, until they release their liquid and the pan dries out, about 10 minutes. Stir in the garlic and cook until fragrant, less than 1 minute. Scrape the contents of the pan into a large food processor. Reserve the pan, no matter its condition.

6. Use a slotted spoon to fish the porcinis (and any bits) out of the soaking liquid (reserve that liquid). Squeeze the porcinis dry by handfuls over the bowl of reserved liquid, then add the porcini to the food processor. Add the shiitake mushrooms. rosemary, thyme, salt, and red pepper flakes. Process until coarsely ground, about like ground meat.

7. Set the saucepan or sauté pan back over high heat. Pour in the Marsala and bring to a full boil, scraping up any browned bits still in the pan. Boil until the liquid has been reduced by half, about 8 minutes.

8. Measure the mushroom liquid and add enough water to bring it to 4 cups. Stir this mushroom broth and the tomato paste into the reduced Marsala until smooth. Bring to a full simmer. Stir in the mushroom mixture from the food processor and bring back to a simmer. Cover, reduce the heat to low, and simmer slowly until thickened like a traditional ragù, not soupy at all, about 30 minutes.

9. Bring a large pot of water to a boil over high heat. Add the pasta and cook about 3 minutes from the moment it hits the water, stirring occasionally. Drain in a colander set in the sink. Twirl the pasta on serving plates and spoon the mushroom ragù on top.

NOTES

● Those eggs must be at room temperature to meld properly with the flour and make tender pasta. Leave them out on the counter for 20 minutes before making the pasta.

● There should never be any need to salt the water in which you cook pasta. The sauce should have enough salt to season the dish properly. And while we're at it, there's absolutely no call for oiling the cooking water. You just end up with oily noodles.

● Check the reserved mushroom soaking liquid to see if there's any grit in the bowl. If so, line a colander with a single layer of cheesecloth or a large coffee filter, set a bowl underneath, and strain the liquid to remove that grit.

A MENU

FIRST SMALL PLATE: Tomato Gelée, Pistachio Shortbread (page 67)

SECOND SMALL PLATE: Asparagus Spears, Pickled Radicchio (page 40)

PASTA: Kamut Pappardelle, Mushroom Ragù

DESSERT: Strawberries drizzled with syrupy, aged balsamic vinegar and sprinkled with ground black pepper

POUR

A luscious, bold, red Barolo to keep the flavors earthy, with a balanced acidity to bring the pasta itself forward in the heavy sauce

Fettuccine, Curried Chickpeas, Dried Apricots

8 SERVINGS

A last-minute dish, this one's a mash-up of dried spices, fresh ingredients, and dried fruit. It's a wild range: from coriander to pecans, nutmeg to chickpeas, cinnamon to scallions. The key to bringing those disparate tastes together is the pecan oil, something of a luxury. It's sweet and satisfying. Just wait until you use the leftover oil to make a pecan pie or a simple vinaigrette! Trouble is, pecan oil doesn't move off the shelf all that often and so can be rancid by the time it gets into your cart at the store. Open it up the moment you get home and make sure it smells like pecans, neither acrid nor tangy. If it's rancid, take it back for a full refund. Store an opened bottle or can in your refrigerator for up to 3 months.

2 cups canned chickpeas, drained and rinsed

1 cup chopped dried apricots

2 teaspoons ground coriander

1 teaspoon ground cinnamon

1 teaspoon ground cumin

1 teaspoon ground ginger

½ teaspoon ground turmeric

½ teaspoon salt

¼ teaspoon freshly grated nutmeg

Up to ¼ teaspoon cayenne pepper

1 cup roasted pecan oil

2⅔ cups chopped pecan pieces

2 pounds fresh spinach fettuccine, cooked and drained according to the package instructions

1 cup thinly sliced scallions, dark green parts only

1 tablespoon finely grated orange zest

1. Mix the chickpeas, apricots, coriander, cinnamon, cumin, ginger, turmeric, salt, nutmeg, and cayenne in a large bowl. Set aside.

2. Heat the oil in a very large, deep skillet over medium heat. Add the pecans and cook, stirring all the while, until fragrant and lightly browned, about 4 minutes. Add the chickpea mixture and stir over the heat for 1 minute.

3. Stir in the pasta, scallions, and orange zest. Toss over the heat for 30 seconds before plating.

▶ AHEAD

● Mix the chickpeas, apricots, and spices up to 6 hours in advance. Store, covered, at room temperature.

▶ MORE

Follow this flavorful dish with this palate cleanser: Smash about 2 tablespoons softened orange sorbet and ½ ounce (1 tablespoon) Aperol in a highball glass or a tall, narrow glass. Top with a splash (1 to 2 ounces) of chilled prosecco.

▶ GARNISH

Serve with grilled lemon wedges.

▶ NOTES

● If you don't have a large, deep skillet, you might have to divide this dish between 2 smaller skillets and cook both at the same time.

● Most fresh fettuccine is made with eggs—however, there are fresh eggless versions available in some high-end supermarkets, if you'd like to turn this dish vegan.

▶ A MENU

FIRST SMALL PLATE: Masa Tarts, Caramelized Garlic Custard, Radish Slaw (page 79)

SECOND SMALL PLATE: Walnuts, Peas, Daikon, Butter, Tomatoes (page 52)

PASTA: Fettuccine, Curried Chickpeas, Dried Apricots

DESSERT: Fleur de Sel Caramels (page 279) and aged Amontillado sherry

▶ POUR

An unoaked Chardonnay for apricot and citrus notes without any complicated tobacco undertones

Soba Noodles, Edamame, Kumquats

8 SERVINGS

We love zippy kumquats and salty edamame, both excellent snacks. And we love them even more together in a single dish, a smack of sour against sweet. We've matched them with firm, almost nutty soba noodles in a melded sauce that's still pretty bright in its flavors but has also tamed the expected clash of those paired flavors to give it a wonderfully sophisticated finish.

2 cups frozen edamame, thawed

21 ounces dried soba noodles (two 300-gram packages)

6 tablespoons fresh lime juice

¼ cup soy sauce

2 tablespoons finely grated palm sugar or packed light brown sugar

2 teaspoons tamarind paste (see page 187)

2 tablespoons toasted sesame oil

6 scallions, thinly sliced

1 tablespoon minced garlic

6 ounces fresh shiitake mushrooms, stems discarded, caps thinly sliced

8 kumquats, thinly sliced and seeded

1. Set up a bowl of ice water. Bring a large saucepan of water to a boil over high heat. Add the edamame and blanch for 2 minutes. Use a slotted spoon to transfer them to the ice water. Stir well, then drain in a colander set in the sink. Dump the edamame into a large bowl and set aside.

2. Add more ice to that bowl of water. Bring the saucepan of water back to a boil over high heat. Add the soba noodles, stir well, and cook until tender but with some bite at the center of each noodle, about 3 minutes. Use a slotted spoon to transfer the noodles to the ice water. Add some more ice and set aside.

3. Whisk the lime juice, soy sauce, palm sugar, and tamarind paste in a small bowl until the sugar dissolves. Drain the noodles in a colander set in the sink and transfer to a large bowl.

4. Set a large wok over high heat for a few minutes, then add the oil. Immediately add the scallions and garlic and stir-fry for 1 minute. Add the shiitakes and edamame and stir-fry for 1 minute.

5. Add the lime juice mixture. Bring to a full simmer, stir-frying until bubbling and the vegetables are coated in sauce, about 2 minutes. Scrape the contents of the wok over the noodles and toss gently. Divide among serving plates or mound on a large platter. Top with kumquats.

AHEAD

• The edamame can be blanched up to 8 hours in advance. Store, covered, at room temperature.

• The lime juice mixture can be whisked together up to 6 hours in advance. Store, covered, at room temperature.

• The noodles can be boiled up to 2 hours in advance. Store in their ice water on the counter. Drain and heat in a microwave on high for 20 to 30 seconds to take off any chill.

LESS

Look for ready-to-eat, fresh, shelled edamame in the produce section; they needn't be blanched.

A MENU

FIRST SMALL PLATE: Roasted Radishes, Their Greens, Browned Butter (page 35)

SECOND SMALL PLATE: Kohlrabi, Enoki, Peanuts, Grilled Scallions (page 59)

PASTA: Soba Noodles, Edamame, Kumquats

DESSERT: Dried figs, dates, and dark chocolate

POUR

A sweet, low-alcohol Moscato d'Asti, often served at dessert, but here a tangerine-and-honey match to the sweet-and-sour sauce

Rice Noodles, North African Ragù

6 SERVINGS

This heavily spiced stew of tomatoes, peas, and sugar snaps is a light and flavorful way to bring summer to the table. With flavors reminiscent of a tagine, the sauce is served over rice noodles, a somewhat chewy textural contrast to those crunchy vegetables. Cook them in step 3 as little as possible so they stay toothsome, just warmed through and barely softened.

⅓ cup olive oil

1½ cups chopped yellow onion

1 tablespoon minced garlic

1 tablespoon minced fresh ginger

1 teaspoon ground coriander

1 teaspoon ground cumin

½ teaspoon ground cardamom

½ teaspoon ground cinnamon

½ teaspoon salt

¼ teaspoon ground cloves

Up to ¼ teaspoon cayenne pepper

1 can (14.5 ounces) crushed tomatoes (about 1¾ cups)

2 tablespoons packed dark brown sugar

12 ounces baby zucchini, cut into ½-inch-thick rounds (about 1½ cups)

6 ounces sugar snap peas, trimmed and cut into ½-inch pieces (about 1½ cups)

1 cup frozen green peas, thawed

1 pound moderately wide (about ½ inch) dried rice noodles

1. Set a large saucepan over medium heat for a couple of minutes, then swirl in the oil. Add the onion and cook, stirring often, until translucent and softened, about 5 minutes. Stir in the garlic and ginger; cook, stirring often, for 1 minute.

2. Stir in the coriander, cumin, cardamom, cinnamon, salt, cloves, and cayenne; cook until fragrant, about 1 minute, stirring almost constantly. Stir in the tomatoes and brown sugar and bring to a simmer. Cover, reduce the heat to low, and simmer slowly for 15 minutes.

3. Stir in the zucchini, sugar snaps, and green peas. Cook until crisp-tender, stirring often, no more than 3 minutes. Set the ragù aside, covered.

4. Soak the noodles in a large bowl of warm tap water for 10 minutes. Meanwhile, bring a large pot of water to a boil over high heat. Drain the noodles, then add them to the pot. Boil until chewy-tender, 2 to 3 minutes. Drain again, then divide them among bowls and ladle the ragù on top.

▌ AHEAD

● Make the ragù through step 2 up to 24 hours in advance. Store, covered, in the refrigerator and warm, covered, over medium heat before serving.

▌ LESS

Substitute 1½ tablespoons tikka or Kashmiri masala blend for the spices. Check to see if you need to add salt to those spice blends.

▌ GARNISH

Sprinkle black sesame seeds over each serving.

▌ A MENU

SMALL PLATE: Chickpea Blini, Curried Sweet Potatoes (page 74)

SALAD: Apple Slaw, Fried Chickpeas (page 108)

PASTA: Rice Noodles, North African Ragù

DESSERT: Pecan Baklava, Fennel Syrup (page 245)

▌ POUR

A velvety Semillon, particularly from Oregon, with crisp minerality and honeysuckle notes to work against the big palette of spices

Leek/Gorgonzola Lasagna

8 SERVINGS

This was the first recipe we wrote out for this book. The dish proved a winner at a dinner party among committed carnivores, even a couple who run a grass-fed beef farm! The basic flavor fusing—spunky blue cheese with sweet leeks and fragrant nutmeg—actually sparks new accents among the ingredients, downright umami bits with faint, sweet notes, mostly because of the way the oven's heat takes the edge off the ingredients to allow them a better marriage than mere proximity. Sure, there's plenty of Gorgonzola here. But it doesn't power up over everything else. The leeks are poached whole and then layered with the pasta and sauce. You'll need a sharp knife to cut it into squares without tearing the leeks.

▶ AHEAD

● Braise the leeks up to 2 days in advance. Store on a covered plate in the fridge.

● Make the sauce up to 4 hours in advance. Keep it covered on the back of the stove and reheat over low heat before using.

▶ NOTES

● Large fresh lasagna sheets are available at high-end markets and specialty Italian grocery stores. They're often made to the exact size of a 9 x 13-inch baking dish. If not, you'll need to slice them down to the right size to fit. And if they're small, you'll need to double the number of large, cutting them to piece together and fit each layer.

● If you can't find fresh pasta sheets, use 3 dried lasagna noodles for every fresh pasta sheet. Boil and drain the dried pasta according to the package instructions. (And one caveat: Do not use no-boil noodles for this fairly low-moisture casserole.)

● Don't bake the casserole any longer than suggested—and don't let it sit out on the counter too long. It can dry out.

3 cups dry vermouth

3 cups vegetable broth

10 fresh sprigs thyme

6 large leeks (about 2½ pounds), white and pale green parts only, halved lengthwise and washed carefully

4 tablespoons (½ stick) unsalted butter

5 tablespoons all-purpose flour

2 cups dry but light white wine, such as a Pinot Blanc

2 cups whole or low-fat milk

2 ounces Gorgonzola cheese

½ teaspoon salt

½ teaspoon freshly grated nutmeg

½ teaspoon freshly ground black pepper

3 to 6 large fresh lasagna sheets (see Note)

⅔ cup coarsely ground toasted walnuts

2 ounces Parmigiano-Reggiano cheese, finely grated (about ½ cup)

1. Bring the vermouth, broth, and thyme sprigs to a simmer in a large, high-sided sauté pan or skillet over high heat. Add the leeks, cover, reduce the heat to low, and simmer slowly until very tender, about 1 hour. Carefully remove the leeks from the pan with a large spatula. Drain them on a plate lined with paper towels.

2. Melt the butter in a large skillet or sauté pan over medium heat. Whisk in the flour until a light paste forms. Drizzle in the wine, whisking all the while, until smooth. Whisk in the milk and cook, whisking all the while, until thickened and bubbling, about 2 minutes. Crumble in the Gorgonzola, and add the salt, nutmeg, and pepper, whisking until smooth.

(continued)

3. Position the rack in the center of the oven and heat to 350°F.

4. Blot the leeks dry. Bring a large pot or Dutch oven of water to a boil over high heat. Add the fresh lasagna sheets one at a time for 2 minutes, fishing each out with a big strainer or even the handle of a wooden spoon. Rinse in a colander with cool water, then continue boiling more pasta.

5. Spread a thin layer of the Gorgonzola sauce in the bottom of a 9 x 13-inch baking dish. Top with a layer of pasta, cutting to fit as necessary. Spread a thin layer of the sauce over the noodles, then top with half the leeks, fanning them out as necessary. Sprinkle with half the nuts. Repeat: more pasta, another thin layer of sauce, the rest of the leeks, the rest of the nuts. Top with a third pasta layer, the remainder of the sauce, and the grated Parmesan.

6. Cover and bake for 20 minutes. Uncover and continue baking until lightly browned and bubbling, about 15 more minutes. Cool on a wire rack for 5 to 10 minutes before slicing into squares to serve.

▶ A MENU

FIRST SMALL PLATE: Squash Noodles, Almond Chimichurri (page 45)

PASTA: Leek/Gorgonzola Lasagna

SECOND SMALL PLATE: Tomato Gelée, Pistachio Shortbread (page 67)

DESSERT: Summer Pudding, Black Currants, Blackberries (page 263)

▶ POUR

Brut rosé champagne for sweet, slightly acidic bubbles to further balance the blue cheese

Pear/Parmesan Lasagna

8 SERVINGS

Yes, pears and Parmigiano-Reggiano are a classic match: sweet with salty, floral with slightly sour. But baked together, they become nearly irresistible. We put them in a buttery lasagna, designed to be the end of a meal after several smaller courses. But don't expect a goopy casserole. There's no ricotta sauce, so the sweet and intense flavors are actually a bit summery, despite the seemingly autumnal palette of pears and cheese. In fact, we think of this dish as September heaven: a recipe to celebrate the last of the tomatoes and the first of the fall fruits. (And by the way, the real key to the dish's success, the little secret buried in the recipe, is in the outrageous pairing of butter and roasted hazelnut oil.)

- 5 tablespoons unsalted butter, plus more for the baking dish
- 1 medium yellow onion, finely chopped
- 1½ pounds tomatoes, peeled (see page 171), seeded, and chopped
- ½ teaspoon salt
- ½ cup fruity white wine, such as Riesling

- 2 large Anjou or Bartlett pears (about 12 ounces each), peeled, cored, and cut crosswise into ¼- to ½-inch-thick slices
- 3 tablespoons roasted hazelnut oil
- 2 large or 4 small fresh lasagna sheets (see page 147)
- ¼ pound Parmigiano-Reggiano cheese, thinly shaved

AHEAD

- The tomato sauce can be made up to 2 days in advance. Store, covered, in the refrigerator, but heat over medium-low heat to a slow simmer before using.

- The pears can be roasted up to 8 hours in advance. Store, covered, at room temperature.

- The lasagna can be built up to 2 hours in advance. Store, covered, at room temperature, until baking.

GARNISH

Sprinkle a light dusting of ground cinnamon over each serving. Better yet, grate a cinnamon stick on a Microplane, allowing you to control just a smattering of the spice for each plate.

NOTES

- Baking the lasagna covered keeps it soft and rich, rather than condensed and browned.

- Aluminum foil should not sit against an acidic sauce. Thus, a layer of parchment paper adds protection before the casserole is sealed.

1. Melt the butter in a large saucepan over low heat. Add the onion and cook slowly, stirring often, until softened, about 15 minutes.

2. Stir in the tomatoes and salt. Cover, keep the heat at low, and simmer slowly, stirring occasionally, until the tomatoes begin to break down, about 30 minutes.

3. Pour in the wine. Cook, uncovered, stirring often, until the tomatoes are quite soft, about 15 minutes. Use an immersion blender to puree the sauce right in the pan. (Or pour the contents of the pan into a large blender, cool for 10 minutes, cover, and blend until smooth. Be sure to remove the center knob from the lid and cover the lid with a clean kitchen towel to keep the blender from spewing the warm ingredients over the kitchen.)

4. Position the rack in the center of the oven and heat to 400°F. Toss the pears and oil in a large roasting pan. Bake, stirring occasionally, until soft and lightly browned, about 30 minutes. Leave the oven on and reduce the temperature to 350°F.

5. Bring a large pot or Dutch oven of water to a boil over high heat. Add a noodle sheet, boil for 2 minutes, then lift out and into a colander with a strainer or the handle of a wooden spoon. Rinse with cool water. Continue boiling the remaining sheet(s).

6. Butter a 9 x 13-inch baking dish. Lightly coat the bottom with ½ cup tomato sauce. Cover the bottom of the dish with a pasta sheet (or 2 if using the small sheets), then top with the pears and Parmesan, spreading them in an even layer across the casserole. Top with the remaining pasta sheet(s), then the rest of the sauce.

7. Cover with parchment paper, then foil. Bake until bubbling and hot, about 40 minutes. Cool on a wire rack for 10 minutes before cutting into squares to serve.

▶ **A MENU**

SALAD: Fava Bean/Sugar Snap Salad, Warm Breadcrumbs (page 103)

PASTA: Pear/Parmesan Lasagna

LARGE PLATE: Cauliflower Strudel, Cranberry Chutney (page 226)

DESSERT: Chocolate/Tallegio Panini, Caramel Dipping Sauce (page 241)

▶ **POUR**

A fruit-forward but dry Côtes du Roussillon red wine for a light tonality that won't muddle the buttery sauce

Baked Macaroni/Mushrooms/Cashews

8 SERVINGS

A vegan version of mac and cheese, this casserole is spiked with many more vegetables than more standard recipes, mostly for contrasting textures and flavors, ones that help rein in the richness of the creamless creamy sauce, made from rich coconut milk and cashews. Sure, this one's pure comfort food. It's a great way to end a more down-home menu. And there'll probably be leftovers. Who wouldn't want them for lunch the next day? Or for that matter, who wouldn't want this casserole on an average weeknight after work?

1¾ cups regular or light coconut milk

¾ cup roasted, unsalted cashews

½ cup nutritional yeast (see page 19)

1 pound dried elbow macaroni

½ cup almond oil, divided, plus more for greasing

4 cups thinly sliced yellow onions (about 2½ large)

½ pound cremini mushrooms, thinly sliced

¼ pound fresh shiitake mushrooms, stems discarded, caps thinly sliced

1 cup dry white wine, such as Viognier, divided

1 cup fresh or thawed frozen green peas

¼ cup all-purpose flour

2 cups unsweetened almond milk

2 tablespoons vegan Worcestershire sauce

1 tablespoon Dijon mustard

1 teaspoon dried thyme

1. Place the coconut milk, cashews, and nutritional yeast in a large blender. Cover and blend until as smooth as possible, turning off the machine and scraping down the interior of the canister several times.

2. Bring a large saucepan of water to a boil over high heat. Add the macaroni, stir well, and cook until almost al dente, some resistance still in each piece of pasta, 4 to 5 minutes. Drain in a colander set in the sink.

> AHEAD

● Blend the coconut milk puree up to 8 hours in advance. Store, covered, in the refrigerator.

● Cook the vegetables in steps 4 and 5 up to 4 hours in advance. Store, covered, at room temperature.

● Cook the macaroni up to 2 hours in advance. Rinse with cool water to prevent sticking and store in the colander at room temperature.

> NOTE

● Finding vegan Worcestershire sauce can be a challenge, although it's available at most high-end supermarkets.

3. Position the rack in the center of the oven and heat to 375°F.

4. Set a large skillet over medium-low heat for a minute or so, then pour in ¼ cup of the almond oil. Add the onions, reduce the heat much further, cover, and cook slowly, stirring often, for 40 minutes. Uncover and continue cooking, stirring often, until browned, caramelized, and sweet, about 20 minutes. If the onions begin to burn, reduce the heat even further. Scrape the onions into a large bowl.

5. Add both kinds of mushrooms to the skillet, increase the heat to medium, and cook, stirring often, until they begin to brown, about 15 minutes. Pour ½ cup of the wine into the skillet, increase the heat to medium-high, and boil, stirring often to scrape up browned bits in the skillet, until the liquid has been reduced to a thick glaze, about 3 minutes. Scrape the contents of the skillet into the bowl with the onions Add the peas and stir well.

6. Set that same skillet back over medium heat. Add the remaining ¼ cup almond oil, then the flour. Whisk until the two form a thick paste, about 30 seconds. Whisk in the remaining ½ cup wine in a slow, steady stream, then whisk in the almond milk. Continue cooking, whisking all the while, until the mixture bubbles and thickens a bit, about 1 minute. Pour in the coconut milk puree, the Worcestershire sauce, mustard, and thyme. Whisk until bubbling and somewhat thickened, 2 to 3 minutes. Scrape this mixture into the bowl with the onions and mushrooms, then add the cooked macaroni and stir well to combine.

7. Oil the bottom and sides of a 9 x 13-inch baking dish. Spread the macaroni mixture into it. Bake until lightly browned and bubbling at the edges, about 25 minutes. Serve piping hot, dishing up individual servings or bringing the hot casserole right to the table.

▶ A MENU

FIRST SMALL PLATE: Shredded Beets, Capers, Avocados (page 50)

PASTA: Baked Macaroni/Mushrooms/Cashews

SECOND SMALL PLATE: Crunchy Runner Beans, Pickled Shallots (page 43)

DESSERT: Canadian ice wine and chocolate-covered almonds

▶ POUR

A dry but chilled Tavel rosé, a robust, mineral-rich acidity to complement the casserole

Fig/Olive Ravioli, Cardamom/Orange Flower Cream

8 SERVINGS/16 RAVIOLI

Imagine this: a thick, salty, sticky filling for ravioli, made from a sweet and briny concoction bound with balsamic vinegar, balanced by a rich sauce studded with cardamom and brightened with orange flower water. The results are dramatic, modernist cuisine—but understandable, too.

- 6 fresh green or yellow figs, preferably Calimyrna, Sierra, or Kadota, stemmed (about 5 ounces)
- ½ cup pitted green olives
- 2 tablespoons aged balsamic vinegar
- 1 large or 2 small fresh lasagna sheets (see Note)
- ¼ cup olive oil, plus more for greasing
- ¼ cup all-purpose flour
- ½ cup dry vermouth
- 1½ cups whole or low-fat milk
- 1½ ounces Parmigiano-Reggiano cheese, finely grated (about 6 tablespoons)
- ½ teaspoon ground cardamom
- ½ teaspoon freshly ground black pepper
- ¼ teaspoon orange flower water

1. Process the figs, olives, and vinegar in a food processor to a coarse paste.

2. Lay the pasta sheet(s) on a clean, dry work surface. Slice into thirty-two 1½-inch squares. Top 16 of the squares with 1 tablespoon filling each. Wet the edges of those squares, then top with the remaining 16 squares. Press to seal.

3. Position the rack in the center of the oven and heat to 350°F. Lightly oil a 9 x 13-inch baking dish.

4. Bring a large pot or Dutch oven of water to a boil over high heat. Boil the ravioli for 3 minutes from the time they enter the water. Use a slotted spoon to remove them in batches, then line these in the baking dish in one layer with slightly overlapping edges.

5. To make the sauce, heat the oil in a medium saucepan over medium heat. Whisk in the flour just until a paste, then whisk in the vermouth until smooth. Whisk in the milk in a slow, steady stream and continue whisking until the mixture thickens and bubbles, about 5 minutes. Whisk in the cheese, cardamom, pepper, and orange flour water. Pour this mixture over the ravioli in the baking dish.

6. Bake until browned and bubbling, about 35 minutes. Transfer the baking dish to a wire rack and cool for 5 minutes before dishing it up, two ravioli per serving.

AHEAD

- Make the ravioli up to 6 hours in advance before boiling; lightly flour a large lipped baking sheet, set them on it, seal with plastic wrap, and refrigerate.

GARNISH

Sprinkle a few black cardamom seeds over the servings.

NOTES

- Look for orange flower water in large baking aisles or in kitchenware stores.

- In some ways, cardamom has become the new cinnamon, a spice used over and over in baked desserts. But when you put it against orange flower water, you'll again understand its savory roots.

- You should be able to make this dish using one large 9 x 13-inch pasta sheet, from a 12- to 16-ounce package. You need a total of 72 square inches to make the 16 ravioli.

- The ravioli cannot be baked in advance since the sauce is fairly thin and won't stand up to reheating.

- This dish could be a main course, but it would probably serve four.

A MENU

SMALL PLATE: Baked Artichokes, Dulse Flakes, Pine Nuts (page 61)

SALAD: Brussels Sprout/Fennel Salad, Kumquats (page 102)

PASTA: Fig/Olive Ravioli, Cardamom/Orange Flower Cream

DESSERT: Pecan/Coconut Cake, Orange Marmalade (page 269)

POUR

A Bandol rosé that offers a full-palette complexity of jammy, red-wine notes *and* the lighter finish of a more traditional rosé

Curried Spaetzle, Ginger Broth

6 SERVINGS

A German favorite, these little dribs and drabs of chewy dough (*SHPET-zuhl*) are here spiced with a fiery Thai curry paste and moistened with rich coconut milk. To give this half Europe/half Asia concoction a culinary context on the plate, those spaetzle are immersed in a spicy but stomach-calming broth, then topped with toasted coconut for some all-important crunch.

6 cups vegetable broth, divided

¼ cup julienned fresh ginger

3 tablespoons finely grated palm sugar

1 medium garlic clove, smashed

1½ cups all-purpose flour

1 teaspoon salt

½ cup plus 2 tablespoons regular or light coconut milk

2 large eggs, at room temperature and lightly beaten

2 tablespoons Thai yellow curry paste (see page 184)

6 tablespoons unsweetened coconut flakes, toasted

1. Stir 4 cups of the broth, the ginger, palm sugar, and garlic in a large saucepan and bring to a simmer over medium heat, stirring until the sugar dissolves. Cover, reduce the heat to low, and simmer slowly for 30 minutes.

2. Set a fine-mesh sieve over a large bowl and strain the broth mixture into the bowl. Discard the solids, pour the strained liquid back into the saucepan, and stir in the remaining 2 cups broth. Keep warm, covered, over very low heat.

3. Mix the flour and salt in a large bowl. Whisk in the coconut milk, eggs, and curry paste until a soft, wet dough forms.

4. Bring a large pot of water to a boil over high heat. Use a spaetzle maker (see Note) to form the tiny grains and drop them into the water. Cook until they float, about 1 minute.

5. Fish the spaetzle out with a slotted spoon and divide them among 6 deep bowls. Pour 1 cup warmed broth into each bowl and top each bowl with a tablespoon of coconut.

AHEAD

● Prepare the broth up to 1 day in advance. Store, covered, in the fridge, then warm over low heat.

● Boil the spaetzle up to 2 hours in advance. Spread them on a large baking sheet, cool for 20 minutes, then cover with plastic wrap and store at room temperature. However, they will get gummier the longer they sit.

NOTES

● If you don't want the trouble of making julienned ginger, grate it through the large holes of a box grater.

● In a can of coconut milk, the solids will have separated from the liquid. Stir those solids back into the liquid.

● Palm sugar, sometimes called jaggery, is an Asian and African staple, a sugar made from date concentrate, cane juice, and/or palm sap.

● If you don't have a spaetzle maker, put about one-fourth of the spaetzle dough on a cutting board, then use a knife to chip off pellets into the boiling water below, no more than 1 inch long and ¼ inch wide, most of them irregular and tiny. You'll need to work in batches so that the spaetzle are not boiled too long and turn gummy.

A MENU

FIRST SMALL PLATE: Asiago Cookies, Tahini/Lentil Cream (page 89)

SECOND SMALL PLATE: Jerusalem Artichoke Fritters, Cranberries, Almonds (page 73)

PASTA: Curried Spaetzle, Ginger Broth

DESSERT: Lemon Cream Donuts (page 277)

POUR

An Oregon Zinfandel with its sturdy emphasis on chocolate over berries

Orecchiette, Cauliflower, Raisins, Olives

8 SERVINGS

Here's another pasta dish that could become a final course in a longer meal. It's fairly simple, the roasted flavors a mix of salty and sweet, rosemary and raisin. The oven melds those disparate elements without muffling them, resulting in unexpected comfort food. The servings are not big enough to be an entrée on their own but are correctly sized if a few smaller plates have come before. In fact, this recipe makes a great lunch on the weekend, with nothing more than a glass of iced tea on the side.

1 large cauliflower head (about 2 pounds), stemmed and cut into smaller florets

1 cup halved, pitted black olives

½ cup olive oil

2 tablespoons minced fresh rosemary leaves

1 pound dried orecchiette

½ cup golden raisins

1 cup dry white wine, such as Chardonnay

2 ounces Parmigiano-Reggiano cheese, finely grated (about ½ cup)

1 teaspoon freshly ground black pepper

½ teaspoon freshly grated nutmeg

1. Position the rack in the center of the oven and heat to 400°F.

2. Stir the cauliflower, olives, oil, and rosemary in a large roasting pan until the cauliflower is coated in herbs and oil. Roast, tossing once, until the cauliflower is lightly browned and crisp-tender, about 20 minutes.

3. Meanwhile, bring a large pot of water to a boil over high heat. Stir in the orecchiette and boil until almost al dente, a little firmness at the center of each piece, about 5 minutes. (You'll only know by taking one out and tasting it.) Add the raisins and boil for 1 minute. Drain in a colander set in the sink.

4. Stir the wine into the hot roasting pan, scraping up any browned bits in the pan. Add the pasta, raisins, Parmesan, pepper, and nutmeg. Toss well before plating.

▷ AHEAD

● Make the entire dish up to 1 hour in advance. Store at room temperature.

▷ LESS

Use 8 cups precut cauliflower florets, available in the produce section. Cut any larger florets into bits no more than 1½ inches each.

▷ GARNISH

Sprinkle servings with minced parsley leaves, more shaved cheese, and/or red pepper flakes.

▷ NOTES

● Orecchiette are small rounds of pasta, said to resemble little ears. By the way, we've made this dish with regular and whole-grain orecchiette, both to good success.

● Boiling the raisins not only warms them up, it also plumps them.

▷ A MENU

FIRST SMALL PLATE: Blue Cheese Cheesecake, Walnuts, Dill (page 86)

SECOND SMALL PLATE: Steamed Artichokes, Red Peppers, Basil (page 42)

PASTA: Orecchiette, Cauliflower, Raisins, Olives

SOUP: Pear Soup, Ginger, Buttery Leeks (page 129)

DESSERT: Olive Oil/Vin Santo Cake, Pine Nuts, Dried Apples (page 265)

▷ POUR

A chilled, dry, white Rueda with melon notes amid the underlying minerality that will balance the casserole's inherent sweetness

Gnocchi, Shallots, Harissa

8 SERVINGS

Harissa is a North African, chile-based condiment. Our version is looser than standard preparations, more sauce than spread. When added to these potato dumplings and caramelized shallots, it adds up to a wild fusion of flavors, from Tunisia through Italy and then on to Latin America—since we use chocolaty pasillas as the chiles in the harissa. Those chiles give the sauce an almost Oaxacan mole quality. Nothing here stands on tradition. You might want a simple, cooling salad right after this course—nothing more than, say, cold sliced cucumbers, dressed with rice vinegar, a smattering of sugar, and some flaked sea salt. Or a simple main course with plenty of acidity among its flavors to lift up everyone's taste buds.

▶ **AHEAD**

● Make the sauce up to 3 days in advance. Store, covered, in the refrigerator, but allow to come back to room temperature before using.

● Roast the shallots up to 6 hours in advance. Store at room temperature, but warm in a 300°F oven for 10 to 15 minutes while you boil the gnocchi.

● Make the gnocchi up to 6 hours in advance. Arrange them in a single layer on a rimmed baking sheet, cover tightly with plastic wrap, and refrigerate until you're ready to boil them.

▶ **GARNISH**

Sprinkle toasted pepitas (hulled pumpkin seeds) and/or toasted black sesame seeds over the servings.

HARISSA

- 4 dried pasilla chiles
  Boiling water
- 2 large red bell peppers
- ¼ cup olive oil
- 1 cup chopped shallots
- 1 tablespoon minced garlic
- 1 teaspoon ground caraway
- 1 teaspoon ground coriander
- 1 teaspoon ground cumin
- ¼ cup red wine vinegar
- ½ teaspoon salt

GNOCCHI AND SHALLOTS

- 4 pounds russet (baking) potatoes
- 12 large shallots, peeled and quartered
- ½ cup olive oil
- 4 large egg yolks
- 1 tablespoon salt
- 2¼ to 3 cups all-purpose flour, plus more for dusting
- 3 ounces Pecorino Romano cheese, finely grated (about ¾ cup)

1. To make the harissa: Stem and seed the pasillas, then tear them into large pieces. Cover with boiling water in a large bowl. Soak for 20 minutes to soften.

2. Meanwhile, char the bell peppers over an open gas flame or on a large baking sheet 4 to 6 inches from the broiler, turning often. Set the blackened peppers in a bowl and seal with plastic wrap—or place them in a paper bag and seal tightly.

3. Drain the chiles, then put them in a large blender. Peel off as many of the blackened bits as you can from the bell peppers, then stem, seed, and core them. Put these into the blender as well.

4. Set a large skillet over medium heat for a few minutes. Swirl in the oil and add the shallots. Cook, stirring often, until softened, about 5 minutes. Stir in the garlic, caraway, coriander, and cumin and cook until fragrant, about 1 minute.

5. Turn off the heat and pour in the vinegar, scraping up any browned bits in the skillet. Scrape the contents of the skillet into the blender. Add the salt as well. Cool for 10 minutes, then cover and pulse repeatedly until smooth, scraping down the inside of the canister at least once.

6. To make the gnocchi: Position the rack in the center of the oven and heat to 375°F. Bake the potatoes on the oven's rack until soft and tender, about 1 hour. At the same time, mix the shallots and the oil in a large roasting pan. Bake until soft and slightly browned, about 20 minutes, tossing occasionally. Transfer the shallots to a wire rack to await the assembly of the dish.

7. Transfer the potatoes to a wire rack to cool for about 1 hour, until just a bit warm and easily handled. Peel the potatoes and put the flesh through a potato ricer and into a large bowl.

8. Stir the yolks and salt into the riced potatoes, then add 2¼ cups flour. Mix to form a soft dough. Add more flour as necessary to get a consistency that definitely holds together but is soft, not sticky.

9. Turn the dough out onto a dry, clean work surface that's been dusted with flour. Knead until soft and smooth, about 3 minutes. Divide the dough into 8 balls. Roll one ball under your palms into a rope about 16 inches long. Cut the rope crosswise into 1-inch pieces. Roll each piece up a floured fork to create a small set of indentations around about three-quarters of the dough. Set aside and continue rolling, cutting, and making more gnocchi, dusting the work surface with flour only as needed to keep the dough from sticking.

10. Bring a large pot of water to a boil over high heat. Drop one-third of the gnocchi in and cook until they float, about 2 minutes. (Working in batches prevents crowding and mitigates drastic temperature fluctuations.) Use a slotted spoon to fish the gnocchi out of the water and drain thoroughly in a colander. Repeat with the two remaining batches, one at a time.

11. Add the gnocchi to the warm roasting pan with the shallots. Once all the gnocchi have been boiled, toss the contents of the pan gently with the pecorino. To serve, divide the gnocchi and shallots among 8 serving plates, then dollop each with the harissa sauce. Or spread the gnocchi and shallots on a big platter and spoon the harissa sauce down the center of the platter.

NOTES

- Pasilla chiles (pah-SEE-yah) are long, thin, dried chiles, sometimes called chiles negros (or "black chiles"). Technically pasillas should be dried chilaca chiles, but in North America they're often the cheaper, dried poblanos, which have a far less complex, more acidic taste. Look for the real thing in Latin American supermarkets—and ask questions. A pasilla should be fingerlike with a chocolate aroma, not at all citrusy.

- Only a russet potato has the right level of starch to make tender gnocchi.

- You'll need a potato ricer to complete this dish to success. It's a specialty tool—available at kitchenware stores and online—that pushes cooked potato through dozens of little holes to create fine, fragile threads. Yes, you can scoop the white flesh out of the skin and mash it with a pastry cutter or even a fork, but we find the gnocchi are never quite as tender as those made with a ricer.

- Rather than using a fork, buy a ridged gnocchi board for rolling them.

A MENU

SOUP: Cucumber Soup, Basil, Buttermilk (page 123)

PASTA: Gnocchi, Shallots, Harissa

LARGE PLATE: Ratatouille Crudo (page 171)

DESSERT: Coconut Cheesecake Flan (page 273)

POUR

Sparkling mineral water to clean the palate without any added flavor contrasts

Sweet Potato/Amaretti Gnocchi, Sage Butter

8 SERVINGS

Although these surprising gnocchi are made with sweet potatoes and crumbled Italian cookies, their success is still dependent on the russet potatoes in the batch. Those latter will add enough starch to hold the dumplings together. The gnocchi's natural sweetness is balanced with a fairly classic butter sauce, laced with sage for a Thanksgivingish take on the palette. All in all, this dish is pretty indulgent, even if the portions are moderately sized. It probably shouldn't end a meal—or at least not come right before dessert. Instead, consider these a first (or second) plate with a larger main-course event in the offing.

▶ AHEAD

● Make the gnocchi through step 3 up to 6 hours in advance. Arrange them in a single layer on a rimmed baking sheet, cover tightly with plastic wrap, and refrigerate until you're ready to boil them.

▶ NOTE

● Amaretti are tiny, hard, Italian macaroons, made with bitter almonds and/or apricot pits. Look for them in specialty stores among the international cookies.

2 pounds orange-fleshed sweet potatoes

1 pound russet (baking) potatoes

4 large egg yolks

5 to 6 cups all-purpose flour, plus more for dusting

½ cup finely ground amaretti cookies

1 teaspoon salt

16 tablespoons (2 sticks) unsalted butter, cut into chunks

2 tablespoons minced fresh sage

1 teaspoon freshly ground black pepper

¼ teaspoon freshly grated nutmeg

1. Position the rack in the center of the oven and heat to 375°F. Roast the sweet and russet potatoes on a large baking sheet until tender, about 1 hour. Cool on a wire rack until easily handled, about 30 minutes. Peel the potatoes and put them all through a potato ricer and into a large bowl.

2. Stir the egg yolks into the potatoes until creamy. Add 4 cups of flour, the ground amaretti, and salt. Stir to form a soft dough, adding more flour as necessary to get the dough to cohere, probably a cup more, maybe even more than that depending on the day's humidity, the moisture content of the flour, and even the residual moisture content of the baked potatoes.

3. Dust a clean, dry work surface with flour. Divide the dough into 8 equal balls. Roll one under your palms into a rope about 12 inches long. Cut the rope crosswise into 1-inch pieces, like small pillows. Continue making the remainder from subsequent ropes.

(continued)

4. Bring a large pot of water to a boil over high heat. Drop one-third of the gnocchi in and boil until tender, about 5 minutes. (Working in batches prevents crowding and mitigates drastic temperature fluctuations.) Use a slotted spoon to lift them out of the water and drain completely in a colander. Repeat with the two remaining batches, one at a time.

5. Divide the butter between two large skillets and melt each over medium heat. Divide the sage, pepper, and nutmeg between the skillets. Stir well and add half the gnocchi to each skillet. Fry, tossing occasionally, until lightly browned and crisp on at least one side, about 3 minutes.

6. To serve, divide all the gnocchi among serving plates, scraping any dribs of buttery sauce in the pan over each serving.

A MENU

LARGE PLATE: Goat Cheese Fondue, Grilled Bread, Pears (page 173)

PASTA: Sweet Potato/Amaretti Gnocchi, Sage Butter

SALAD: Watermelon Panzanella, Capers, Basil (page 118)

DESSERT: Fresh juicy peaches with shot glasses of amaretto

POUR

Either chilled prosecco to offer palate-cleansing bubbles or a hearty California Syrah to match the depth of the butter sauce

Polenta, Chestnuts, Balsamic Vinegar, Roasted Radicchio

8 SERVINGS

The technique for traditional polenta is notorious: You need to stand at the stove and stir. Forever. That's hardly conducive to a happy host of a dinner party. Still, we don't want to give up on this creamy favorite, especially when its naturally sweet corn flavors can work so well in a lineup of other dishes for the evening. So we want to advocate for a simpler slow-cooker version. It's more efficient but still quite tasty, particularly with chestnuts and sage in the mix. The bitter radicchio, roasted to sweetness with wine and balsamic vinegar, marks the contrast and brings out the sweetness of the corn even more.

3 cups vegetable broth

1 cup rustic, coarse-grained polenta, preferably whole-grain (see Note)

1½ cups jarred roasted chestnuts, finely chopped

1 tablespoon minced fresh sage

½ teaspoon freshly grated nutmeg

2 medium radicchio heads, cut into quarters

6 tablespoons olive oil

¼ cup dry but fruit-forward red wine, such as Zinfandel

½ teaspoon salt

½ teaspoon freshly ground black pepper

2 tablespoons aged balsamic vinegar

2 teaspoons sugar

1. Mix the broth, polenta, chestnuts, sage, and nutmeg in a 4- to 6-quart slow cooker. Cover and cook on high for 1 hour. Stir well, then continue cooking on high, stirring two more times, until smooth and creamy, about 30 minutes.

2. Meanwhile, position the rack in the center of the oven and heat to 400°F.

3. Set the radicchio quarters in a large roasting pan. Drizzle the olive oil and wine over them and sprinkle with salt and pepper. Roast for 15 minutes, nudging the quarters once to make sure they're not sticking. Sprinkle with the vinegar and sugar and roast until tender and glazed, about 5 minutes longer.

4. To serve, divide the polenta among 8 plates. Top each serving with a radicchio quarter plus some of the pan juices.

AHEAD

- Roast the radicchio quarters up to 2 hours in advance. Store at room temperature.

- The polenta will keep warm in the slow cooker for 2 hours. However, it can begin to stiffen, so stir in a little more broth to loosen it up before serving.

MORE

Stir ¼ cup mascarpone into the polenta before serving.

GARNISH

Fry slivered garlic in olive oil in a medium skillet over medium heat until browned and blistered, about 2 minutes. Spoon out the garlic bits and set them onto the servings.

NOTES

- Look for coarse, whole-grain polenta from suppliers like Anson Mills (either in stores or on the web). Most of the polenta produced in North America is made from a refined version of corn.

- Don't skimp on that balsamic vinegar. It should be the best you can afford.

A MENU

FIRST SMALL PLATE: Fiddlehead Tacos, Almond Romesco (page 70)

SECOND SMALL PLATE: Warm Buffalo Mozzarella, Yellow Tomato Sauce (page 39)

THIRD SMALL PLATE: Roasted Grapes/ Olives (page 37)

PASTA: Polenta, Chestnuts, Balsamic Vinegar, Roasted Radicchio

DESSERT: Chocolate Pots de Crème (page 253)

POUR

An aged red Nebbiolo with its undertones of violets, truffles, and prunes

Pear Risotto, Gorgonzola, Dill

6 SERVINGS

Although pears and blue cheese are a classic pairing, we match them with lemon zest and shallot as well as sweet, creamy, medium-grain white rice for more depth and contrast. We wouldn't end a meal with a dish like this one because the flavors are intense but pretty rustic. They seem as if they're leading to the next course. Still, this new take on the classic might be a great way to start the meal—or a hearty course after the starter and before a larger plate. Risotto traditionally involves plenty of stirring over the heat. However, we do have a way around that problem: Check "Less."

5 cups vegetable broth

1½ cups pear nectar

1 tablespoon finely grated lemon zest

1 tablespoon minced dill fronds

4 tablespoons (½ stick) unsalted butter, cut into small bits

1 large shallot, peeled and thinly sliced

1½ cups Arborio rice

½ cup dry vermouth

2 Comice pears, peeled, cored, and diced

2 ounces Parmigiano-Reggiano cheese, finely grated (about ½ cup)

3 ounces Gorgonzola cheese, crumbled

1. Combine the broth, nectar, lemon zest, and dill in a large saucepan. Bring to a very low simmer over medium-high heat, then reduce the heat and keep warm without bubbling.

2. Melt the butter in a large, high-sided sauté pan or skillet over medium heat. Add the shallot and cook, stirring often, until softened, about 4 minutes. Add the rice and stir over the heat for 1 minute to toast. Pour in the vermouth, bring to a full simmer over medium-high heat, and cook, stirring often, until the pan is almost dry.

3. Add the pears and ¾ cup of the warm broth mixture. Reduce the heat to low and cook, stirring all the while, until the pan is almost dry. Then add more broth mixture in ¾-cup increments, stirring all the while. The heat should be low enough that you're adding more broth mixture every 3 to 5 minutes. Keep working at it until the rice is tender, the sauce has thickened around it, and the broth mixture is used up, between 30 and 40 minutes. Stir in the Parmigiano-Reggiano.

4. To serve, divide among 6 serving plates. Crumble Gorgonzola over the top of each serving.

LESS

To make risotto in a pressure cooker, reduce the broth to 3 cups and the nectar to 1 cup. Follow this recipe through step 2, using the uncovered pressure cooker to cook and reduce the various ingredients. Then add the liquid and the pears, cover, and bring to high pressure over high heat. Adjust the temperature to keep the pressure constant and cook at high pressure for 8 minutes. Remove the pan from the heat and use the quick-release method to open the cooker (see the instruction manual for your model). Place the cooker back over medium heat, add the Parmesan, and stir until thick and creamy, about 2 minutes. Crumble the Gorgonzola on top of the servings.

GARNISH

Snip chives over each serving.

NOTES

● Arborio rice is a medium-grained rice, prized for its starchy chew.

● The pears should smell sweet and ripe. If not, they'll contribute nothing to the final dish.

● Lest it overpower the other ingredients, the Gorgonzola only stands in for part of the full complement of cheese.

A MENU

PASTA: Pear Risotto, Gorgonzola, Dill

SALAD: Grapefruit/Avocado Salad, Pistachios (page 100)

LARGE PLATE: Tomatoes, Mushrooms, Phyllo Nests (page 208)

DESSERT: Chocolate Chip Cookies, Maple, Tahini, Dates (page 236) and Fennel/Cardamom Pears (page 247; omit the Ginger Mascarpone)

POUR

A classic, Oregon Pinot Noir to offer moderated sweetness and fruity acidity

Barley Risotto, Peas, Camembert

8 SERVINGS

Rustic meets chic. Here's an over-the-top take on a rice-less version of risotto, made with chewy hull-less barley, which becomes a creamy, whole-grain base for sweet peas and a very creamy, pungent cheese. There's really no way to make this dish in advance, so your timing will have to be more exact, keeping the barley at a simmer during the first course and then disappearing to the kitchen to finish off this incredible bit of decadence.

- 4 tablespoons (½ stick) unsalted butter, cut into small bits
- 2 large yellow onions, chopped
- 2 cups hull-less barley
- 1 tablespoon minced fresh sage
- 1 tablespoon fresh thyme leaves
- 1 teaspoon freshly ground black pepper
- 1 cup dry vermouth
- 8 cups vegetable broth
- 2 cups fresh or thawed frozen green peas
- 4 ounces Camembert cheese, rind removed and the cheese cut into little bits

1. Melt the butter in a large pot or Dutch oven over medium heat. Add the onions, reduce the heat to medium-low, and cook, stirring often, until soft and beginning to turn sweet, about 10 minutes.

2. Stir in the barley, sage, thyme, and pepper. Cook for 1 minute, stirring constantly. Then pour in the vermouth. Continue cooking, stirring often, until the vermouth has been absorbed, about 3 minutes.

3. Pour in the broth and bring to a simmer. Cover, reduce the heat to low, and simmer slowly for 1 hour.

4. Uncover the pot and continue cooking, stirring constantly, until most of the liquid has been absorbed and the mixture is creamy, about 25 minutes. Stir in the peas and Camembert. Cover and let stand off the heat for 5 minutes. To serve, mound the mixture onto small serving plates.

▶ MORE
Drizzle 1 teaspoon truffle oil over each serving.

▶ NOTE
● Hull-less barley is the only whole-grain barley sold in North America. It's chewy and earthy. Hull-less barley is a special hybrid, developed so the hulls pop off the grains at harvest, leaving all the bran and germ intact. Look for it in health food stores or at upscale markets that carry a large selection of whole grains—or, of course, online.

▶ A MENU
FIRST SMALL PLATE: Potato/Cucumber Mille-Feuille (page 84)

PASTA: Barley Risotto, Peas, Camembert

SECOND SMALL PLATE: Roasted Grapes/Olives (page 37)

DESSERT: Cassis wine (not crème de cassis) and candied orange peels

▶ POUR
A rich, robust, earthy, raisiny Châteauneuf-du-Pape to contrast with the barley and bring the truffles back to the fore of the mix

LARGE PLATES

Let's say your vacation starts tomorrow. (It could happen.) You pack your bags and head out early in the morning. Over the course of the trip, you may have wonderful little detours, but Zion National Park awaits. Or Prince Edward Island. Or Paris.

A dinner party is like that. You're headed to the main course—or as we call it, the large plate. Yes, you can make a meal out of several small plates (or a vacation out of the detours). But those events are probably the exception, not the rule.

Large plates don't necessarily mean big servings. In fact, most of the portion sizes in this chapter are more modest when compared with standard main-course recipes, mostly to keep this part of the meal from overwhelming everyone at a multicourse feast. But large plates are still large—that is, in the scope of their palettes. We're way beyond flavor juxtaposition here. We're aiming for *depth*—not earthy or savory necessarily, and not just good brown-

ing with layered sauces, but rather a coherent tonality that pings flavor highs and lows in each forkful. Sure, proper caramelization is part of depth. But so's lemon juice— especially when the two are melded in a baked casserole, not just set against each other like toasty croutons in a vinaigrette.

Our small plates, salads, and almost all the soups have skimmed the taste buds, a fizz of the basic flavors that are as tantalizing as they are satisfying. These main courses move toward saturation, as if you pushed the tastes of a dish through a high-contrast filter and ended up with a palette that's darker *and* brighter, bolder and more subtle. Gone are the matchups of sweet and sour or earthy and spicy. Those basic

elements of flavor are not just shacked up. They're married.

As we've implied, we planned these meals with a long-standing culinary rule: First courses are about ingredients; main courses, about technique. So we feel free to expand these recipes into the full set of cooking methods, several in one dish: browning, basting, braising, baking, grilling. Heat makes the marriage (in cooking and elsewhere).

Take heart: These recipes are not complicated. Most do require terraced techniques: Sear this, wilt that, then braise it together. We're using heat for a greater purpose: not just to blanch vegetables to bring out their sweetness. Rather, we're using heat to affect, alter, and realign the flavors themselves.

That said, some of these recipes also use Asian bottled condiments. They're like a quick sauce in a jar, the long melding over heat done for you. And some of these recipes do indeed offer simple additions to the plate like salsas or easy sauces that give the blended flavors a little spark, pulling them out of the murk. For example, when we mix masa and Brie to make dense, chewy arepas (that is, South American corn-cake buns), we top them with an asparagus salsa to make sure there's some vinegar on the plate to help the Brie/corn mélange stay appetizing and interesting over the course of the, well, course.

At a carnivore's table, a big joint of meat or a couple of whole steamed fish would now make an appearance. With vegetarian fare, we must take the naturally bright flavors of our ingredients and their more expansive textural range and then recraft those in ways that mute extraneous notes and build to a common, blended finish. In the small plates and salads, we celebrated spikes and flourishes. Now we'll work to calm them down *and* to intensify the foundational, savory notes. We love the vinegar in that asparagus salsa for the arepas, but we used less than we would have had it been part of a first course.

Even this late in the meal, it's important to remember the point of a dinner party. When you've got the large plates down on the table and you're back in your place among your guests, the point is *not* the food. What you serve is just the scenery for your relationships, like what you see out of the car window on vacation. No doubt about it, good food will highlight the laughter, the closeness, and the affection. It will even bring them to the light in surprising ways. Cook well but be ready for that, the best part of the evening.

PACING THE MAIN COURSE

At most multicourse dinner parties, appetites will flag—usually, around 9:30 p.m. at our table. There's already been plenty of food and drink, but the main course is yet to come. Here's how we get around the inevitable problem:

1. **Hold back on the wine during the course that precedes the large plate.** No doubt about it, wine is filling. You don't have to be stingy, but don't refill the glasses quite so often. And make sure the water glasses are always full.

2. **Bump the music.** If you've got a playlist, the tunes should rise to something livelier or fuller at this point in the evening. In our house, we switch from 1940s standards to more modern lounge, from French jazz to something a little more techno. Or we switch from Haydn string quartets to Ravel piano waltzes.

3. **Serve less and offer seconds.** While many of these large-plate recipes offer small servings, some yield a 9 x 13-inch casserole. You needn't finish it. Leftovers are terrific. Who wants to cook on the day after? But remember that even the smaller scale offerings are palate-saturating because of their emphasis on depth. If you see appetites already flagging, offer smaller tastes. A main course is tricky: You want enough so no one goes away hungry but not too much because dessert is in the offing. You'll need to discover the balance.

Ratatouille Crudo

6 SERVINGS

Let's start our large plates with a surprise. Raw vegetables are often thought of as strictly appetizer fare. But with careful attention to a full scope of flavors, even they can be morphed into a main course. Although we are striving for depth at this point in the meal's arc, vegetarian (and vegan) dishes shouldn't try to run from their roots. They should still highlight *the vegetables*, not try to fake them into something meatish. Given all that, we can't imagine a better main course than this one. Rather than a heavy, stewed ratatouille, we deconstructed the standard to reveal its more elemental flavors, wrapping summery tomatoes, bell peppers, and plenty of herbs with grilled eggplant slices and raw zucchini strips to make pouches of an intense flavor range on each plate.

1 large eggplant	2 teaspoons capers, rinsed and minced
¼ cup olive oil	2 teaspoons fresh thyme leaves
3 medium globe or beefsteak tomatoes, peeled (see Note)	1½ tablespoons red wine vinegar
1 red or yellow bell pepper, chopped	1 teaspoon minced fresh rosemary
¼ cup minced yellow onion	½ teaspoon salt
¼ cup minced fresh basil	2 large zucchini
1 tablespoon minced garlic	

1. Slice off a bit of the stem end of the eggplant and cut it lengthwise into 6 slices about ½ inch thick (see Note). Rub these with the oil.

2. Prepare a grill for high-heat, direct cooking (or heat a large grill pan over medium-high heat until smoking). Add the eggplant slices and cook, turning once, until soft and well marked, about 8 minutes. Transfer to a cutting board.

3. Cut the peeled tomatoes into quarters and gently squeeze out the seeds and their pulp over the sink. Chop the tomatoes and add them to a large bowl. Stir in the bell pepper, onion, basil, garlic, capers, thyme, vinegar, rosemary, and salt. Toss gently but well.

AHEAD

- Grill the eggplant slices up to 2 days in advance. Store, covered, on a plate in the refrigerator.

- Omitting the salt and vinegar, stir the tomato mixture together up to 4 hours in advance and store, covered, at room temperature. Add the salt and vinegar just before you make the packets.

- Make the packets up to 1 hour in advance. Store, lightly covered, at room temperature.

GARNISH

Sprinkle the servings with freshly grated lemon zest. Surround the servings with a few purchased pickled onions.

NOTES

- To cut the eggplant: Cut a small slice off the thick, bulbous end so the eggplant will stand up. Then, to get even slices, slice off the sides of the thicker, bulbous end to make a straight shot down the vegetable for slicing. If you're concerned about getting 6 slices from one eggplant, buy two. You'll have some left over, but better safe than sorry.

- To peel tomatoes: Set them in a large heatproof bowl, cover with boiling water, and set aside just until the skin breaks, 30 seconds to 1 minute. Use a fork to spear the tomatoes out of the water. Cool on the counter until easily handled, about 5 minutes. Wash your hands so you can use them to peel off the loosened tomato skins.

- An outdoor grill offers the highest, best heat for eggplant slices. But for the best color and texture in a grill pan indoors, consider weighting the eggplant down with a large, heavy skillet.

(continued)

4. Use a vegetable peeler to make long, thin strips from the zucchini, running the tool down the length of the vegetable and letting the strips fall onto a cutting board until you're down to the seeds on all sides. (Discard the seedy cores.)

5. To assemble the dish, lay an eggplant slice on a clean, dry work surface. Overlap 4 or 5 zucchini strips perpendicular to the eggplant slice and at its center (see the photograph on page 170). Place ½ cup tomato mixture on top of the zucchini strips in the center of the eggplant slice. Fold the zucchini strips up and over the filling to enclose it, then fold the eggplant slice up and over the zucchini strips to make a packet. Turn upside down and transfer to a serving plate. Repeat, making the remaining portions.

▌ NOTES *(continued)*

● Although this dish is best in the summer when tomatoes are at their peak, substitute 1 pound cherry tomatoes in the winter for a burst of sunshine at your table. There's no need to skin those cherry tomatoes; just slice them in half and remove as many of the seeds as possible.

▌ A MENU

FIRST SMALL PLATE: Crunchy Runner Beans, Pickled Shallots (page 43)

SECOND SMALL PLATE: Roasted Cipollini Onions, Fava Beans Two Ways (page 56)

LARGE PLATE: Ratatouille Crudo

DESSERT: Olive Oil/Vin Santo Cake, Pine Nuts, Dried Apples (page 265)

▌ POUR

A big, fruit-forward California Zinfandel, preferably an old-vine Zin, to balance the dish's acidity with its sweet cherry and blackberry notes

Goat Cheese Fondue, Grilled Bread, Pears

8 SERVINGS

Goat cheese adds its characteristic, savory flare to a simple fondue. But you don't want to push it too far—you don't want to use *only* soft, fresh chèvre. Instead, a goat Gouda will have more maturity with caramel and honey accents in its decidedly umami flavors. That goat-y goodness is best balanced with simple, fresh ingredients in a fondue—just rosemary and black pepper here. Once you've got the fondue ready, you'll also need to bring the whole fandango to the table: the pot, fondue forks, plates, and lots of napkins.

Olive oil, for greasing the grill pan

16 slices (½-inch-thick) country-style bread, such as a boule or miche

1 cup dry white wine, such as Chardonnay

1 cup heavy cream

1 teaspoon minced garlic

1 teaspoon minced fresh rosemary

1 teaspoon freshly ground black pepper

10 ounces semifirm goat Gouda, shredded through the large holes of a box grater

1 tablespoon all-purpose flour

11 ounces soft goat cheese (or chèvre)

4 ripe but still firm pears, cored and cut into wedges

1. Oil a large grill pan and set over medium-high heat until smoking. Add the bread and grill, turning once, until hot, crunchy, and well marked, about 3 minutes. Transfer to a wire rack.

2. Mix the wine, cream, garlic, rosemary, and pepper in a large saucepan. Bring to the barest simmer over medium-low heat, stirring often.

3. Toss the Gouda and flour in a bowl. Whisk the Gouda into the hot cream mixture until melted. Crumble in the soft goat cheese and whisk until smooth.

4. Pour the mixture into a fondue pot at the center of the table. Light the candle or flame underneath, then serve with the grilled bread and sliced pears for dipping.

AHEAD

- Grill the bread up to 2 hours in advance. Store uncovered on the wire rack at room temperature.

- Prepare the pears up to 2 hours in advance, but submerge in a bowl of cold water with 1 to 2 tablespoons lemon juice to keep them from browning. Drain and pat dry before serving.

MORE

When the fondue is almost all gone, lower the heat as much as possible and crack a large egg or two into the pot. Scramble the eggs gently over the flame, scraping the burned cheese from the sides and into the mixture.

NOTES

- Semifirm (sometimes called "young") goat Gouda is very white, not yellow like the Gouda from cow's milk (because goats digest all the beta-carotene in their food). Do not use hard, dry, aged goat Gouda.

- A hot fondue pot can leave a mark on a wooden table. Have table pads under the tablecloth or hot pads under the pot.

- If your table is large, invest in two smaller fondue pots and split the recipe between them.

A MENU

SMALL PLATE: Jerusalem Artichoke Fritters, Cranberries, Almonds (page 73)

SALAD: Brussels Sprout/Fennel Salad, Kumquats (page 102)

LARGE PLATE: Goat Cheese Fondue, Grilled Bread, Pears

DESSERT: Almond/Cardamom Biscotti (page 238)

POUR

A crisp, light Sauvignon Blanc with rose and violet notes among its bright acidity

Ricotta/Spinach Dumplings, Parmesan Cream Sauce

6 SERVINGS

Winter weekends are made for dinner parties. As the sun sets early and the darkness creeps over our yard, we banish the cold by lighting the candles and serving hearty, warming fare like this casserole. The tender, spiced, even lemony dumplings are baked in a simple cream sauce that emphasizes their luxurious texture while softening some of the sweetness. There's not much more to do except spoon out servings onto plates. It's best minutes out of the oven, so plan your timing carefully.

> ### AHEAD

Complete the recipe through step 6 up to 2 hours in advance. Store, lightly covered, at room temperature.

> ### GARNISH

Although we're generally not fans of side dishes at dinner parties, this casserole could use a little contrast at the table. Accompany the servings with grilled asparagus spears, drizzled with a flavorful but light vinaigrette.

> ### NOTE

● Make sure the lemon zest is in fine bits. If you don't use a small-bored Microplane to grate the zest, mince it on a cutting board to ensure no one ends up with a big thread in a single dumpling.

- 1 box (10 ounces) frozen chopped spinach, thawed
- ½ pound regular or part-skim ricotta cheese
- ¼ pound Pecorino Romano cheese, finely grated (about 1 cup)
- 3 large egg yolks, at room temperature
- ¾ cup semolina flour, plus more for rolling
- 1 tablespoon minced fresh chives
- 1 tablespoon minced dill fronds
- ½ teaspoon finely grated lemon zest
- ½ teaspoon salt
- ¼ teaspoon freshly grated nutmeg
- 1 teaspoon freshly ground black pepper, divided
- 1 tablespoon unsalted butter
- 1 tablespoon all-purpose flour
- 1 cup whole or low-fat milk
- 2 tablespoons dry white wine, such as California Chardonnay
- 2 ounces Parmigiano-Reggiano cheese, finely grated (about ½ cup)

1. Squeeze the thawed spinach by the handful over the sink to remove excess moisture, then crumble it into a large bowl.

2. Stir in the ricotta, Pecorino, egg yolks, semolina, chives, dill, lemon zest, salt, nutmeg, and ½ teaspoon of the pepper to form a wet but coherent dough. Cover and refrigerate for 2 hours.

3. Spread some semolina flour on a large plate. Use damp, clean hands to form the dough into 24 balls the size of a golf ball, rolling them one by one in the semolina to coat thoroughly before setting them on a large rimmed baking sheet.

(continued)

4. Bring a large pot of water to a boil over high heat. Working in batches, add 5 or 6 dumplings to the boiling water and boil for 10 minutes. Use a slotted spoon to scoop them out, drain them, and transfer to a 9 x 13-inch baking dish. Repeat with the remaining dumplings.

5. Position the rack in the center of the oven and heat to 375°F.

6. To make the sauce, melt the butter in a medium skillet over medium heat. Whisk in the flour until a creamy paste. Slowly whisk in the milk in a steady, fine stream until the paste has dissolved. Whisk in the wine and continue whisking over the heat until thickened and bubbling, 3 to 4 minutes. Whisk in the Parmesan, then pour this sauce over the dumplings in the baking dish. Sprinkle the remaining ½ teaspoon pepper over the casserole.

7. Bake until lightly browned and bubbling, about 20 minutes. Cool for 5 to 10 minutes before serving.

▶ A MENU

SALAD: Roasted Pears, Fig Caponata (page 110)

SOUP: Gazpacho Shooters (page 126)

LARGE PLATE: Ricotta/Spinach Dumplings, Parmesan Cream Sauce

DESSERT: Fresh berries

▶ POUR

A full-bodied, vibrant Pinot Gris from Oregon with notes of melon and pears to brighten the dumplings' flavors

Asparagus/Morel Sauté, Poached Eggs

8 SERVINGS

This dish is for spring evenings when wool sweaters have given way to cotton. These vegetables are the first signs of better weather in New England. After our winters, they're the most anticipated culinary bits. They're melded into a rather quick ragù, the base for poached eggs.

4 tablespoons (½ stick) unsalted butter

1 large leek (white and pale green part only), halved lengthwise, carefully washed, and thinly sliced

16 morel mushrooms, brushed clean (see Note) and halved lengthwise

24 thin asparagus spears, cut into 1-inch pieces

2 tablespoons minced fresh tarragon leaves

½ teaspoon salt

½ teaspoon freshly ground black pepper

⅓ cup dry white wine, such as Chardonnay

3 tablespoons heavy cream

½ cup grated Gruyère cheese

8 large eggs

1. Position the rack in the center of the oven and heat to 400°F.

2. Melt the butter in a large ovenproof skillet over medium heat. Add the leeks and cook, stirring often, until softened, about 4 minutes. Add the morels and asparagus and cook, still stirring often, just until the asparagus is crisp-tender, about 4 minutes.

3. Stir in the tarragon, salt, and pepper, and cook a few seconds, then pour in the wine, stirring well to get any browned bits off the bottom of the skillet. Cook, stirring fairly frequently, until the liquid has reduced to about half its original volume, about 4 minutes.

4. Stir in the cream and sprinkle the mixture with the Gruyère. Slip the skillet into the oven and bake until the cheese has melted and even browned a little, about 10 minutes. Remove from the oven and set aside.

5. Fill a third of a Dutch oven with water and bring to a simmer over high heat. Reduce the heat so the water barely bubbles. Crack an egg into a custard cup or ramekin and slip the egg into the water. Repeat with 1 or 2 more eggs. Cook until the whites are set but the yolks are soft, about 3 minutes. With a slotted spoon, transfer the eggs to a plate lined with paper towels. Continue poaching more eggs. To serve, spoon the warm vegetable mixture onto 8 serving plates. Set a poached egg on each plate.

▶ AHEAD

● Prepare the vegetable mixture through step 3 up to 2 hours in advance. Store, covered, at room temperature. Bring the mixture back to a low simmer before continuing on.

▶ GARNISH

Lay tiny, tender sprigs of fresh herbs around the plate and on top of the dish itself: chervil, parsley, chives, and/or dill.

▶ NOTE

● Morels can be loaded with grit. To clean them, set them in a paper bag, seal, and shake vigorously, thereby removing some of the internal dirt. Lift the mushrooms out of the bag, leaving the dirt behind, and drop them in a bowl of cool water. Stir vigorously, then set aside for a few minutes before lifting them out of the water to dry thoroughly on paper towels.

▶ A MENU

SMALL PLATE: Shredded Beets, Capers, Avocados (page 50)

PASTA: Soba Noodles, Edamame, Kumquats (page 143)

LARGE PLATE: Asparagus/Morel Sauté, Poached Eggs

DESSERT: Fig Galette, Honey Cream (page 248)

▶ POUR

A fairly exuberant, almost unbalanced California Syrah to offer peppery olive accents to this creamy dish

Braised Kabocha Squash, Scallions, Miso

8 SERVINGS

Even when we're marrying flavors, rather than just aligning them, we don't have to be overly fussy with the ingredients themselves. Here's a simple, mild, sweet stew to follow a more complicated starter, particularly something with fiery or bitter ingredients like chiles or chard. The miso will slowly permeate the sweet squash, rendering it almost briny but with a slightly fermented flavor that's offset by plenty of peppery scallions and a fairly large amount of ginger—and thus spotlight a large range of flavors in each spoonful. The serving size is fairly small here. The flavors are so pronounced that a little will go a long way. If you're worried, offer a couple of small plates before this main course.

¾ cup vegetable broth

6 tablespoons white miso paste (see page 115)

6 tablespoons mirin

¼ cup peanut oil

12 medium scallions, thinly sliced

3 tablespoons minced fresh ginger

4 teaspoons minced garlic

2 medium kabocha squash, peeled and cubed (about 12 cups)

1. Position the rack in the center of the oven and heat to 325°F.

2. Whisk the broth, miso paste, and mirin in a bowl until well combined.

3. Set a large Dutch oven or cast iron casserole over medium heat for a few minutes. Add the oil, then the scallions. Cook, stirring often, until wilted, about 2 minutes. Stir in the ginger and garlic and cook a few seconds until aromatic. Stir in the squash. Pour in the broth mixture, increase the heat to high, and bring to a simmer, stirring occasionally.

4. Cover the pot and slip it into the oven. Bake until the squash is tender, about 30 minutes. Serve in shallow bowls.

AHEAD

• Make this dish 24 hours in advance. Store, covered, in the refrigerator. Reheat, covered, in a 300°F oven until warm, about 20 minutes. (Do not stir for fear of breaking up the squash.)

MORE

Mix 1 cup purchased seaweed salad (preferably dressed wakame salad) with 6 cups cooked short-grain brown rice (from about 3 cups raw rice). Make a bed of this combo for the stew.

GARNISH

Sprinkle black sesame seeds over each serving.

NOTES

• Kabocha is a variety of winter squash, sort of like a squat pumpkin but green skinned, not orange. The flesh, however, is yellow to orange—and quite sweet. If you can't find kabocha, substitute diced, peeled, and seeded butternut squash.

• If peanut allergies are a concern, substitute untoasted sesame oil, always available at Asian supermarkets.

A MENU

SMALL PLATE: Pulled Vegetable Sliders (page 76)

SALAD: Peanut Chaat, Cardamom Yogurt (page 107)

LARGE PLATE: Braised Kabocha Squash, Scallions, Miso

DESSERT: Porter Pie, Graham Cracker Crust, Meringue (page 260)

POUR

A light, sweet Beaujolais—not a Beaujolais Nouveau, but rather a low-tannin wine from Gamay grapes—that offers complex sweetness with hints of petunias, cherry pits, and raspberries

Grilled Cauliflower, Thai Chili Sauce, Sweet Potato Puree

8 SERVINGS

Although we're not much into meatish fakes, you can indeed turn a firm, large cauliflower into steaks (of a sort) that deserve a knife and a fork. Rather than grill them outdoors, we've headed to the stove because we feel the sear from the skillet, followed by the more gentle heat of the oven, creates the best overall texture. We also let an Asian condiment do a lot of the work in balancing the flavors. Since this dish is a big finish to a meal, the courses that come before should be light and simple but with spiky, hot, or salty flavors so this plate doesn't come out of the blue.

▶ AHEAD

● Make the sweet potato puree up to 4 hours in advance. Store, covered, on the back of the stove.

▶ GARNISH

Combine equal parts panko breadcrumbs and coarsely ground gingersnap cookies to sprinkle over each serving.

▶ NOTES

● Thai sweet chili sauce is the dipping sauce of choice for spring rolls in Thai restaurants—and available in almost all larger supermarkets. It's a thickened concoction of vinegar, sugar, and chiles, sometimes with aromatic vegetables in the mix.

● There will inevitably be leftover cauliflower that is not cut into steaks. Save it in the fridge and use it in a day or two to make an easy dinner like Orecchiette, Cauliflower, Raisins, Olives (page 156).

PUREE

- 1 tablespoon roasted walnut oil
- ½ cup chopped yellow onion
- 1 tablespoon minced fresh ginger
- ½ teaspoon salt
- ½ teaspoon freshly ground black pepper
- 2½ pounds sweet potatoes, peeled and cut into ½-inch cubes
- ½ cup unsweetened apple cider

STEAKS

- 2 large cauliflower heads (about 2 pounds each)
- ¼ cup peanut oil (or perhaps a little more)
- ¾ cup Thai sweet chili sauce, such as Mae Ploy

1. To make the puree: Set a large saucepan over medium heat for a couple of minutes, then add the walnut oil. Dump in the onion, ginger, salt, and pepper. Cook, stirring often, until the onion softens, about 5 minutes. Add the sweet potatoes and stir over the heat for 1 minute. Pour in the cider and bring to a simmer. Cover, reduce the heat to low, and simmer until the sweet potatoes are tender, about 25 minutes.

2. Transfer the contents of the saucepan to a large food processor and process until smooth, scraping down the bowl at least once.

3. To make the steaks: Position the rack in the center of the oven and heat to 375°F.

(continued)

4. Trim the green leaves off the cauliflower heads, then slice them each in half through the stem. Starting at the cut side of each cauliflower half, make ½-inch-thick slices for as long as the slices will hold together. You should end up with about 4 slices per head (or 2 slices per half a head).

5. Set a large cast iron skillet over medium heat for a few minutes. Swirl in 1 tablespoon peanut oil, then slip some of the cauliflower slices into the skillet, probably no more than 2 slices. Cook, turning once, until browned, even blistered a bit, about 8 minutes. Transfer to a large rimmed baking sheet, add another tablespoon of peanut oil to the skillet, and continue frying the rest in more batches as necessary.

6. Once all the cauliflower slices are on the baking sheet, brush them with the chili sauce. Bake until tender and bubbling at the edges, about 10 minutes.

7. To serve, divide the sweet potato puree onto the serving plates and top each with a cauliflower steak.

◗ A MENU

FIRST SMALL PLATE: Roasted Grapes/ Olives (page 37)

SECOND SMALL PLATE: Masa Tarts, Caramelized Garlic Custard, Radish Slaw (page 79)

SOUP: Plum Soup, Cinnamon, Cloves (page 121)

LARGE PLATE: Grilled Cauliflower, Thai Chili Sauce, Sweet Potato Puree

DESSERT: Orange/Coconut Bundt (page 268)

◗ POUR

A lemony, balanced Pinot Grigio to bring the high flavor notes in the dish back into focus

Stir-Fried Bok Choy, Dried Mushrooms, Preserved Black Beans

6 SERVINGS

Spicy and aromatic, this quick stir-fry is a straightforward presentation of vegetables without fuss. It highlights the fresh greens while muting their slight bitterness with Asian condiments (like hoisin sauce and black bean chili paste) alongside earthy, almost musky mushrooms. They're the easiest way to build a layered set of fused flavors! This dish is best as a light main course to mark the end of a set of bolder small plates. (It would also make a great weeknight supper for four, no dinner party in sight!)

8 large dried shiitake mushrooms or other large dried Chinese black mushrooms

Boiling water

¼ cup soy sauce

2 tablespoons hoisin sauce

2 tablespoons Asian black vinegar, preferably Taiwanese

2 tablespoons Shaoxing wine

2 teaspoons sugar

2 tablespoons peanut oil

4 scallions, thinly sliced

1 tablespoon minced fresh ginger

1 tablespoon black bean chili paste

8 cups baby bok choy, well rinsed

1. Set the mushrooms in a big heatproof bowl and cover with boiling water. Soak for 20 minutes. Drain in a colander set in the sink, then stem and quarter the mushrooms.

2. Whisk the soy sauce, hoisin sauce, black vinegar, Shaoxing, and sugar in a bowl.

3. Set a large wok over medium-high heat for a couple of minutes, then swirl in the oil. Add the scallions, ginger, and black bean paste and stir-fry until aromatic, about 1 minute.

4. Add the mushrooms and stir-fry for 1 minute. Then add the bok choy and stir-fry until slightly wilted, about 4 minutes.

5. Pour in the soy sauce mixture and bring to a full simmer, tossing and stirring all the while. Continue cooking until the bok choy stems are crisp-tender, about 2 minutes.

AHEAD

- Soak, stem, and quarter the mushrooms up to 4 hours in advance. Store at room temperature.

- Whisk the soy sauce mixture together up to 2 hours in advance.

MORE

Serve over cooked long-grain white rice—or short-grain brown rice.

GARNISH

Pass a variety of Asian vinegars to splash on servings: red, black, rice, and coconut vinegar.

NOTES

- Bok choy can be sandy. To remove the grit, clean the sink, stopper it, and fill with cool water. Submerge the bok choy, agitate, and soak for 10 minutes. Skim the bok choy out of the water.

- Dried black mushrooms can also be sandy. Run your finger under their gills after they've been rehydrated to feel for any grit. If you notice any, run the mushrooms under tap water to clean.

- Black bean chili paste is a spicy brew with preserved black beans.

- Shaoxing is a Chinese rice wine, prized in cooking.

A MENU

SOUP: Pear Soup, Ginger, Buttery Leeks (page 129)

SMALL PLATE: Tomato Gelée, Pistachio Shortbread (page 67)

LARGE PLATE: Stir-Fried Bok Choy, Dried Mushrooms, Preserved Black Beans

DESSERT: Coconut Cheesecake Flan (page 273)

POUR

A Chinese beer

Stewed Butternut Squash, Coconut Milk, Warm Spices

8 SERVINGS

This comforting but decidedly spicy stew would be quite a treat on a fall evening: lots of late-season vegetables, a Southeast Asian broth, and plenty of finishing aromatics to bring the flavors back into balance. The dish would even be a welcome part of a Thanksgiving table. The homemade spice paste is nothing like any store-bought version of Thai curry paste. It's aromatic without being too fiery, fragrant but without being sweet, a complex blend of spices and aromatics (including a serrano chile). You'll make more than required for a single recipe. Save it and add it to vegetable soups and stews with coconut milk in the mix for plenty of aromatic heat.

1 fresh lemongrass stalk, white part only, peeled

1 serrano chile, quartered and seeded

1 garlic clove

2 whole cloves

1 tablespoon cumin seeds

1 tablespoon ground turmeric

1 teaspoon ground coriander

1 teaspoon ground cinnamon

1½ tablespoons coconut oil

1 large yellow onion, halved then thinly sliced into half-moons

¼ cup minced fresh ginger

2⅔ cups regular or light coconut milk

¾ cup dry vermouth

2 medium butternut squash, peeled, seeded, and cubed (about 9 cups)

¾ pound thinly sliced cremini mushrooms

2 medium red bell peppers, chopped

6 tablespoons minced fresh basil

1½ tablespoons grated palm sugar or packed light brown sugar

1½ tablespoons fresh lime juice

1½ tablespoons soy sauce

) AHEAD

● Make the lemongrass paste up to 1 week in advance. Store, covered, in the refrigerator. Or freeze for up to 3 months.

) LESS

Use store-bought Thai yellow curry paste. However, it may be far more hot than aromatic. If desired, add the stated amounts of ground coriander and cinnamon to the pot to enhance it.

) MORE

Serve over cooked short-grain white rice (aka sushi rice).

) NOTES

● The amount of lemongrass paste you use should be based on your ability to tolerate heat. If you're concerned, use less the first time, maybe only 1 tablespoon, just to get the hang of the flavors.

● Coconut oil is solid at room temperature. You may need to dig it out of the jar, sort of like digging out candle wax.

● The butternut squash should be cut into 1-inch cubes. Otherwise, it will take too long to get tender. If you buy prepared butternut squash in the produce section's refrigerator case, you'll mostly likely have to cut the chunks down to size.

1. Crush the lemongrass in a mortar with a pestle to a paste—or grind in a mini food processor or a clean spice grinder. Add the chile, garlic, cloves, cumin seeds, turmeric, coriander, and cinnamon; grind to a grainy, dry paste. (If you're using a mini food processor, scrape down the bowl after pulsing the machine to make sure everything's getting ground.) Scrape the paste into a small plastic or glass container.

2. Melt the coconut oil in a large pot over medium heat. Add the onion and ginger. Cook, stirring often, until soft and fragrant, about 5 minutes. Add *up to* 3 tablespoons of the lemongrass paste (see Note) and cook about 1 minute, stirring all the while.

3. Pour in the coconut milk and vermouth and stir to combine, scraping up any browned bits from the bottom of the pot as the liquids come to a simmer. Add the squash, mushrooms, and bell peppers. Stir well and bring to a simmer.

4. Cover, reduce the heat, and simmer slowly for 15 minutes. Stir in the basil, sugar, lime juice, and soy sauce. Cover and continue simmering, stirring occasionally, until the squash is tender, about 15 minutes.

▶ A MENU

FIRST SMALL PLATE: Mushroom Bao (page 94)

SECOND SMALL PLATE: Parsnip Flans (page 64)

LARGE PLATE: Stewed Butternut Squash, Coconut Milk, Warm Spices

DESSERT: Sliced pears and shaved Parmigiano-Reggiano drizzled with honey

▶ POUR

A sweet, fragrant Riesling or Spätlese to cool down the palate and balance the many spices

Asparagus Stir-Fry, Tamarind Paste, Coconut Rice

8 SERVINGS

This surprisingly light dish rounds out our collection of five Asian-inspired main courses, each an attempt to use simple, purchased condiments to merge disparate flavors without too much work. Of all these large-plate recipes, this one best delivers the promise of spring. The tender asparagus is used in a quick, sweet-and-sour stir-fry to become the topping for rice cooked in coconut milk. The surprise here may be the way the sour tamarind paste balances the searingly hot sambal oelek. Most of us think of balancing hot with sweet (and indeed, there is brown sugar here), but a sour counterpoint pushes a dish to a more savory finish, something often missing in recipes that call for chiles or chile pastes. Although this main course does seem to call to spring, you don't have to time it to the seasons, since asparagus shows up in our supermarkets all year long. However, those fall and winter spears can be quite tough. Trim off any thick ends, then shave the spears with a vegetable peeler down to no more than a ¼-inch diameter at the base.

▶ AHEAD

● Blanch the asparagus up to 4 hours in advance. Once cooled and drained, store, covered, at room temperature.

▶ MORE

To take this dish over the top, use white asparagus spears. You needn't trim these down, especially since they're more fragile. Instead, just avoid very fat ones—or blanch these for 4 minutes to assure they're tender.

▶ NOTE

● Tamarind paste—sometimes labeled as tamarind concentrate—is the juice of the fruit boiled down to a sweet-and-sour, sticky paste. Look for it among East Indian, Latin American, or even Southwestern condiments at the store.

2 pounds thin asparagus spears, cut into 2-inch pieces (about 8 cups)

2 cups long-grain white rice, preferably jasmine rice

2¼ cups water

1¾ cups regular or light coconut milk

1 tablespoon minced fresh ginger

4 kaffir lime leaves

½ teaspoon salt

2 tablespoons peanut oil

3 tablespoons minced shallot

3 tablespoons peeled, minced fresh lemongrass, white part only

1 tablespoon minced garlic

1½ tablespoons sambal oelek (see page 59)

1 tablespoon grated palm sugar or packed light brown sugar

½ tablespoon tamarind paste (see Note)

1. Blanch the asparagus in a big saucepan of boiling water for 2 minutes (timed from when the asparagus goes into the water). Drain in a colander set in the sink, then rinse thoroughly with cool tap water to stop the cooking. Drain completely.

(continued)

2. Mix the rice, water, coconut milk, ginger, lime leaves, and salt in a large saucepan and bring to a boil over medium-high heat, stirring occasionally. Cover, reduce the heat to low, and simmer until the rice is tender and almost all the liquid has been absorbed, about 16 minutes. Let the pan stand off the heat, covered, for 15 minutes.

3. Meanwhile, set a large wok over high heat until smoking. Swirl in the oil, then add the shallot, lemongrass, and garlic. Stir-fry for 30 seconds, then add the sambal, sugar, and tamarind paste. Stir-fry until aromatic, about 30 seconds. Add the asparagus and toss over the heat for 1 minute, just until coated and hot.

4. To serve, fluff the rice in the saucepan with a fork to separate the grains, then mound on a serving platter or individual plates. Top with the asparagus mixture, making sure you get every drop of the sauce in the wok.

▶ **A MENU**

SMALL PLATE: Kohlrabi, Enoki, Peanuts, Grilled Scallions (page 59)

SALAD: Wedge, Ginger, Miso (page 115)

LARGE PLATE: Asparagus Stir-Fry, Tamarind, Coconut Rice

DESSERT: Chocolate Pots de Crème (page 253)

▶ **POUR**

An IPA or amber ale to offer some slightly bitter, cooling fizz against the fiery stir-fry—or else a California Zinfandel with present, summer-y sweet notes

Vegetable Kebabs, Saffron Oil, Quinoa Pilaf

8 KEBABS

You'll get raves for a platter of these tasty but simple skewers, especially after they're coated in this most flavorful oil. But the real winner here is the pilaf underneath: earthy but a little sour, nutty but moderately bright. Lentils du Puy, also called "green French lentils," are particularly earthy and chewy, a good contrast to the grassy quinoa in the mix. This dish can be a go-to main course for a dinner party on the deck.

3 tablespoons sherry vinegar

½ teaspoon saffron

½ cup peanut oil

PILAF

1⅓ cups lentils du Puy

2 tablespoons roasted walnut oil

1 medium leek (white and pale green part only), halved lengthwise, carefully washed, and thinly sliced

¼ cup pine nuts, chopped

¼ cup dried currants

1 teaspoon dried oregano

1 teaspoon dried thyme

½ teaspoon salt

½ teaspoon freshly ground black pepper

1 bay leaf

¾ cup white or red quinoa

1½ cups vegetable broth

⅓ cup minced fresh cilantro leaves

2 tablespoons fresh lemon juice

KEBABS

8 cipollini onions

8 cremini mushrooms

8 canned artichoke hearts, rinsed

4 small Japanese eggplants (about 4 ounces each), cut into 2-inch pieces

4 yellow pattypan squash (about 8 ounces each), quartered through the stems

▶ AHEAD

● Make the saffron oil up to 1 day in advance. Store, covered, at room temperature.

● Make the pilaf up to 4 hours in advance. Store, covered, at room temperature.

▶ NOTES

● Most quinoa now sold in modern packaging has been rinsed to remove a bitter compound on the grain. But check the label carefully. If it says to rinse the quinoa, by all means do so in a fine-mesh sieve over the sink.

● It's a myth that you must soak bamboo skewers. Yes, for bigger cuts of meat that stay over the heat for prolonged periods of time, it may be necessary. But not for vegetable kebabs that are done in no time. The skewers will burn a bit, but the extra effort isn't warranted.

1. Microwave the vinegar in a small bowl on high for 30 seconds, then stir in the saffron. Let stand for 30 minutes, then stir in the peanut oil.

2. To make the pilaf: Bring a large saucepan of water to a boil over high heat. Add the lentils, reduce the heat to medium, and simmer until tender, about 18 minutes. Drain in a colander set in the sink.

3. Set that same saucepan back over medium heat for a couple of minutes. Swirl in the walnut oil, then add the leek. Cook, stirring often, until softened, about 5 minutes. Stir in the pine nuts, currants, oregano, thyme, salt, pepper, and bay leaf. Cook, stirring constantly, for 1 minute. Stir in the quinoa and cook, stirring often, for 1 minute.

4. Pour in the broth and bring to a boil. Cover, reduce the heat to low, and simmer until the liquid has been absorbed, about 18 minutes. Set the covered saucepan off the heat for 5 minutes before stirring in the cilantro and lemon juice as well as the tender drained lentils.

5. To make the kebabs: Bring a large pot of water to a boil over high heat. Add the onions and blanch for 1 minute from when they take a dive into the water. Drain in a colander set in the sink, then run cool tap water over them to stop the cooking. Drain completely.

6. Thread each of eight 10-inch bamboo skewers with the onion, mushroom, artichoke heart, eggplant, and squash.

7. Prepare a grill for high-heat, direct cooking (or heat a grill pan over medium-high heat until smoking). Grill the skewers, turning occasionally with tongs and brushing with the saffron oil, until browned and tender, about 10 minutes.

8. To serve, mound the pilaf on a serving platter or individual serving plates. Top with the skewers.

▶ A MENU

SMALL PLATE: Baked Artichokes, Dulse Flakes, Pine Nuts (page 61)

SALAD: Watercress/Celery Root Salad, Za'atar (page 116)

LARGE PLATE: Vegetable Kebabs, Saffron Oil, Quinoa Pilaf

DESSERT: Pecan Baklava, Fennel Syrup (page 245)

▶ POUR

A Bandol rosé, a contrast in itself with its bright minerality and sturdy, jammy flavors, to accent the sweet notes in a mostly savory dish

Zucchini Pancakes, Yellow Pepper Relish

6 SERVINGS

No, it's not breakfast for dinner. These are savory pancakes, laced with cheese and lemon zest, topped with a vinegary, spicy relish. Don't worry: You won't be standing in the kitchen over a hot stove at the main course. You can even make these pancakes in advance. All in all, this may be the most host-friendly recipe in the chapter. What's more, these cakes provide an appealing, welcome crunch at the end of the meal. We can't really top such promise.

RELISH

- 2 yellow bell peppers, cut into quarters
- 1 small yellow onion
  Boiling water
- ½ cup cool water
- ½ cup plus 2 tablespoons distilled white vinegar
- 3 tablespoons sugar
- ¼ teaspoon salt
- ¼ teaspoon red pepper flakes

PANCAKES

- 3 medium zucchini (about 7 ounces each)
- 1 very small yellow onion (about 3 ounces)
- 2 large eggs, at room temperature and well beaten in a small bowl
- 1½ cups panko breadcrumbs
- ½ cup regular or part-skim ricotta cheese
- ½ cup finely ground almonds
- 1 ounce aged Asiago cheese, finely grated (about ¼ cup)
- 1 teaspoon finely grated lemon zest
- 1 teaspoon dried thyme
- ½ teaspoon salt
- ½ teaspoon freshly ground black pepper
  Peanut or canola oil, for frying

▌ AHEAD

● Prepare the relish up to 4 hours in advance. Store in the covered saucepan at room temperature. Or make it up to 1 week in advance, scrape it into a glass or plastic container, and refrigerate.

● Make the pancakes up to 4 hours in advance. Store, uncovered, in the refrigerator on a baking sheet. Warm in a 350°F oven for 15 to 20 minutes.

▌ NOTE

● Keep rewetting your hands as you form the pancakes in step 6. Doing so will keep the batter from sticking (too much) to your fingers. Or just drop the required amount into the skillet and use the bottom of a measuring cup to press it into a pancake.

▌ MORE

Smear some kidney bean puree (page 194) on each plate before adding the pancakes and relish.

1. To make the relish: Shred the bell peppers and onion with the large holes of box grater or in a food processor fitted with shredding blade. Place in a large heatproof bowl, cover with boiling water, and soak for 5 minutes. Drain in a colander set in the sink.

2. Place the peppers and onion in a medium saucepan. Stir in the cool water and ½ cup of the vinegar. Bring to simmer over high heat. Remove from the heat, cover, and let stand for 10 minutes. Drain in a colander set in the sink.

3. Return the peppers and onion to the saucepan. Stir in the remaining 2 tablespoons vinegar, the sugar, salt, and red pepper flakes. Bring to a simmer over medium-high heat. Reduce the heat to low and simmer, stirring often, for 10 minutes, or until thickened like marmalade. Set aside, uncovered, off the heat.

4. To make the pancakes: Grate the zucchini and onion through the large holes of a box grater. Squeeze the mixture dry by small handfuls over the sink.

5. Separate the strands, put them in a big bowl, and stir in the eggs, panko, ricotta, almonds, Asiago, lemon zest, thyme, salt, and black pepper until a coherent if wet dough forms.

6. Pour about ¼ inch oil into a large skillet and set over medium heat until faint ripples mark the oil's surface. Scoop up ¼ cup of the batter and form into a ½-inch-thick patty between wet, clean hands. Slip into the oil, then make a few more patties, never crowding the skillet. Fry, turning once, until crisp and browned, about 8 minutes. Transfer to a wire rack and continue making more. Serve two per person with the relish dotted on top.

▶ A MENU

SOUP: Cucumber Soup, Basil, Buttermilk (page 123)

SALAD: Beet/Orange Salad, Spicy Gingerbread Croutons (page 104)

LARGE PLATE: Zucchini Pancakes, Yellow Pepper Relish

DESSERT: Summer Pudding, Black Currants, Blackberries (page 263)

▶ POUR

A Blanc de Blancs from Champagne with its citrus and apricot accents

Kale/Apple Stew, Kidney Bean Puree

6 SERVINGS

Here's a big range of cooking techniques: caramelizing the onions, wilting the kale, roasting the apples, pureeing the kidney beans. It'll all add up to a pronounced flavor range: the earthy and bitter kale mellowed by the fragrant apples (with some help from sweet beets); the classic French combo of thyme and allspice made slightly sweeter with the addition of pecans; and the sweet beans whirred into rich coconut milk for a more savory take on a standard bean puree. On the plate, that puree actually darkens the flavors in the stew a bit, creating a sophisticated finish in a fairly complicated dish.

PUREE

- 4 cups canned kidney beans, drained and rinsed
- ¼ cup regular or light coconut milk
- ½ teaspoon ground cumin

STEW

- 5½ tablespoons olive oil, divided
- 3 large yellow onions, thinly sliced (about 4 cups)
- 2 large, firm, moderately tart apples, such as Pippins, peeled and cut into eighths
- 3 medium beets, peeled and cut into eighths
- ½ teaspoon salt
- ½ teaspoon freshly ground black pepper
- 1 pound kale, stemmed and chopped (about 8 packed cups)
- ½ cup moderately dry white wine, such as Semillon
- ½ teaspoon ground allspice
- ½ teaspoon dried thyme
- 1½ tablespoons white wine vinegar
- ⅓ cup pecan pieces

AHEAD

● The puree can be made up to 6 hours in advance. Store, covered, at room temperature.

● The stew can be made up to 2 hours in advance. Store, covered, at room temperature. Warm, covered, in a 400°F oven for 10 minutes before serving.

GARNISH

Top with crumbled, store-bought kale chips.

NOTES

● After 30 or 40 minutes, the onions will be golden, even lightly brown, with just enough residual bite to stand up to the kale and beets.

● The kale stew on its own would be a great starter—or perhaps a second course between the starter and the main event.

1. To make the puree: Process the beans, coconut milk, and cumin in a large food processor until smooth. Scrape into a large bowl and set aside.

2. To make the stew: Set a large pot or Dutch oven over medium-low heat for a couple of minutes, then add 3 tablespoons of the oil. Dump in the onions and reduce the heat to low. Cook, stirring occasionally but more and more as the onions break down, until caramelized and sweet, 30 to 40 minutes. If they turn a very dark brown, remove the pot from the heat for a minute or so and reduce that heat even further when they return to it.

3. Meanwhile, position the rack in the center of the oven and heat to 400°F. Toss the remaining 2½ tablespoons oil with the apples, beets, salt, and pepper in a large roasting pan. Bake, stirring occasionally, until soft and lightly browned, about 40 minutes.

4. Stir the kale into the onions and cook, stirring all the while, until slightly wilted, about 1 minute. Stir in the wine, allspice, and thyme. Cover and simmer, stirring occasionally, until the kale is tender, about 10 minutes.

5. Remove the roasting pan from the oven and immediately stir in the vinegar, scraping up any browned bits on the bottom. Scrape the kale, onions, and any oil from the pot into the roasting pan and stir in the pecans.

6. To serve, spread a little kidney bean puree on serving plates, preferably making a circle with a hole at the center. Mound the kale mixture into the center of the plates.

▌A MENU

SMALL PLATE: Red Cabbage Pot Stickers, Raisin Chipotle Dip (page 92)

SALAD: Grapefruit/Avocado Salad, Pistachios (page 100)

LARGE PLATE: Kale/Apple Stew, Kidney Bean Puree (page 194)

DESSERT: A platter of dried fruit and nuts

▌POUR

A hearty red from the Portuguese Ribatejo (or Tejo) region with leathery rusticity to bring this high-flying dish back to earth

Buttery Black-Eyed Pea Stew, Fried Corn Cakes

8 SERVINGS

A creamy, vegetable-rich stew with a crunchy corn cake—what could be a better match? We call these sorts of dishes *complicated simplicity*. They're also the essence of what we believe dinner-party main-course fare should be, the flavors thickly layered but softened a bit and very smooth. The cakes are pretty easy to prepare—and the black-eyed peas, garlic, and other ingredients in the stew just need time over the heat to meld properly. Consider this one our take on new Southern cuisine. It feels as if you spent all day preparing it. You didn't. You needn't tell.

▶ AHEAD

● Fry the corn cakes up to 2 hours in advance. Store on the wire rack. Warm on a baking sheet in a 350°F oven for 10 minutes.

● Make the stew up to 2 hours in advance. Store, covered, at room temperature in its pan. Reheat over low heat until bubbling, stirring often, before serving.

▶ GARNISH

Sprinkle minced parsley leaves over the servings.

▶ NOTE

● There's no salt in the corn cake recipe because canned chopped chiles are well stocked with sodium.

CORN CAKES

- 2 cups fresh or thawed frozen corn kernels
- ¾ cup heavy cream
- ½ cup canned chopped mild green chiles
- 6 tablespoons unsalted butter, melted and cooled a few minutes
- 2 large eggs, at room temperature and lightly beaten
- 1 cup yellow cornmeal
- ½ cup all-purpose flour
- Corn oil, for frying

STEW

- 4 tablespoons (½ stick) unsalted butter
- 2 medium yellow onions, chopped
- 1 large red bell pepper, chopped
- 4 medium celery stalks, chopped
- 2 teaspoons minced garlic
- 3 tablespoons all-purpose flour
- 1 teaspoon dried sage (do not use rubbed sage)
- 1 teaspoon dried thyme
- ½ teaspoon sweet paprika
- ½ teaspoon salt
- ¼ teaspoon celery seeds
- ¼ teaspoon freshly grated nutmeg
- Up to ¼ teaspoon cayenne pepper
- 2 cups vegetable broth
- 5 cups black-eyed peas, thawed frozen or rinsed canned
- ½ cup heavy cream

1. To make the corn cakes: Stir the corn, cream, chiles, butter, and eggs in a large bowl until well combined. Stir in the cornmeal and flour to make a soft but rich batter, like a thick pancake batter.

(continued)

2. Heat a large nonstick skillet over medium heat. Coat the skillet lightly with oil. Scoop up a scant ¼ cup of the batter and drop it into the skillet. Add a few more, spacing them apart, then use the back of a metal spatula or pancake turner to flatten them to 3½-inch rounds. Cook, turning once, until browned and set, about 4 minutes. Transfer to a wire rack and continue making more cakes until you have 16 in all, adding a little oil before each batch and never crowding the skillet.

3. To make the stew: Melt the butter in a large, high-sided sauté pan over medium heat. Add the onions, bell pepper, celery, and garlic. Cook, stirring often, until softened, about 10 minutes.

4. Meanwhile, stir the flour, sage, thyme, paprika, salt, celery seeds, nutmeg, and cayenne in a small bowl.

5. Whisk the spiced flour mixture into the onion mixture and cook for 30 seconds, whisking all the while. Whisk in the broth until the flour dissolves, bring to a simmer, and continue whisking until thickened and bubbling, about 2 minutes.

6. Stir in the black-eyed peas and cream and bring back to a simmer, stirring often. Cover, reduce the heat to low, and simmer to meld the flavors, about 15 minutes, stirring occasionally.

7. To serve, ladle the stew into shallow soup bowls and top each with two corn cakes.

▶ A MENU

FIRST SMALL PLATE: Grilled Leeks, Hazelnuts, Lemon (page 38)

SECOND SMALL PLATE: Portobello Confit, Pickled Ramps (page 66)

LARGE PLATE: Buttery Black-Eyed Pea Stew, Fried Corn Cakes

DESSERT: Pumpkin Pie Tamales (page 256)

▶ POUR

An oaked Chardonnay for bright, floral notes with vanilla and butter accents

Millet/Brown Rice Casserole, Antipasti

8 SERVINGS

Antipasti? Before the pasta? Among the large plates? Well, not really. This casserole's definitely a main course, an end stop to the evening's savory lineup. But it uses items off an antipasti platter (or the antipasti bar at your supermarket) to morph two ancient grains into complex comfort food. This dish would be best after a light small plate or two, each big on fresh vegetable flavors, probably tending a little to the sour side for good contrast.

3 tablespoons olive oil

1 medium leek (white and pale green parts only), halved lengthwise, carefully washed, and thinly sliced

8 ounces cremini mushrooms, thinly sliced

2 teaspoons minced garlic

1 cup short-grain brown rice, such as brown sushi rice

½ cup millet

¾ cup dry white wine, such as Chardonnay

1 tablespoon minced fresh rosemary

1 tablespoon fresh thyme leaves

½ teaspoon fennel seeds

½ teaspoon red pepper flakes

½ teaspoon salt

2 cups frozen artichoke heart quarters, thawed (about one 9-ounce box)

1 cup thinly sliced sun-dried tomatoes

½ cup thinly sliced pitted green olives

3 cups vegetable broth

1. Position the rack in the center of the oven and heat to 350°F.

2. Set a 4- to 6-quart round or oval cast iron casserole over medium heat for a few minutes, then swirl in the oil. Add the leek and cook, stirring often, just until softened, about 2 minutes. Add the mushrooms and cook, stirring frequently, until they release their liquid and the pan is dry again, about 5 minutes. Stir in the garlic and cook for 30 seconds.

3. Add the rice and millet and cook for 30 seconds to toast the grains. Pour in the wine and bring to a simmer, scraping up any browned bits in the pot. Stir in the rosemary, thyme, fennel, red pepper flakes, and salt. Then add the artichoke heart quarters, sun-dried tomatoes, and olives.

4. Pour in the broth; bring to a full simmer, stirring often. Cover and bake until nearly all the liquid is absorbed, about 1 hour. Turn the oven off and leave the covered casserole in it for 1 hour before serving.

MORE

Add up to ¼ cup toasted pine nuts to the casserole.

NOTE

● Although there is a range of cast iron casserole dishes you can use, the 4-quart model will treat the rice and millet the best, allowing minimum evaporation as the grains become tender.

A MENU

FIRST SMALL PLATE: Chestnut/Cashew/Porcini Pâté (page 75)

SECOND SMALL PLATE: Roasted Grapes/Olives (page 37)

LARGE PLATE: Millet/Brown Rice Casserole, Antipasti

DESSERT: Walnut/Honey Semifreddo, Pomegranate Molasses (page 257)

POUR

A white Friuli with lots of bright, spiky, floral notes that have been mellowed by the mildly acidic finish

Brie Arepas, Asparagus Salsa

8 SERVINGS

Arepas are small corn cakes, common in Colombia and Venezuela. Here, we've shifted them from the New World back to the Old. To France, in fact. We've stuffed them with Brie before frying them to crisp and irresistible. The pairing of corn (or masa) and Brie is stunning: sweet, sour, pungent, and creamy, all at once. We've then taken the whole dish over the top with a fresh, crunchy salsa made from raw asparagus and tomatoes with garlicky aromatics, a spiky way to add depth and dimension to the cakes.

▶ **AHEAD**

● The salsa can be made up to 6 hours in advance. Store, covered, at room temperature.

● The stuffed arepas can be made up to 2 hours in advance. Store, covered, in the refrigerator until you're ready to fry them.

▶ **NOTES**

● Masarepa is a ground cornmeal specifically designed to create arepas. You cannot substitute masa harina. Look for masarepa at almost all Latin American markets.

● Don't use a runny, ripe Brie. Instead, you want a slice with firm edges so that the cheese is easier to work with.

● Seal the edge of each arepa so no cheese leaks out. Pinch the edges.

SALSA

- 1 pound pencil-thin asparagus spears, cut into ¼-inch pieces
- 16 cherry tomatoes, chopped
- ¼ cup minced red onion
- ¼ cup minced cilantro leaves
- 1 tablespoon fresh lime juice
- 1 teaspoon minced garlic
- 1 teaspoon minced seeded jalapeño chile
- ½ teaspoon ground cumin
- ½ teaspoon salt

AREPAS

- 3¾ cups warm water
- 3 cups masarepa (see Note)
- ½ tablespoon salt
- 1 pound firm Brie, rind removed
- Corn oil, for frying

1. To make the salsa: Set up a large bowl of ice water. Bring a large pot of water to a boil over high heat. Add the asparagus pieces and blanch for 1 minute from the time they enter the water. Use a slotted spoon to transfer them to the ice water and cool before draining in a colander set in the sink. Mix the asparagus with the tomatoes, onion, cilantro, lime juice, garlic, jalapeño, cumin, and salt in a large bowl.

2. To make the arepas: Stir the water, masarepa, and salt in a large bowl to form a thick batter. Set aside for 5 minutes as the moisture is absorbed into the masa mixture. Turn out onto a clean, dry work surface. Knead just a little, about 30 seconds, to form a coherent, uniform, if sticky, dough.

3. Scoop up ⅓ cup of the dough and divide this amount in half. Roll each half into a ball between your palms. Flatten each ball into a 3-inch round on a clean, dry work surface. Flatten 1½ tablespoons Brie into a disk just shy of 3 inches in diameter. Set the Brie on top of one round of dough and top with the second. Seal the edges all around. Set aside and continue making more until you have 16 stuffed arepas.

4. Set a large baking sheet on the center rack of the oven and heat to 200°F.

5. Heat a large nonstick skillet or well-seasoned cast iron skillet over medium heat. Pour in enough oil to coat the skillet well, then add several of the stuffed arepas. Fry, turning once, until browned and crisp, about 8 minutes. Transfer to the baking sheet in the oven to keep warm and continue frying more arepas.

6. To serve, place 2 arepas on each plate and top with the asparagus salsa.

▶ A MENU

PASTA: Drunken Spaghetti, Pine Nuts, Parsley (page 137)

FIRST SMALL PLATE: Roasted Radishes, Their Greens, Browned Butter (page 35)

SALAD: Fava Bean/Sugar Snap Salad, Warm Breadcrumbs (page 103)

LARGE PLATE: Brie Arepas, Asparagus Salsa

DESSERT: Chocolate Chip Cookies, Maple, Tahini, Dates (page 236) with glasses of whole milk

▶ POUR:

A chilled, sweet/tart Chablis with apple and herbal accents to smooth out any rough edges in the salsa

Coconut Tofu, Sour Beans

8 SERVINGS

Tofu may seem like a natural in a vegetarian main course, but it's actually a bit challenging. The point of tofu, after all, is its texture: soft, firm, chewy, cheesy, or silken, depending on the variety. But its legendary blandness presents a culinary problem. We solve that here by poaching firm tofu in coconut milk, then setting it on top of a hot-and-sour mix of fresh long beans (sort of like green beans on steroids with less sweetness and a more grassy taste). The poaching liquid then gets reduced into a sauce for the plates. All in all, it's a very aromatic dish, a fiery spark that rings the flavor changes from sour to earthy. It's probably not a dish you want to serve on its own on a weeknight. Instead, it marks a wide scope of flavors for the end of a set of plates at your dinner party.

2 pounds firm tofu, drained and cut into 8 large squares or rectangles

1¾ cups regular coconut milk (do not use light)

3 cups distilled white vinegar

1½ cups water

1½ pounds Chinese long beans, cut into ⅛-inch pieces

2 tablespoons peanut oil

3 medium scallions, thinly sliced

1 tablespoon minced fresh ginger

1 teaspoon minced garlic

½ teaspoon red pepper flakes

½ teaspoon Sichuan peppercorns

¼ teaspoon cardamom seeds

3 tablespoons soy sauce

2 tablespoons Asian black vinegar

1 tablespoon demerara sugar (see Note)

AHEAD

- The tofu can be poached up to 2 hours in advance. Store in its poaching liquid in the skillet, covered, at room temperature.

- The beans can be stir-fried up to 1 hour in advance. Store, uncovered, in their wok at room temperature. Reheat quickly over high heat, tossing constantly.

MORE

Offer bowls of cooked short-grain white rice alongside each serving. Or dress that rice with a little rice vinegar and a pinch of sugar, then top it with toasted sesame seeds and serve as a small follow-up, cool-down bowl to this main course.

GARNISH

Sprinkle minced cilantro leaves over each serving.

NOTES

- Chinese long beans are a specific varietal of legumes, each pod up to half a yard long, grown to be eaten with the seeds inside. If you can't find long beans, substitute green beans, although the dish's finish will be less grassy and decidedly sweeter.

- Demerara sugar is a coarse-grained, crunchy, unrefined sugar, primarily extracted from sugar cane, not sugar beets. It's prized for its slightly musky sweetness.

1. Line a large cutting board or baking sheet with paper towels. Set the tofu pieces on top, then put a layer of paper towels over them and a second cutting board on top. Weight the top cutting board down by placing a heavy saucepan or a couple of cans on top. Set aside at room temperature for 30 minutes.

2. Bring the coconut milk to a simmer in a large skillet over medium-high heat. Slip the tofu in a single layer into the skillet, then reduce the heat to low and simmer very slowly, uncovered, for 30 minutes. Set aside.

3. Bring the distilled white vinegar and water to a boil in a large saucepan over high heat. Add the beans and blanch for 1 minute from the time the beans hit the liquid. Drain in a colander set in the sink but do not rinse.

4. Set a large wok over medium-high heat for a few minutes, then add the peanut oil, followed quickly by the scallions, ginger, garlic, red pepper flakes, Sichuan peppercorns, and cardamom seeds. Stir-fry for 1 minute.

5. Add the drained beans and stir-fry for 1 minute. Pour in the soy sauce and black vinegar; stir in the sugar. Bring to a full simmer and cook, stirring often, until slightly thickened, about 2 minutes.

6. To serve, divide the beans among the plates; set one piece of tofu on each pile of beans. Bring the coconut milk to a boil in the skillet, now set over high heat. Boil until reduced and slightly thickened, about 3 minutes. Drizzle 1 to 2 tablespoons around each plate.

▷ A MENU

FIRST SMALL PLATE: Asiago Cookies, Tahini/Lentil Cream (page 89)

SECOND SMALL PLATE: Cauliflower Grains, Cucumber, Parsley (page 53)

LARGE PLATE: Coconut Tofu, Sour Beans

DESSERT: Fleur de Sel Caramels (page 279)

▷ POUR

A rich, sweet, balanced Gewürtzraminer to balance the heat and add floral accents ·

Ginger Falafel, Wasabi Cream

8 SERVINGS

These crunchy bits of chickpea dough make a wonderful, moderately sized last course, aromatic and fresh in themselves, made even better with this nose-spanking dip. Although it's a fairly simple dish—and the technique of deep-frying takes care of melding all those spices in no time—you'll discover that the textural contrast of crunch and cream is a great way to mark the end of a dinner party (at least before the dessert). This dish should follow first courses with milder, sweeter flavors.

1 pound dried chickpeas

½ cup loosely packed fresh cilantro leaves

½ cup thinly sliced scallions

5 tablespoons minced fresh ginger

6 peeled garlic cloves

3 tablespoons soy sauce

1 teaspoon baking powder

2 cups regular or low-fat sour cream

½ cup rice vinegar

4 teaspoons wasabi paste

Olive oil, for frying

1. Soak the chickpeas in a bowl of cool water for 24 hours at room temperature.

2. Drain and rinse in a colander set in the sink. Pour the chickpeas into a large food processor and add the cilantro, scallions, ginger, garlic, soy sauce, and baking powder. Process to a thick, grainy, coarse paste, scraping down the bowl's interior occasionally.

3. Whisk the sour cream, rice vinegar, and wasabi paste in a medium bowl until creamy. Cover and refrigerate for at least 1 hour to blend the flavors.

4. Pour about 3 inches oil into a large, deep saucepan. Clip a deep-frying thermometer to the inside of the pan and heat the oil over medium heat to 350°F. Set a fine-mesh wire rack over paper towels.

5. Form the chickpea mixture into thirty-two 1¼-inch balls. Slip several into the hot oil, just enough that there's room to spare around them. Fry, turning occasionally, until crisp and browned, about 5 minutes. Adjust the heat so the oil's temperature remains fairly constant. Use a slotted spoon to transfer the balls to the wire rack. Continue frying more falafel.

6. To serve, smear some wasabi cream on 8 serving plates and top each with 4 falafel.

▶ AHEAD

● Make the wasabi cream up to 24 hours in advance. Store, covered, in the refrigerator.

● Make the chickpea batter up to 1 hour in advance. Store in the covered food processor bowl at room temperature.

▶ GARNISH

Sprinkle diced, seeded cucumber and diced red bell pepper around the plates.

▶ A MENU

FIRST SMALL PLATE: Asparagus Spears, Pickled Radicchio (page 40)

SECOND SMALL PLATE: Squash Noodles, Almond Chimichurri (page 45)

PASTA: Orecchiette, Cauliflower, Raisins, Olives (page 156)

LARGE PLATE: Ginger Falafel, Wasabi Cream

DESSERT: Dark chocolate squares and port

▶ POUR

A Sauvignon Blanc to lend lots of balanced, fruit-laced, grapy acidity to the dish's spiky flavors

Vegetable/Lentil Balls, Brown Rice Pilaf

8 SERVINGS

Unlike the falafel in the previous recipe, these crunchy, savory spheres are baked, not fried, until deliciously crisp. They're made from lentils and stocked with plenty of vegetables. They're also set atop a moist pilaf, sort of like a rice casserole with basil and tomatoes in the mix. Despite its humble look, it's a relatively sophisticated main course that can be made mostly in advance, then baked at the last minute.

▶ AHEAD

● Make the veggie balls up to 24 hours in advance without baking them. Store, covered, on their baking sheet in the refrigerator.

● Make the pilaf up to 30 minutes in advance. Store, covered, at room temperature.

▶ GARNISH

Sprinkle more finely grated Parmigiano-Reggiano around the servings, as well as minced basil leaves.

PILAF

- ¼ cup olive oil
- 1 large onion, chopped
- 1 cubanelle or Italian frying pepper, stemmed, seeded, and chopped
- 2 cups long-grain brown rice, preferably brown basmati
- 3½ cups canned diced tomatoes
- 3 cups water
- ½ cup loosely packed fresh basil leaves, chopped
- ½ teaspoon salt
- ½ teaspoon freshly ground black pepper

VEGETABLE BALLS

- 2 cups lentils du Puy (aka green French lentils)
- ¼ cup olive oil, plus lots more for greasing
- 1 large yellow onion, chopped
- 1 large fennel bulb, trimmed and chopped

- ½ pound fresh shiitake mushrooms, stems discarded, caps thinly sliced
- 1 tablespoon minced fresh rosemary
- 1 tablespoon fresh thyme leaves
- 1 teaspoon minced garlic
- 1 teaspoon fennel seeds
- 3 large eggs, at room temperature and lightly beaten
- ½ cup Parmigiano-Reggiano cheese, finely grated (about 2 ounces)
- ½ cup panko breadcrumbs
- ½ cup packed fresh parsley leaves
- ½ cup chopped toasted pecans
- 3 tablespoons tomato paste
- 1 teaspoon salt
- ½ teaspoon freshly ground black pepper

1. To make the pilaf: Heat the oil in a large saucepan or Dutch oven over medium heat. Add the onion and cubanelle pepper and cook, stirring often, until softened, about 5 minutes. Stir in the rice and cook, stirring constantly, for 1 minute. Add in the tomatoes, water, basil, salt, and black pepper. Stir well and bring to a boil. Cover, reduce the heat to low, and simmer until the rice is tender and almost all the liquid has been absorbed, about 50 minutes. Set aside, covered, for up to 30 minutes.

2. To make the vegetable balls: Bring a large pot of water to a boil over high heat. Add the lentils, stir well, reduce the heat to medium, and boil until very soft, about 30 minutes. Drain in a colander set in the sink and transfer to a large bowl.

3. Heat the oil in a large skillet over medium-low heat. Add the onion and fresh fennel and cook, stirring often, until softened, about 15 minutes. Add the mushrooms and cook, stirring often, until somewhat softened, even a little browned, about 5 minutes. Stir in the rosemary, thyme, garlic, and fennel seeds. Cook about 2 minutes, stirring all the while, then scrape the contents of the skillet into the bowl with the lentils. Cool for 15 minutes.

4. Stir in the eggs, cheese, panko, parsley, pecans, tomato paste, salt, and pepper until well combined. Working in batches, scrape about one-third of the contents of the bowl into a large food processor and puree until smooth, scraping down the interior of the bowl at least once per batch. Scrape the puree into a second bowl and continue processing more in batches until finished.

5. Position the rack in the center of the oven and heat to 400°F. Oil a large rimmed baking sheet very generously.

6. Use wet, clean hands to form the puree into 32 oversized golf balls. Set these on the prepared baking sheet and roll them around to coat all sides in the oil. Bake, turning once, until browned and firm, about 20 minutes. Cool on the baking sheet for 5 minutes.

7. To serve, divide the pilaf among 8 serving plates and top each with 4 veggie balls.

▶ A MENU

FIRST SMALL PLATE: Steamed Artichokes, Red Peppers, Basil (page 42)

SECOND SMALL PLATE: Blue Cheese Cheesecake, Walnuts, Dill (page 86)

LARGE PLATE: Vegetable/Lentil Balls, Brown Rice Pilaf

DESSERT: Fennel/Cardamom Pears, Ginger Mascarpone (page 247)

▶ POUR

A hearty Super Tuscan (or a more economical Chianti Classico) for a long, almost savory finish with balanced tannins that will connect the vegetable balls more closely to the pilaf

Tomatoes, Mushrooms, Phyllo Nests

6 SERVINGS

Although many of our larger main courses are more rustic and free form—and so look more in keeping with their deeper, more wide-ranging, and even free-form flavor spectrum—we do occasionally go for elegance this late in the meal. These crunchy nests of phyllo dough hold a fairly straightforward mixture of roasted vegetables. It's spiky and even a little sour if served hot, or it can taste softer and more balanced if served at room temperature.

8 ounces fresh shiitake mushrooms, stems discarded, caps thinly sliced

3 cups grape tomatoes (about 1½ pints)

2 large shallots, thinly sliced and separated into rings

1 tablespoon minced garlic

½ tablespoon minced fresh sage

1 teaspoon salt

½ teaspoon freshly ground black pepper

6 tablespoons olive oil

8 ounces frozen vegan phyllo dough, thawed (do not unroll)

Olive oil cooking spray

1. Position the rack in the center of the oven and heat to 400°F.

2. Mix the mushrooms, tomatoes, shallots, garlic, sage, salt, and pepper in a large roasting pan. Drizzle with the oil and toss well. Roast, tossing once, until soft and a bit browned, about 20 minutes. Cool in the pan on a wire rack for 10 minutes. Leave the oven on and reduce the temperature to 375°F.

3. Cut the rolled up sheets of phyllo dough into ¾-inch-wide strips, like a thick chiffonade. Unravel these strips, put them in a big bowl, and spray repeatedly with olive oil spray, tossing gently, until evenly coated.

4. Coat a large rimmed baking sheet with olive oil spray. Divide the phyllo strips into 6 piles on the sheet and spread each pile to form a nest 5 to 6 inches in diameter with slightly mounded sides. Bake until browned and crisp, about 12 minutes. Cool on the baking sheet on a wire rack for at least 10 minutes.

5. To serve, place one nest on each serving plate and top with a rounded ⅓ cup of the mushroom mixture.

▶ AHEAD

● Make the nests up to 4 hours in advance, provided the day's not humid. Store, uncovered, at room temperature.

● Roast the mushroom mixture up to 2 hours in advance. Store, uncovered, at room temperature.

▶ GARNISH

Sprinkle finely grated orange zest over each serving.

▶ NOTES

● Some phyllo dough is made with butter—and thus isn't vegan. Read the package labels to make sure.

● If you want to do without an aerosol spray can, buy an olive-oil pump-style sprayer, specifically designed to replicate the canned product without the chemical solvents and aerosols.

▶ A MENU

SMALL PLATE: Parsnip Flans (page 64)

SALAD: Watermelon Panzanella, Capers, Basil (page 118)

LARGE PLATE: Tomatoes, Mushrooms, Phyllo Nests

DESSERT: Chocolate/Taleggio Panini, Caramel Dipping Sauce (page 241)

▶ POUR

A robust, chewy Cabernet Franc blend, with its strawberry and vanilla notes, to foreground the dish's sweetness

Beet Tian, Walnuts, Oranges

8 SERVINGS

This is really a torqued take on a tian, more stocked with vegetables than most recipes. It also has a bolder mix of flavors from walnuts to dill, orange juice to Parmigiano-Reggiano, beet greens to parsley. A tian is Old World fare, a layered vegetable casserole, most often bound together with eggs; its name stands for both the food prepared and the round piece of cookware it's cooked in. Even if you don't have a traditional tian dish, a high-sided, round, sauté pan will work—or a round, cast iron casserole. The results are a savory main course, sort of like a pumped-up frittata, but denser in texture with lots sweet vegetables and savory aromatics in every bite.

- 8 medium beets (about 2 pounds), peeled and cut into 1-inch chunks
- 3 tablespoons olive oil, plus more for greasing
- 1 tablespoon minced garlic
- ½ teaspoon red pepper flakes
- 4 cups packed washed and stemmed beet greens
- ½ cup orange juice
- 1 tablespoon white balsamic vinegar
- ¾ cup chopped toasted walnuts
- ½ cup chopped fresh parsley leaves
- 3 tablespoons minced dill fronds
- 1 tablespoon finely grated orange zest
- 1 teaspoon salt
- 8 large eggs, at room temperature
- 2 ounces Parmigiano-Reggiano cheese, finely grated (about ½ cup)

1. Position the rack in the center of the oven and heat to 400°F. Wrap the beet pieces tightly in a foil packet and roast until tender, about 1 hour. Leave the oven on and reduce the temperature to 375°F. Dump the beets into a big bowl and cool for 30 minutes.

2. Set a large skillet over medium heat for a few minutes, then swirl in the oil. Add the garlic and red pepper flakes; cook, stirring often, until the garlic begins to brown, about 1 minute. Stir in the beet greens and cook, tossing often with kitchen tongs, until beginning to soften, about 2 minutes. Cover and continue cooking until wilted, about 2 minutes.

AHEAD

- Roast the beets up to 24 hours in advance. Store in their foil packet in the refrigerator.

LESS

Look for already-cooked beets in shrink-wrap packages in your market's produce section. These may be slightly smaller than standard "medium" beets, so get the proper weight (rather than the number of beets).

MORE

The plates seem to call out for a little baby arugula and mâche salad, dressed with a bright, lemony vinaigrette.

NOTES

- As you squeeze out the moisture in step 3, move the greens still in the skillet to the side so they're not being doused with the released liquid.

- A tian can be served warm or at room temperature, depending on its desired effect. If the course before has been cold or room temperature, the tian should be warm. But if a hot course comes first, a room-temperature tian may be just the thing. In any event, a tian will not cut well when hot. It needs to cool down for 15 minutes to condense for a good structure.

3. Pick up the greens by small amounts with kitchen tongs and squeeze them over the skillet to remove excess moisture, then set them on a cutting board. (Reserve the liquid in the skillet.) When all the greens are on the cutting board, cool a few minutes before chopping into small bits. Add to the bowl with the beets.

4. Bring the liquid in the skillet back to a simmer over medium-high heat and stir in the orange juice and vinegar. Boil, stirring occasionally, until reduced to a thick glaze, about 3 minutes. Scrape this glaze into the bowl with the beets and greens. Add the walnuts, parsley, dill, orange zest, and salt. Toss well.

5. Beat the eggs in a large bowl with a whisk or an electric mixer at medium speed until uniform and creamy. Stir in the Parmesan, pour over the beet mixture, and toss well.

6. Oil a 10-inch round cast iron casserole or a high-sided ovenproof sauté pan. Pour in the egg mixture, smoothing out the ingredients so they are evenly distributed. Bake, uncovered, until puffed, browned, and set, about 45 minutes. Cool for 15 minutes on a wire rack before slicing into wedges.

▶ **A MENU**

SOUP: Garlic Soup, Gruyère, Cognac (page 130)

SALAD: Apple Slaw, Fried Chickpeas (page 108)

LARGE PLATE: Beet Tian, Walnuts, Oranges

DESSERT: Strawberry/Black Pepper Cake, Chocolate Balsamic Glaze, Vanilla Gelato (page 270)

▶ **POUR**

An Australian Shiraz with bold fruit flavors and spicy accents, our favorite match to eggs

Red-Braised Tofu, Mushrooms, Scallions

8 SERVINGS

After vegetables or other ingredients are long stewed in high-quality soy sauce, they take on a reddish tint—and thus the name sometimes given to more classic versions of this Asian braise: "red cooking" or "red cooked" (depending on how you translate the Chinese characters). Soy sauce is the star of the dish, so go beyond a standard bottling. Head to an Asian market, where you'll find an astounding array, many of them murky or earthy, with plenty of lip-smacking umami notes. Look for a heavily flavored soy sauce, sometimes called "dark soy sauce," or even try a rich, Japanese *saishikomi* ("twice-brewed"). In any event, the sauce should coat the inside of the bottle as you turn it. Avoid both mushroom soy or the so-called thick soy sauce, a specialty item so thick it *appears* to have been congealed with cornstarch.

3 cups vegetable broth	2 tablespoons minced garlic
¾ cup soy sauce	2 tablespoons minced fresh ginger
6 tablespoons Shaoxing wine (see page 183)	½ pound fresh shiitake mushrooms, stems discarded, caps thinly sliced
1½ tablespoons sambal oelek	
1 tablespoon sugar	1½ tablespoons rice vinegar
¼ cup peanut oil	1½ tablespoons arrowroot
8 scallions, thinly sliced	2 pounds extra-firm silken tofu (see Note), cut into 1-inch cubes
4 carrots, minced	

1. Whisk the broth, soy sauce, Shaoxing, sambal, and sugar in a large bowl until the sugar dissolves.

2. Set a large pot or Dutch oven over medium heat for a few minutes, then swirl in the oil. Add the scallions, carrots, garlic, and ginger and cook, stirring often, just until the scallion greens have wilted, about 2 minutes. Add the mushrooms and cook, stirring all the while, for 2 minutes. Pour in the broth mixture and bring to a full simmer. Cover, reduce the heat to low, and simmer slowly for 15 minutes.

3. Whisk the vinegar and arrowroot in a small bowl. Stir this slurry into the pot and continue cooking, stirring often, until the mixture thickens. Add the tofu, stir gently, cover, and simmer very slowly for 10 minutes to heat through.

MORE

Serve the stew over cooked medium-grain white rice.

GARNISH

Sprinkle white sesame seeds over each serving.

NOTES

● Extra-firm silken tofu is something of a specialty product. In North America, it's most commonly available in shelf-stable, aseptic packaging. We like its texture because it has some chew while still being very luxurious. If you are unable to find extra-firm or firm silken tofu, do not substitute soft silken tofu. Instead, use firm standard tofu (for a slightly spongier consistency but a better result that soft silken tofu).

● If carrots are thoroughly washed for dirt, there's no need to peel them when they're stewed, braised, or baked in recipes like these.

A MENU

SMALL PLATE: Red Cabbage Pot Stickers, Raisin Chipotle Dip (page 92)

SALAD: Brussels Sprout/Fennel Salad, Kumquats (page 102)

LARGE PLATE: Red-Braised Tofu, Mushrooms, Scallions

DESSERT: Fig Galette, Honey Cream (page 248)

POUR

A Viognier with distinct pollen and lavender notes to lift this aromatic stew off its earthy base

Stuffed Poblanos, Sweet Potatoes, Walnut Cream

6 SERVINGS

Here's what you'll do: Stuff poblano chiles, top them with a rich nut cream, and bake the casserole into bubbling bliss. In other words, you'll also create a sophisticated main course in rather modest servings. (Those big flavors can become too heavy in larger amounts.) We've put this dish among the large plates, despite its being one chile per person, because its palette is definitely main-course-centric: bold, ample, and satisfying. It almost says *we've arrived at the top* out loud!

---

2 pounds medium sweet potatoes (about 4)

1 canned chipotle chile in adobo sauce, minced

½ teaspoon ground cinnamon

½ teaspoon ground cumin

1 teaspoon salt, divided

6 large poblano chiles

1½ cups walnut pieces

2 tablespoons chopped shallot

½ cup olive oil

½ teaspoon freshly ground black pepper

1. Position the rack in the center of the oven and heat to 375°F.

2. Bake the sweet potatoes on a rimmed baking sheet until soft, about 1 hour. (Leave the oven on.) Cool on a wire rack for at least 15 minutes. Peel the potatoes and mash in a large bowl with the chipotle chile, cinnamon, cumin, and ½ teaspoon salt.

3. Meanwhile, char the poblanos over an open flame until blackened on all sides, turning often. (Or set them on a large rimmed baking sheet 4 to 6 inches from a heated broiler and broil until blackened on all sides, turning occasionally.) Place the chiles in a bag and seal or set them in a large bowl and cover with plastic wrap. Set aside for 20 minutes.

4. Peel the chiles, cut off the stems, and gently remove the seeds and membranes inside with a small spoon. Fill each poblano with one-sixth of the sweet potato mixture, setting them in a 9 x 13-inch baking dish as you finish them. Cover the dish with foil and bake until hot, about 30 minutes.

5. Meanwhile, place the walnuts, shallot, olive oil, pepper, and the remaining ½ teaspoon salt in a large blender. Cover and blend until fairly smooth, turning the machine off and scraping down the inside of the canister a few times.

6. To serve, place a stuffed poblano on each serving plate. Top with walnut cream.

▶ **AHEAD**

● Stuff the poblano chiles up to 6 hours before baking. Store, covered, at room temperature.

● Make the walnut cream up to 4 hours in advance. Store, covered, in the blender canister in the refrigerator. Pour into a small bowl and microwave on high in 10-second increments until room temperature.

▶ **GARNISH**

Sprinkle pomegranate seeds and toasted pepitas (hulled pumpkin seeds) over each serving.

▶ **NOTE**

● Don't toast the walnuts before blending them. The oils will begin to morph in the heat and the ensuing cream will not be as rich.

▶ **A MENU**

SALAD: Bulgur Salad, Roasted Cherry Tomatoes, Basil Confetti (page 113)

SMALL PLATE: Fiddlehead Tacos, Almond Romesco (page 70)

LARGE PLATE: Stuffed Poblanos, Sweet Potatoes, Walnut Cream

DESSERT: Espresso/Chocolate Bundt, Ginger/Whisky Sauce (page 266)

▶ **POUR**

A berry-stocked Pinot Noir for rich excess in the glass that can compete with what's on the plate

Tortilla Casserole, Eggplant, Cheddar

8 SERVINGS

Who said dinner party fare can't be goopy like the best cheesy casseroles? No, you probably don't want to serve this dish at a formal dinner party, but it will certainly bring *oohs* and *aahs* to a more informal affair, a few friends around the table. Or you might consider this as your go-to dish for a big holiday meal like Thanksgiving. It's a fairly simple mix of ingredients, leaving its focus on the outstanding sauce made from the New Mexico reds.

12 dried New Mexico red chiles, stemmed and seeded

3 tablespoons olive oil, plus more for greasing

1 large yellow onion, chopped

2 teaspoons minced garlic

4 cups vegetable broth

1 tablespoon minced fresh oregano leaves

1 teaspoon salt

One 4-inch cinnamon stick

4 medium eggplants (about 12 ounces each), stemmed, peeled, and cut into ½-inch-thick slices

14 corn tortillas

2 cups grated Cheddar cheese (about ½ pound)

1. Toast the chiles in a dry skillet over medium heat, turning occasionally, until fragrant, about 4 minutes. Transfer to a large bowl. Keep the skillet over medium heat.

2. Add the oil to the hot skillet, then the onion. Cook, stirring often, until soft, about 4 minutes. Add the garlic and cook, stirring all the while, for 1 minute.

3. Pour in the broth and stir well. Add the oregano, salt, cinnamon stick, and the toasted chiles. Bring to a simmer, then cover, reduce the heat to low, and simmer until the chiles are very soft, about 20 minutes.

AHEAD

● Build the casserole up to 1 day in advance before baking. Store, covered, in the refrigerator. Bake it straight from the fridge but add 10 minutes to the baking time.

MORE

Increase the variety of chiles in the mix: Substitute one or a combination of mulato, ancho, or pasilla chiles for half the New Mexico reds.

GARNISH

Top servings with dollops of sour cream and diced mango.

4. Remove the cinnamon stick. Use an immersion blender to puree the sauce in the pan (or pour the sauce into a large blender, cool for 10 minutes, then remove the center knob in the lid, cover the opening with a clean kitchen towel, and blend until smooth). Set aside.

5. Generously oil a large grill pan and set it over medium-high heat until smoking. Add the eggplant rounds, as many as will fit without crowding. Weight them down with the bottom of a heavy skillet (or a panini press) and grill, turning once, until softened and marked, about 8 minutes. Transfer the rounds to a cutting board and continue grilling more, oiling the pan again if any begin to stick.

6. Position the rack in the center of the oven and heat to 350°F.

7. Meanwhile, build the casserole. Smear ½ cup of the chile sauce in the bottom of a 9 x 13-inch baking pan. Top with about one-third of the tortillas, tearing them to make an even, overlapping layer. Smear with one-third of the remaining sauce, then lay half the eggplant rounds over the sauce. Top with half the Cheddar. Make another layer with half the remaining tortillas, half the remaining sauce, the rest of the eggplant, and the rest of the cheese. Top with the remainder of the tortillas and the remainder of the sauce.

8. Cover with parchment paper, then seal with foil. Bake until bubbling, about 40 minutes. Cool for 5 minutes before cutting into wedges to serve.

▌ A MENU

SMALL PLATE: Wilted Chard, Pistachios, Lovage (page 47)

SOUP: White Gazpacho, Fried Fennel Seeds (page 125)

LARGE PLATE: Tortilla Casserole, Eggplant, Cheddar

DESSERT: Big Pretzels, Coconut Dulce de Leche Fondue (page 242)

▌ POUR

An oaky Tempranillo, moderately full-bodied with more tannins than acids to provide complex, spicy, and even savory notes

Zucchini Casserole, Mashed Potatoes

8 SERVINGS

A vegan take on shepherd's pie, this savory casserole is winter fare. The zucchini ragù is the real star, layered with roasted eggplant slices and then baked under coconut-spiked mashed potatoes. If you haven't tried dill and cinnamon together, now's your chance, each one softening the other into a sophisticated pairing. The servings are large—maybe larger than you'll need. Frankly, we like to make extra of a casserole like this because leftovers are such a gift on the day after a dinner party.

- 3 large eggplants (about 1 pound each), stemmed and cut into ¼- to ½-inch-thick rounds
- 2 tablespoons olive oil, plus more for greasing and brushing
- 1 medium yellow onion, chopped
- 2 large zucchini (about 10 ounces each), shredded through the large holes of a box grater and squeezed to remove excess moisture
- 1½ cups dry red wine, such as Pinot Noir
- ⅓ cup tomato paste
- 2 tablespoons minced dill fronds
- 1 teaspoon ground cinnamon
- 2½ pounds russet (baking) potatoes, peeled and cut into 1-inch cubes
- ⅔ cup regular or light coconut milk
- ⅔ cup vegetable broth
- 1 teaspoon salt
- ½ teaspoon freshly ground black pepper
- 2 cups chopped toasted walnuts

1. Position the racks in the top and bottom third of the oven (or do the best you can dividing your oven into thirds). Heat to 375°F.

2. Grease 2 large rimmed baking sheets with oil. Lay the eggplant slices evenly across them. Brush the slices with oil, then turn them over and brush again. Bake until tender, about 20 minutes. Transfer to a wire rack to cool. (Leave the oven on and move one of the racks back to the center.)

AHEAD

- Make the eggplant slices and zucchini mixture up to 24 hours in advance. Cover tightly and refrigerate.
- Build the casserole up to 6 hours in advance. Cover loosely with plastic wrap and refrigerate before baking.

MORE

Use an electric mixer to mash the potatoes so they're smooth and pipe them on top of the casserole from a pastry bag fitted with a star or round tip.

3. Set a large saucepan over medium heat for a few minutes, then pour in the 2 tablespoons oil. Add the onion and cook, stirring often, until softened, about 4 minutes. Add the zucchini shreds and cook for 2 minutes, stirring frequently.

4. Pour in the wine. Stir in the tomato paste, dill, and cinnamon. Bring to a full simmer, then cover, reduce the heat to low, and simmer until the vegetables are tender, about 15 minutes.

5. Set up a vegetable steamer over 1 or 2 inches of simmering water. Add the potatoes, cover, and steam until tender, about 20 minutes. Drain and transfer the potatoes to a large bowl. While still hot, use a potato masher or an electric mixer at medium speed to mash the potatoes with the coconut milk, broth, salt, and pepper until creamy.

6. Build the casserole. Lay one-third of the eggplant slices in a 9 x 13-inch baking dish, overlapping a little but creating an even layer. Top with half the zucchini mixture, then half the walnuts. Lay half the remaining eggplant slices on top, then spread the remaining zucchini mixture and nuts over these. Finally, top with the remaining eggplant slices and smooth the mashed potatoes over the casserole.

7. Bake the casserole until bubbling and lightly browned, about 45 minutes. Cool for 5 minutes before bringing to the table or dishing up individual servings.

A MENU

SMALL PLATE: Roasted Brussels Sprouts, Farro, Apricots (page 54)

LARGE PLATE: Zucchini Casserole, Mashed Potatoes

DESSERT: Steamed Pudding, Chocolate Sauce (page 274)

POUR

A Greek rosé, such as Agiorgitiko, for lots of sunshiny acidity with distinctly herbal notes

Basmati Rice, Cashews, Spring Vegetables

6 SERVINGS

In many ways the opposite of the preceding recipe, this not-gooey, fresh casserole is our take on biryani, a legendary dish for which there are probably as many versions as there are cooks in India. Ours is not swimming in broth; and the spices are more warming than fiery. But you have a part in this, too. We encourage you to find fresh spring vegetables and develop a signature mix that'll afford the most vibrant flavors to bring the sweet rice back into balance in the dish. This is also one of the few dishes that we believe *must* be served family-style, with caramelized onions and cashews scattered over the top. Set it in the center of the table or serve it from the sideboard. Either way, it's a big finish with a full range of lighter flavors.

1 tablespoon cider vinegar

1 teaspoon garam masala

1 teaspoon ground cumin

½ teaspoon ground cinnamon

¼ teaspoon saffron

¼ teaspoon ground cloves

¼ teaspoon cayenne pepper

⅓ cup vegetable oil

1 large yellow onion, grated through the large holes of a box grater

1 tablespoon minced fresh ginger

2 teaspoons minced garlic

1½ cups canned tomato puree

½ cup regular coconut milk (do not use light)

3 cups quick-cooking spring vegetables (such as peas, asparagus, sugar snaps, baby zucchini, cauliflower florets), cut into ½-inch pieces

½ cup minced fresh cilantro leaves

1 teaspoon salt

6 cups cooked long-grain white rice, preferably basmati

2 tablespoons olive oil, plus more for greasing

1 medium yellow onion, halved and thinly sliced into half-moons

½ cup chopped toasted, unsalted cashews

AHEAD

- Prepare the spice paste up to 2 days in advance. Store, covered, at room temperature.

- Build the casserole up to 6 hours before baking. Store, covered, in the refrigerator. Bake it straight from the fridge but moisten the dish with ¼ cup vegetable broth and add 10 minutes to the baking time.

MORE

Serve with grilled or warmed na'an, roti, paratha, or even fried puri. Also—and perhaps essentially—make a simple raita from plain yogurt, minced seeded cucumber, a little minced onion, ground coriander, and salt. And to take that raita over the top, add oil-fried mustard or cumin seeds. Use the raita as a sauce on the side of the plate.

NOTES

- You'll get 6 cups cooked long-grain rice from about 2½ cups raw rice, depending on its moisture content from long storage.

- You'll only need to chop the vegetables that are themselves larger than ½ inch. So no chopping peas! The point is to get a mélange that replicates the flavors of the season, based on what's fresh at your market.

- Because of the way the rice will continue to soak up all available moisture in the casserole, this dish is best if eaten hot from the oven, cooled just a few minutes so the liquids have a chance to "set up" in the casserole.

1. Stir the vinegar, garam masala, cumin, cinnamon, saffron, cloves, and cayenne in a small bowl until a paste. Set aside.

2. Position the rack in the center of the oven and heat to 350°F. Lightly grease a 9 x 13-inch baking dish with olive oil.

3. Heat the 1/3 cup vegetable oil in a large skillet over medium heat, then add the grated onion. Cook, stirring often, until it begins to brown, about 5 minutes. Add the ginger and garlic and cook for 1 minute, stirring all the while.

4. Scrape the prepared spice paste into the skillet and cook until fragrant, about 1 minute, still stirring all the while. Stir in the tomato puree and coconut milk. Bring to a full simmer, stirring up any browned bits in the skillet. Stir in the spring vegetables and cook, stirring often, until just tender, about 3 minutes. Remove the skillet from the heat and stir in the cilantro and salt.

5. Pack half the rice into the prepared baking dish, making an even, smooth layer. Top with the vegetable mixture, again smoothing it out to be fairly flat. Seal with the remaining rice. Cover and bake until hot and steaming, about 30 minutes.

6. Meanwhile, set a large skillet over medium-high heat for a few minutes, then swirl in the 2 tablespoons olive oil. Add the sliced onion and cook, stirring occasionally, until very dark, even a little crispy, about 8 minutes.

7. Remove the casserole from the oven and cool for 10 minutes on a wire rack. Turn the casserole upside down onto a large serving platter and remove the baking dish. Spread the browned onions and cashews across the top to serve.

A MENU

FIRST SMALL PLATE: Stewed Giant Lima Beans, Dandelion Greens, Feta (page 60)

SECOND SMALL PLATE: Blistered Butter Beans, Pecans, Fennel (page 46)

LARGE PLATE: Basmati Rice, Cashews, Spring Vegetables

DESSERT: Banana Shortbreads, Peanut Cream, Grape Granita (page 251)

POUR

A crisp, cold Chenin Blanc with a sweet/tart pop to assure that this dish stays focused on spring

Bolita Bean Stew, Fall Vegetables, Lemony Breadcrumbs

8 BIG SERVINGS

Here's a vegetarian version of cassoulet. Where's the duck confit? The sausage? Nowhere. And they needn't make an appearance. After all, cassoulet is a *bean* dish, not a meat dish. Its technique is all about building a big casserole with plenty of aromatics. (Those meatish items were just supposed to be kitchen leftovers anyway.) Here, we hold our notion in extremis. We don't use any faked meat or soy sausage. Instead, we put the beans with the tomatoes as the foundation for a well-stocked, root vegetable casserole with a savory, crunchy topping. Yes, you'll make extra. You'll want leftovers.

▶ AHEAD

● Boil the beans up to 24 hours in advance. Stove, covered, in the refrigerator, but allow to come back to room temperature before using.

● Roast the root vegetables up to 6 hours in advance. Store, uncovered, at room temperature.

● Make the tomato and bean mixture up to 2 hours in advance. Store, covered, at room temperature.

● Make the breadcrumb mixture up to 2 hours in advance. Store, covered, at room temperature.

▶ NOTES

● Creamy bolita beans are a Southwestern favorite, like a better (ahem) version of pinto beans. If you can't find them, either in the store or from a mailorder supplier, substitute dried Great Northern beans.

● So-called "baby" carrots aren't immature. They're large carrots that have been cut down for snacking. You can use regular carrots here; we used the "baby" ones to make life easier.

● Make sure you use fresh breadcrumbs, not dried. Look for them in the bakery section of your supermarket. Or grind day-old baguette chunks in a food processor to make your own. And make extra. As if a contradiction in terms, fresh breadcrumbs can be frozen in a sealed plastic bag with good results. Use them right out of the freezer.

● Although there's some issue with gastric distress associated with the water the beans have been cooked in, it's dissipated a great deal by the acidic tomatoes and the total fiber content. Besides, that water is so flavorful!

● The baked casserole keeps well for leftovers up to 3 days if stored in the fridge, covered.

- 2 cups dried bolita beans (see Note)
- 2 sprigs (6-inch) fresh rosemary
- 2 sprigs fresh thyme
- 2 small dried hot chiles, such as chiles de àrbol
- 2 bay leaves
- 1 pound parsnips, peeled and cut into 1-inch pieces
- 1 pound "baby" carrots (see Note), halved lengthwise
- 1 pound celery root (aka celeriac), peeled and cut into ½-inch pieces
- 11 tablespoons olive oil, divided
- 1 large yellow onion, chopped
- 1 large fennel bulb, trimmed and chopped
- 1 can (28 ounces) diced tomatoes, drained
- 1 teaspoon salt
- ½ teaspoon freshly ground black pepper
- ½ cup chopped lovage or celery leaves
- 3 cups fresh breadcrumbs
- ¼ cup pine nuts, finely chopped
- ¼ cup Parmigiano-Reggiano cheese, finely grated (about 1 ounce)
- 2 teaspoons finely grated lemon zest

1. Soak the beans in a large bowl of cool water for at least 12 hours and up to 16 hours. Drain in a colander set in the sink.

2. Pour the beans into a large pot and add enough water so it stands 4 inches over them. Stir in the rosemary, thyme, chiles, and bay leaves. Bring to a boil over high heat, stirring a few times. Cover, reduce the heat to low, and simmer until just tender, 1 hour 30 minutes to 2 hours.

(continued)

3. Meanwhile, position the rack in the center of the oven and heat to 400°F. Toss the parsnips, carrots, and celery root with ¼ cup (4 tablespoons) of the oil in a large roasting pan. Roast until browned and soft, about 1 hour 10 minutes, tossing three or four times to prevent sticking and to make various sides of the pieces rest against the hot surface. Cool in the pan on a wire rack for 10 minutes. Leave the oven on but reduce the temperature to 350°F.

4. When the beans are done, set a colander over a bowl set in the sink. Drain the beans, catching the liquid below. Discard the rosemary, thyme, chiles, and bay leaves.

5. Set a very large skillet over medium heat for a couple minutes, then add 3 tablespoons of the oil. Dump in the onion and fennel and cook, stirring often, until very soft, even lightly browned, about 15 minutes.

6. Stir in the tomatoes, salt, and pepper. Cook, stirring often, until the tomatoes soften and begin to break down, about 3 minutes. Stir in the lovage or celery leaves, then stir in the beans.

7. Spoon half the bean and tomato mixture into a shallow, round, 4- to 5-quart flameproof cast iron casserole. Spoon and spread the roasted vegetables over these, then top with the remaining bean and tomato mixture. Pour enough reserved liquid from the beans to come just shy of the top layer of the casserole. Cover the casserole and bake until hot and bubbling, about 45 minutes.

8. Meanwhile, combine the breadcrumbs, pine nuts, cheese, lemon zest, and the remaining ¼ cup oil in a large food processor and process until well blended. Set aside.

9. Transfer the casserole to the stovetop over medium-high heat and bring to a boil. Boil for 2 minutes to reduce excess liquid. Sprinkle the top of the casserole evenly with the breadcrumb mixture while the casserole is still very hot and bubbling. Return to the oven and bake, uncovered, until browned, about 40 minutes. Cool on a wire rack for 10 minutes before dishing up servings or bringing the whole casserole right to the table.

▶ A MENU

SMALL PLATE: Potato/Cucumber Mille-Feuille (page 84)

SOUP: Gazpacho Shooters (page 126)

LARGE PLATE: Bolita Bean Stew, Fall Vegetables, Lemony Breadcrumbs

DESSERT: Lemon sorbet drizzled with aged rum

▶ POUR

A robust, in-your-face Gigondas red for extraordinary, old-fashioned, spicy-berry heft against the beans

Stuffed Escarole, Agrodolce Sauce

8 SERVINGS

This dish is something of a showstopper because, well, who's ever stuffed a whole head of escarole? It's an Italian-inspired meal, sort of a new take on stuffed cabbage, brilliantly sweet-and-sour (thus, agrodolce) with added earthy, even bitter notes from the leafy greens. The servings are not large because the flavors are intense. Half a stuffed head per person is really more than enough, especially at the end of a larger meal. Given that the dish is fabulous without being difficult, consider baking your own bread (see page 27).

4 medium escarole heads

4 cups cooked long-grain white rice, preferably jasmine rice

½ cup toasted pine nuts

½ cup golden raisins

1 teaspoon dried dill

1 teaspoon fennel seeds

½ teaspoon salt

½ teaspoon freshly ground black pepper

3½ cups canned crushed tomatoes

¼ cup balsamic vinegar

2 tablespoons sugar

1. Cut the dark green tops off the escarole heads, leaving a more compact thicket of leaves about 5 inches high. Remove any loose, outer leaves. Carefully rinse the interior of the head between the leaves to remove any sand or grit.

2. Set up a large bowl of ice water. Bring a large pot or Dutch oven of water to a boil over high heat. Submerge 1 escarole head in the water and blanch for 1 minute from the time it enters the water. Use a big slotted spoon to transfer the escarole to the ice water to cool while the water returns to a full boil in the pot. Remove the escarole from the ice water and gently squeeze to remove water. Set aside, add more ice to the bowl, and continue blanching the remaining heads, using this procedure.

3. Mix the rice, pine nuts, raisins, dill, fennel seeds, salt, and pepper in a large bowl.

4. Open up the leaves of one of the heads and fill the center as well as between the larger inner leaves with 1 to 1¼ cups of the rice mixture. Close up the head, then use butchers' twine to hold the head closed, wrapping it around the escarole so the leaves stay shut over the filling without pulling the twine too tight before knotting it. Repeat with the remaining escarole.

(continued)

AHEAD
● Stuff the stuffed escarole heads up to 6 hours in advance. Store, covered, in the refrigerator.

LESS
Pick up a couple of large containers of cooked white rice from a Chinese restaurant.

NOTES
● Since escarole is notoriously gritty deep in its leaves, you'll need to work efficiently but carefully to remove all that muck. Don't pull the leaves too far out or they'll break off.

● About 2 cups raw long-grain white rice will yield about 4 cups cooked.

● When stuffing the escarole, place about half the filling in the center of the head, then begin filling between the leaves around the core from there on out, stopping before you get too far out in the head so that the outer leaves can enclose the inner filling without holding any themselves.

5. Position the rack in your oven so that a large, covered pot can sit in the oven with at least 2 inches of head space. Heat the oven to 350°F.

6. Bring the tomatoes, vinegar, and sugar to a simmer in a large oven-proof pot or Dutch oven over medium-high heat, stirring occasionally.

7. Place the escarole bundles in the tomato mixture. Cover and bake until hot and tender, about 45 minutes. Cool, covered, in the pot for 5 minutes.

8. To serve, slice each stuffed escarole in half through the root, putting each half on a serving plate. Spoon the tomato sauce over and around the escarole halves.

A MENU

SMALL PLATE: Butternut Squash Tart, Toasted Almonds, Roquefort (page 82)

SALAD: Frisée Salad, Smoked Bread Cubes, Poached Egg (page 120)

LARGE PLATE: Stuffed Escarole, Agrodolce Sauce

DESSERT: Apricot No-Cheese Cake (page 262)

POUR

A velvety Pinot Noir with moderately leather tannins to balance the sauce and let the greens come through

Cauliflower Strudel, Cranberry Chutney

8 SERVINGS

Flaky and tender, this strudel definitely signals the savory end of a dinner party. The vegetables are roasted, not braised or stewed, so their caramelized flavors pair well with the sour, strongly spiced chutney, a vinegary dash on the plate. Taken together, they may well represent the largest scope of flavors of any main course in this book.

CHUTNEY

- 3 cups fresh cranberries
- 1 large orange, peeled and cut into supremes (see page 100)
- 1½ cups sugar
- ¼ cup golden raisins
- 3 tablespoons cider vinegar
- ½ teaspoon ground cinnamon
- ½ teaspoon ground ginger
- ¼ teaspoon ground cloves
- ¼ teaspoon salt

STRUDEL

- 4 cups chopped cauliflower florets
- 4 medium shallots, thinly sliced
- 3 tablespoons olive oil
- ¼ cup dry sherry
- ½ cup finely chopped toasted walnuts
- 2 teaspoons fresh thyme leaves
- ½ teaspoon salt
- ½ teaspoon freshly ground black pepper
- ¼ teaspoon celery seeds
  All-purpose flour, for dusting
- 2 large sheets frozen puff pastry dough, thawed (about 1 pound)
- 4 tablespoons (½ stick) unsalted butter, melted and cooled

AHEAD

- Make the chutney up to 2 days in advance. Store, covered, in its pan in the refrigerator, but warm over low heat before serving.
- Roast the vegetables up to 8 hours in advance. When cool, store, covered, at room temperature.
- Assemble the strudels up to 1 hour before baking. Lay a clean, dry kitchen towel over them and store at room temperature.

MORE

Dollop plain Greek yogurt on the servings, then top with the chutney.

NOTE

- For the best taste, use high-quality puff pastry, such as Dufour, or another brand made with butter, not hydrogenated shortening. More standard brands of puff pastry come in larger sheets, some in fact 10 x 15 inches, exactly as called for here. However, those sheets are a bit too thick and should still be rolled to ⅛ inch thick for a crunchier, crisper crust on the dish.

1. To make the chutney: Mix the cranberries, orange supremes, sugar, raisins, vinegar, cinnamon, ginger, cloves, and salt in a large saucepan. Bring to a full simmer over medium-high heat, stirring often. Reduce the heat a bit and simmer, uncovered and stirring often, until the cranberries have burst and the sauce has thickened a bit, about 10 minutes.

2. To make the strudel: Position the rack in the center of the oven and heat to 400°F. Toss the cauliflower and shallots in a large roasting pan with the oil and roast, tossing once, until lightly browned, about 20 minutes. Stir in the sherry and scrape up any browned bits in the pan.

3. Transfer the roasting pan to a wire rack. (Keep the oven on.) Add the walnuts, thyme, salt, pepper, and celery seeds to the roasting pan and stir well. Cool for 30 minutes.

4. Dust a clean, dry work surface with flour. Set a puff pastry sheet on top. Dust the sheet with flour, then roll to 10 x 15 inches, about ⅛ inch thick. Brush with about half the melted butter, then spoon half the filling into a fairly thin line about 1 inch in from one of the longer sides of the rectangle, leaving about 1 inch on each end. Fold the short sides in to close the ends, then roll the sheet up, enclosing the filling. Set on a large baking sheet and repeat, making a second strudel.

5. Bake until golden and puffed, about 35 minutes. Cool on a wire rack for 5 minutes, then slice each strudel into 4 pieces. Transfer these to serving plates. Serve with the warm chutney.

▶ A MENU

SMALL PLATE: Warm Buffalo Mozzarella, Yellow Tomato Sauce (page 39)

PASTA: Pear Risotto, Gorgonzola, Dill (page 164)

LARGE PLATE: Cauliflower Strudel, Cranberry Chutney

DESSERT: Olive Oil/Vin Santo Cake, Pine Nuts, Dried Apples (page 265)

▶ POUR

A crisp, light Viognier, not really chilled, just slightly cooled, maybe on ice for 15 minutes, so the cherry and apricot notes stay at the fore

Stuffed Pears, Wild Rice, Mushrooms

8 SERVINGS

By now, you've probably figured out that we believe pears are the produce section's unused powerhouse in savory, vegetarian dishes. They provide a delicate, floral sweetness, something leafy greens, root vegetables, and mushrooms often lack. You'll want firm, ripe pears for this main course, not so juicy or soft that they fall apart when roasted. You'll stuff them, then slowly caramelize all the flavors in the oven. Once they're ready, use a wide spatula to transfer those pears to the plates gently and carefully. The servings are not large but the flavors are deep, a full stop to a meal.

- 4 tablespoons (½ stick) unsalted butter, divided
- 2 large onions, halved through the root and cut into thin half-moons
- ½ pound cremini mushrooms, trimmed and thinly sliced
- ¼ pound fresh shiitake mushrooms, stems discarded, caps thinly sliced
- 2 tablespoons minced fresh sage
- 3 cups vegetable broth
- 1 cup black wild rice (see Note)
- 1 tablespoon fresh thyme
- ½ cup long-grain white rice, such as jasmine rice
- ½ teaspoon salt
- ½ teaspoon freshly ground black pepper
- 8 large ripe but still firm Comice or Anjou pears
- ½ cup unsweetened apple cider
- ½ cup dry but light white wine, such as Sauvignon Blanc
- 1 large leek (white and pale green part only), halved lengthwise, carefully washed, and thinly sliced

AHEAD

- Make the rice mixture up to 1 day in advance. When cool, store, covered, in the refrigerator. Add a little extra broth to loosen it up before stuffing into the pears.

- Stuff the pears up to 2 hours in advance. Rub each cut pear with lemon juice to prevent discoloration. Store, covered, in their roasting pan at room temperature.

MORE

While beautiful, the pears can seem a little forlorn on the plate. Don't serve them on the biggest plates you have. Or offer each serving with 2 small wedges of Manchego cheese, one drizzled with honey and the other sprinkled with ground Aleppo pepper.

NOTE

- There are actually two types of wild rice: One, which is harvested by hand, is mostly gray or brown in color. The other, harvested by machine, is almost fully black. They require vastly different cooking times. Use only the cultivated, black wild rice for this dish.

1. Melt 2 tablespoons of the butter in a large skillet over medium-low heat. Add the onions, reduce the heat further, and cook, stirring often, until golden and soft, about 25 minutes. Scrape the contents of the skillet into a large bowl.

2. Set the skillet back over medium heat and melt the remaining 2 tablespoons butter in it. Add both kinds of mushrooms and cook, stirring frequently, until they give off their liquid and it reduces to a glaze, about 12 minutes. Stir in the sage and cook for 1 minute. Scrape the contents of the skillet into the bowl with the onions.

3. Bring the broth, wild rice, and thyme to a simmer in a large saucepan over high heat, stirring occasionally. Cover, reduce the heat to low, and simmer slowly for 30 minutes. Stir in the white rice, salt, and pepper. Cover and continue simmering until all the liquid has been absorbed, about 18 minutes. Set aside, covered, for 5 minutes to steam the rice, then scrape the contents of the saucepan into the bowl with the onions and mushrooms. Stir well and cool to room temperature, about 45 minutes.

4. Position the rack in the center of the oven and heat to 350°F.

5. Turning a pear on its side, slice a shallow, thin strip down the pear so that it can sit flat when turned on this side. Turn it over, then slice about a quarter of the total depth of the pear at its fattest part. Use a melon baller to remove the seeds, core, and most of the flesh, leaving about ½ inch of pear flesh under the skin as a shell. Repeat with the remaining pears. Discard the seeds and cores, then chop about 1 cup of the pear flesh and stir it into the rice mixture.

6. Stuff the rice mixture into the pears, mounding it up in each and packing it gently into place. Place the pears stuffing side up in a large roasting pan. Pour the cider and wine around but not on the pears. Scatter the leek around them as well. Cover tightly with foil.

7. Bake until tender and hot, about 45 minutes. Transfer the roasting pan to a wire rack, uncover, and use a large spatula to transfer each pear to a serving plate. Pour the hot juices from the pan into a medium saucepan and bring to a boil over high heat. Boil until reduced by half, about 3 minutes. Drizzle this sauce over the pears on the plates.

▶ A MENU

SMALL PLATE: Raclette/Potato/Pickle Focaccia (page 78)

SOUP: Plum Soup, Cinnamon, Cloves (page 121)

LARGE PLATE: Stuffed Pears, Wild Rice, Mushrooms

DESSERT: Pecan/Coconut Cake, Orange Marmalade (page 269)

▶ POUR

An aged Oloroso (an oaky, dark sherry) to bring tobacco-dense accents to this ephemeral if autumnal dish

Eggplant Wontons,
Tomato Sauce, Gooey Fontina

6 SERVINGS

This one's pure whimsy. It's a deconstructed version of eggplant Parmesan, the wonton wrappers standing in for the pasta. We've set it last among the main courses because it's a tad silly, very labor-intensive, and worth every minute of your time. The simple tomato sauce coats wontons that have been stuffed with eggplants, which are themselves incredible sweet and smoky, given the stovetop roasting technique we employ. The whole mish-mash is topped with cheese and broiled to loveliness. Like nachos? Well, hardly. More like a brand-new take on a cli-chéd classic. Everybody will remember this one.

▶ AHEAD

● Make the tomato sauce up to 24 hours in advance. Store, covered, in the refrigerator and reheat, covered, over medium-low heat until bubbling.

● Stuff the wontons up to 6 hours before baking. Seal the baking sheets with plastic wrap and store in the refrigerator.

▶ NOTE

● If you don't have a gas flame on your range, char the eggplants under a broiler. Position the rack 6 inches from the heating element and heat the broiler. Oil a large rimmed baking sheet. Halve the eggplants lengthwise and set them cut side down on the baking sheet. Broil until the skin is black and crisp and the eggplants themselves are beginning to collapse, about 15 minutes. Remove from the oven and cool to room temperature on the bak-ing sheets. Scrape the flesh from underneath the charred skin and con-tinue with step 5 of the recipe.

2 tablespoons unsalted butter

1 medium yellow onion, chopped

½ cup dry white wine, such as Pinot Grigio

1 can (28 ounces) no-salt-added crushed tomatoes (about 3½ cups)

1 cup loosely packed fresh basil leaves, minced

1 tablespoon honey

½ teaspoon salt

½ teaspoon freshly ground black pepper

2 large eggplants (about 1¼ pounds each)

1 teaspoon fennel seeds

1 teaspoon minced garlic

½ teaspoon red pepper flakes

¼ cup olive oil, plus more for greasing

36 wonton wrappers

¾ pound Fontina cheese, shredded

1. Melt the butter in a large saucepan over medium heat. Add the onion and cook, stirring often, until soft, about 5 minutes.

2. Pour in the wine and simmer until the liquid has been reduced to a glaze, about 3 minutes. Stir in the tomatoes, basil, honey, salt, and pepper. Simmer, uncovered and stirring often, until slightly thick-ened, about 20 minutes. Set aside.

3. Wrap each eggplant in a large sheet of foil, laying the vegetable at one end of a large sheet of foil and then rolling it up so that there are 4 or 5 layers of foil over the eggplant. Seal everything—especially the ends—well.

(continued)

4. Set each eggplant on a stovetop burner grate over an open gas flame (see Note on page 231) for 15 minutes. Turn and continue cooking over the flame for 15 minutes. Transfer the packets to a cutting board, open carefully, and cool for 15 minutes.

5. Remove the squishy eggplants from their packets, stem them, and slit them in half lengthwise. Scoop out the soft flesh and mound it in a fine-mesh sieve set over a bowl. Drain the pulp for 5 minutes, pressing gently with the back of a wooden spoon to release additional liquid. Discard the liquid and put the pulp in a large bowl. Mash with the fennel seeds, garlic, and red pepper flakes.

6. Position the racks in the top and bottom third of the oven (or do the best you can dividing your oven into thirds). Heat to 400°F. Generously grease 2 large rimmed baking sheets with olive oil.

7. Place a wonton wrapper on a clean, very dry work surface. Put about 2 teaspoons eggplant filling in the center of the wrapper, wet two sides with your finger dipped in water, then fold the wrapper over, making a triangle, and press to seal. Place on one of the prepared baking sheets, then soldier on, making 36 stuffed wontons on 2 baking sheets.

8. Brush the wontons on the sheets with the ¼ cup oil. Bake until browned and crisp, about 15 minutes. Cool on the baking sheet on a wire rack for 10 minutes.

9. Move one oven rack so it's 4 to 6 inches from the broiler and heat the broiler. Gather all the wontons onto one baking sheet, overlapping as necessary without stacking them up. Spoon the tomato sauce over them, then top with the cheese. Broil until the cheese melts, about 1 minute. Serve by dividing the wontons and sauce among plates.

▶ A MENU

PASTA: Polenta, Chestnuts, Balsamic Vinegar, Roasted Radicchio (page 163)

SALAD: Roasted Pears, Fig Caponata (page 110)

LARGE PLATE: Eggplant Wontons, Tomato Sauce, Gooey Fontina

DESSERT: Almond/Cardamom Biscotti (page 238) and Vanilla Gelato (page 270)

▶ POUR

A Chianti Classico, because generations of Italian restaurants can't be wrong

FINAL PLATES

They say life's too short so you should eat dessert first. We disagree. No matter the length of life, we still want to eat dessert last. Every great feat deserves a standing ovation. Here's ours. (And now yours.) Whether it's a simple (ahem) vegan caramel or a rock-your-world donut, dessert brings the party to its rightful close.

For a vegetarian celebration, this course is usually the least pressing problem. Aren't most desserts vegetarian already?

Probably. So we decided that our dessert recipes needed to go a step further. About half this chapter is vegan. Unless the dessert was exceptional in some way with cream or eggs, we crafted the recipe without any animal products.

Over the years, we've been turned off by the lackluster, dairy-less offerings. Sure, we love buttercream. And whipped cream. And custard. But sometimes we want a dessert that isn't so heavy. When we do, we're often left with a bowl of berries. That's too bad, because vegan desserts require no extra work. By replacing butter with nut oils or milk with coconut

milk, we can up the flavors without breaking a sweat. In fact, we can offer more flavors per forkful. And that's exactly what we always want to do. Dessert should be loud, the crashing chords at the end of a symphony. The flavors should be pronounced, varied, and differentiated.

Most of these recipes are make-aheads in their entirety. Many are even best if they are made the morning before a dinner party and allowed to "ripen" a bit. Some can be frozen for weeks until you're ready to serve them.

To complement these recipes, we often (but not always) have a dessert wine in the offing. It's under the "Pour" header here. Our favorites, like Canadian ice wines, are sweet and syrupy. But we're

also partial to those that are light and floral, like a late-harvest Riesling or Semillon. But even if we're pouring a special dessert wine, we often have a bottle of red wine open, left over from the main course, since a fruit-forward Zinfandel or Syrah can pair so nicely with a slice of cake or a bit of chocolate bliss.

That said, we've skipped the menus here. These desserts are well represented in our plate schematics throughout the book. Besides, no one would build a meal back from the dessert. Or not often.

A dessert is the last gift you can give. It's often the best memory your friends and family will take home. Who would want to put that out of order, or rush it up front in a meal, or forgo it entirely?

Chocolate Chip Cookies, Maple, Tahini, Dates

36 COOKIES

Long ago, we got bored of those soft, spongy vegan chocolate chip cookies sold at high-end markets. Couldn't someone make a crunchy vegan cookie? Apparently not. So we set out to develop our own. These maple/tahini cookies are already very crisp—but we took the concept a step further. Halfway through baking, we rap the baking sheets against the oven racks, causing the cookies to fall. Crunch heaven. Double the batch if you want. They freeze beautifully.

1¾ cups all-purpose flour	¼ cup mashed pitted dates
1 teaspoon baking soda	½ cup tahini
½ teaspoon salt	½ cup maple syrup
12 tablespoons solid vegetable shortening, preferably expeller-pressed	1 tablespoon vanilla extract
	1 cup semisweet or bittersweet chocolate chips
½ cup packed dark brown sugar	1 cup chopped pecans
½ cup granulated white sugar	

1. Position the racks in the top and bottom third of the oven (or do the best you can dividing your oven into thirds) and heat to 375°F. Line 2 large rimmed baking sheets with parchment paper or silicone baking mats.

2. Whisk the flour, baking soda, and salt in a medium bowl.

3. Use an electric mixer at medium speed to beat the shortening, both sugars, and dates in a large bowl until creamy and thick, about 4 minutes, scraping down the inside of the bowl occasionally with a rubber spatula. Beat in the tahini and maple syrup until smooth, then beat in the vanilla. Turn off the beaters, dump in the flour mixture, then beat at low speed just until combined. Scrape down and remove the beaters. Stir in the chocolate chips and pecans with a wooden spoon.

4. Take 2 tablespoons of dough and roll it into a ball between your clean palms. Set it on one of the prepared baking sheets. Continue rolling more balls, spacing them 2 inches apart on the baking sheets, for about 18 cookies per sheet when you're done.

5. Set the sheets on the two oven racks and bake for 12 minutes. Rap the sheets against the wire rack, then swap them top to bottom and back to front. Continue baking until lightly browned and firm to the touch, about 8 minutes. Cool the baking sheets on a wire rack for 5 minutes, then transfer the cookies to the wire rack to cool completely.

▶ AHEAD

● Store the cooled cookies in a tightly sealed plastic container at room temperature for up to 3 days—or freeze for up to 3 months.

▶ NOTE

● Prechopped baking dates, often sugared and sometimes sold in the baking aisle of large supermarkets, will not mash appropriately for this recipe. You'll need large, moist, pitted dates like Medjools. Or substitute date paste for the mashed pitted dates. Look for date paste in Middle Eastern markets or from online suppliers.

▶ POUR

A rich, dark Cabernet Sauvignon, mostly for dunking

Almond/Cardamom Biscotti

48 BISCOTTI

Although dinner-party desserts are often soft and luxurious, successful offerings sometimes afford a contrast after a main course that has a soft, luxurious consistency. Without a doubt, biscotti have the best bite. They're the ultimate dunking medium to boot. So fill up everyone's glass with red wine. These are made with lots of cornmeal for even more texture.

¾ cup sliced almonds

2 cups all-purpose flour, plus more for dusting

¾ cup sugar

¼ cup medium-grind yellow cornmeal (the supermarket's standard grind)

2 teaspoons baking powder

2 teaspoons black cardamom seeds

½ teaspoon salt

3 large eggs, at room temperature

2 tablespoons almond-flavored liqueur, such as amaretto

1. Position the racks in the top and bottom third of the oven (or do the best you can dividing your oven into thirds) and heat to 325°F. Line 2 large rimmed baking sheets with parchment paper or silicone baking mats.

2. Lightly toast the almonds in a dry skillet over medium-low heat, stirring occasionally, about 5 minutes. Cool for 10 minutes.

3. Meanwhile, whisk the flour, sugar, cornmeal, baking powder, cardamom seeds, and salt in a large bowl.

4. Use an electric mixer at medium speed to beat the eggs and liqueur in a medium bowl until uniform, no whites floating in the mix. Pour this mixture into the flour mixture, add the toasted almonds, and stir into a batter. Dust a clean, dry work surface with flour, then turn the dough out onto it. Knead for 2 minutes, just to combine and smooth. Divide the dough in half and roll each half under your cleaned palms into 12-inch-long logs.

5. Place one log on each of the baking sheets. Bake until puffed and lightly browned, about 30 minutes, turning the pans back to front and switching racks top to bottom halfway through baking. Cool the logs on the baking sheets on a wire rack for 30 minutes. (Keep the oven on.)

6. Gently slice the logs into ½-inch cookies (see Note), cutting them on the diagonal to make fairly long cookies, about 4 to 5 inches each. Fill the baking sheets with these cookies and bake for 5 minutes. Turn the cookies over and bake until dry, about 5 minutes. Transfer to a wire rack and cool to room temperature, about 2 hours.

AHEAD

- Once cooled, the cookies can be stored in a sealed plastic bag or container for up to 2 days on the counter or up to 3 months in the freezer.

NOTES

- Even after 30 minutes, the logs will still be warm and a little fragile, particularly on the "crust" and at the ends. Cup and support the log to hold it together as you gently slice the cookies. A serrated knife works best.

- Since this is a fairly loose dough, use the least amount of flour you can when kneading the dough. You're not kneading to develop the glutens, just to make an even dough.

Maple/Oat Blondies

12 BLONDIES

Bar cookies are a bit of luxury at the end of a meal, something beyond fruit or berries. They're little bits of crunchy, cakey flavor that can be either finger food in front of the fire or a plated affair at the table. By pairing maple syrup with coconut oil in this recipe, we've created a much more complex flavor palette for this down-home American treat. Get the coffee ready.

2 cups all-purpose flour

1 cup rolled oats (do not use steel-cut or quick-cooking)

1 teaspoon baking soda

1 teaspoon ground cinnamon

1 teaspoon salt

12 tablespoons coconut oil, plus more for greasing

½ cup granulated white sugar

½ cup packed light brown sugar

½ cup tahini

½ cup maple syrup

2 tablespoons vanilla extract

1 cup semisweet or bittersweet chocolate chips

1. Position the rack in the center of the oven and heat to 375°F. Melt a little coconut oil in a small bowl in the microwave on high, then brush it on the sides and bottom of a 9 x 13-inch baking dish.

2. Whisk the flour, oats, baking soda, cinnamon, and salt in a medium bowl.

3. Use an electric mixer at medium speed to beat the coconut oil and both sugars in a big bowl until creamy and light, scraping down the inside of the bowl occasionally, about 4 minutes. Beat in the tahini, maple syrup, and vanilla until smooth. Turn off the beaters, dump in the flour mixture, and beat at low speed just until combined. Scrape down and remove the beaters. Stir in the chocolate chips with a wooden spoon.

4. Spread and evenly press the thick batter into the prepared baking dish. Bake until puffed, browned, set to the touch, if still a little soft, about 25 minutes. Transfer to a wire rack and cool to room temperature, about 2 hours. Cut the cake into 12 large bars by making two cuts the long way and three the short way.

▌AHEAD

● Make the blondies a day in advance. Store at room temperature between sheets of wax paper in a sealed, plastic container. Or store them in the freezer for up to 3 months.

▌MORE

If you're not concerned about the fare being vegan, serve with store-bought premium vanilla ice cream. Or make your own Vanilla Gelato (page 270).

▌POUR

A shot of aged Armagnac to complement the tahini

Chocolate/Taleggio Panini, Caramel Dipping Sauce

6 PANINI

Consider these the best grilled cheese sandwiches you've ever tasted. And for dessert, too. They're gooey with Taleggio and still very chocolaty. They're toasted to a crunch, then dipped in a creamy caramel sauce. In other words, s'mores for adults. Nobody will ever forget them.

SAUCE

- ½ cup heavy cream
- 1 cup sugar
- ¼ cup water

PANINI

- 6 slices (2- to 3-inch-wide) ciabatta bread or 6 ciabatta rolls
- 9 ounces Taleggio cheese, rind removed, cut into 6 thin rectangles
- 3 ounces dark chocolate, shaved (about ¾ cup)

1. To make the sauce: Warm the cream in a small saucepan over low heat until steam comes off its surface. Do not boil.

2. Stir the sugar and water in a large saucepan over medium-high heat until the sugar dissolves. Continue cooking until amber, about 3 minutes (see Note). Whisk in the warmed cream. Be careful: The super-hot mixture will foam in the pan. Whisk steadily and exactingly until the sugar is thoroughly dissolved. Cool in the pan for at least 30 minutes.

3. To make the panini: Cut the bread slices in half widthwise or the rolls in half as if to make sandwiches. Make a sandwich with the bread or rolls, using 1 piece of cheese in each and about ½ ounce (or 2 table-spoons) shaved chocolate.

4. Heat a large panini pan (see Note) over medium heat. Add the sandwiches and weight down with the lid. Grill, turning once, until the cheese has melted and the bread is crisp, about 6 minutes. Serve warm with little bowls of the caramel dipping sauce on the side.

▌**AHEAD**

- Make the caramel sauce up to 6 hours in advance. Store, covered, in its saucepan at room temperature. Pour into a small bowl and reheat in the microwave in 10-second bursts, just until warmed, not bubbling.

- Build the sandwiches up to 4 hours in advance. Store, covered, at room temperature before grilling.

▌**NOTES**

- The time it will take the sugar to caramelize can vary, depending on the thickness of the saucepan, the intensity of the heat, and even the day's humidity. Watch carefully that the sugar does not turn dark brown and burn.

- You can also use an electric panini press or even a George Foreman Grill—so long as the lid is attached by an open-jawed hinge that allows that lid to sit flat on the sandwiches. Heat the grill and make at most two of these sandwiches at a time. Since you can't immerse the electric appliances in water to clean them, you might want to give these presses a shot of cooking spray before you add the panini, just to make sure the cheese can be easily cleaned off.

- If you don't have any sort of panini press, set the sandwiches in a large skillet, then set a second, slightly smaller skillet on top, weighting that second skillet down with a large saucepan or a couple of heavy cans.

▌**POUR**

Bourbon, straight up, no fuss, a bit of woody caramel in every sip

Big Pretzels, Coconut Dulce de Leche Fondue

6 SERVINGS

Here's a matchup for dessert heaven: salty pretzels dipped in a creamy coconut sauce that is itself a cross between caramel-rich dulce de leche and a smooth fondue. It may well be one of the finest desserts we've ever concocted, a wonderfully informal end to a plated evening. That sauce, by the way, could be served on its own as a vegan dessert with apple slices for dipping.

PRETZELS

- 1 cup warm water (105° to 115°F)
- 2 tablespoons canola oil, plus more for greasing
- 1 tablespoon malt syrup (see Note)
- 2¼ teaspoons active dry yeast
- 1 teaspoon salt
- 2¾ cups all-purpose flour, plus more for dusting
- ¼ cup baking soda
- 2 tablespoons agave nectar
- 2 tablespoons cool water, plus more for the pot
- 2 tablespoons coarse sea salt

FONDUE

- 3 cans (13.5 ounces each) regular coconut milk (do not use light)
- ⅔ cup packed dark brown sugar
- ½ cup granulated white sugar
- ½ teaspoon salt
- 4½ ounces semisweet or bittersweet chocolate (60% to 80% cacao), chopped
- 1 teaspoon vanilla extract

▶ **AHEAD**

● Make the pretzels ahead (through step 7). Seal them in a plastic bag at room temperature for 1 day or freeze for up to 3 months.

● Make the caramel for the fondue up to 6 hours in advance. Store, covered, at room temperature. Add the chocolate and vanilla, then reheat over low heat, stirring constantly until melted and smooth.

1. To make the pretzels: Stir the warm water, oil, malt syrup, yeast, and salt in a large bowl until the syrup and yeast dissolve. Set aside for 5 minutes until foamy. Meanwhile, dust a clean, dry work surface with flour.

2. Stir the flour into the yeast mixture until a soft dough forms. Turn this mixture out onto the prepared work surface and knead until smooth and satiny, folding the dough over onto itself as you pull, press, and twist it on and against the work surface, about 10 minutes.

3. Oil the inside of a clean, dry large bowl. Set the dough in it, turn the dough over to coat lightly, cover, and set aside in a warm, draft-free place until doubled in bulk, 1 hour 30 minutes to 2 hours.

4. Position the rack in the center of the oven and heat to 450°F. Line a large rimmed baking sheet with parchment paper or a silicone baking mat. Fill a wide, high-sided pot about halfway with water—or so that the water is at least 3 inches deep. Stir in the baking soda until dissolved, then bring to a boil over high heat.

5. Meanwhile, punch down the dough and divide into 6 equal balls. Roll each into a rope 18 inches long. Form these ropes into pretzels: Curve the rope into a fairly tight U, double-twist the U about 2 inches from its two ends, then fold this twisted part and the ends up, over, and into the center of the U itself before sealing the ends against the dough.

6. Reduce the heat so the water simmers slowly. Drop in one or two pretzels (there should be no crowding or overlapping). Simmer for 2 minutes, turning once. Scoop out with a large slotted spoon or large strainer and place on the prepared baking sheet. Continue simmering more pretzels.

7. Whisk the agave nectar and 2 tablespoons cool water in a small bowl smooth. Brush this wash over the pretzels. Sprinkle with coarse salt. Bake until puffed and brown, 12 to 15 minutes. Cool on the baking sheet for 1 minute, then use a wide spatula to transfer the pretzels to a wire rack to cool completely, about 1 hour.

8. To make the fondue: Combine the coconut milk, both sugars, and salt in a large saucepan. Stir over medium heat until the sugar melts and the mixture begins to bubble. Reduce the heat to low and cook, stirring often, for 20 minutes. Then continue cooking, stirring constantly, until golden, thick, and caramelized, 10 to 20 minutes, depending on the heat's intensity and the thickness of the saucepan. Stir in the chocolate and vanilla until melted. Pour into a fondue pot over a small candle or pour into individual dipping bowls to go with the pretzels.

NOTES

● If one pretzel doesn't turn out perfectly, continue on with the rest, letting the dough from the "less-than-the-best" sit for at least 5 minutes before rolling again into a rope.

● If you just don't want to bother making complicated pretzels, it's perfectly acceptable to make pretzel rings—or just 6- to 8-inch-long pretzel sticks. As long as the thickness remains the same, they'll bake in the same amount of time.

● Malt syrup is available at many larger supermarkets and most health food stores. It adds a characteristic, not-too-sweet, wheaty flavor to pretzels. If you can't find any, substitute honey for a less sophisticated finish.

Pecan Baklava, Fennel Syrup

12 PIECES

Pecans and fennel seeds are a great match: the oily, sweet nuts mixed with the bright but slightly murky spice. A little sour sweetness from fresh orange juice brings it all together. We've nixed the melted butter, the standard fat in baklava, and gone for roasted pecan oil, a far more mellow flavor in the mix. Taken together, it's a modernist twist on baklava. It's also a dessert no one can turn down.

▶ AHEAD
● Make the recipe 1 day in advance. Once cooled, store, covered, at room temperature.

▶ GARNISH
Save the orange zest strips from the syrup. Slice them into smaller bits and use them as a topper on each serving.

▶ NOTES
● Phyllo dough is sometimes sold in 1-pound boxes, in which case you'll need three-quarters of the box, and sometimes in ½-pound boxes, in which case you'll need 1½ boxes.

● Most phyllo sold in packages comes in 9 x 13-inch sheets, so there's no cutting required for this recipe. If your sheets are of a different size, you'll need to cut or piece them to make them fit the baking pan in single layers.

SYRUP

- 1 large orange
- 1 cup sugar
- ¾ cup water
- ⅓ cup honey
- 2 teaspoons fennel seeds

BAKLAVA

- 3 cups pecan pieces
- ⅓ cup sugar
- 1 teaspoon ground cinnamon
- ½ teaspoon ground cardamom
- ¼ teaspoon ground cloves
- 1 cup plus 3 tablespoons roasted pecan oil, plus more for the baking dish
- ¾ pound (see Note) frozen phyllo dough, thawed, unrolled, and put under a clean, dry kitchen towel

1. To make the syrup: Use a vegetable peeler to remove the zest from the orange in large strips. Drop these into a large saucepan. Add the sugar, water, honey, and fennel seeds. Stir over medium heat until the sugar dissolves, then increase the heat a little and bring to a boil. Boil for 1 minute, then set aside, covered, in a warm place like the back of the stove while you make the baklava.

2. To make the baklava: Combine the pecans, sugar, cinnamon, cardamom, and cloves in a large food processor and grind until pasty. Add 3 tablespoons of the oil and continue grinding until finely ground but not a paste.

3. Position the rack in the center of the oven and heat to 375°F. Generously grease a 9 x 13-inch baking dish with pecan oil. Pour the remaining 1 cup pecan oil into a small bowl.

(continued)

4. Place 1 sheet of phyllo dough in the baking dish. Brush with some oil. Top with another sheet of phyllo and brush with oil. Repeat the layering and oiling, using about one-third of the total amount of phyllo.

5. Spread half the nut mixture across the phyllo, then repeat step 4, using half the remaining phyllo, oiling each sheet as it gets laid down. Spread this with the remainder of the nut mixture, then use the last of the phyllo to layer on top, brushing each sheet with oil. Use wet hands to press down on the layerings to make them compact without breaking the dough.

6. Use a paring knife to cut a crosshatch pattern of 12 triangles, cutting two-thirds of the way through the baklava in the baking dish. Here's how: First cut the baklava lengthwise in half. Then cut it widthwise into thirds. Then diagonally cut each of the 6 individual sections to create 2 triangles. Bake until browned and crisp, about 30 minutes.

7. Transfer to a wire rack. Strain the warm syrup through a fine-mesh sieve and onto the hot baklava in the pan, coating it evenly and thoroughly. Cool for at least 2 hours before serving.

◗ POUR

A white Port to offer light, bright melon tones to this rather dark flavor palette

Fennel/Cardamom Pears, Ginger Mascarpone

6 SERVINGS

A cold fruit dessert is always refreshing after a multi-course meal, even in the middle of the winter. These poached pears have a savory blend of spices—cardamom + cinnamon + fennel—that gives depth to the sugary syrup and complexity to the ginger-rich cream sauce. Double the recipe if you want breakfast waiting in the fridge the next morning.

MASCARPONE CREAM

- ¾ cup mascarpone, at room temperature
- 1 tablespoon minced fresh ginger
- 1 tablespoon sugar

PEARS

- 4 cups water
- 1 cup sugar
  One 4-inch cinnamon stick
- 6 whole green or white cardamom pods
- 1 teaspoon fennel seeds
- 6 ripe but still firm, medium Bosc pears, cored from the bottom and peeled (stems left on)

1. To make the mascarpone cream: Mix the mascarpone, ginger, and sugar in a small bowl with a fork until creamy. Cover and refrigerate for at least 4 hours.

2. To make the pears: Bring the water, sugar, cinnamon stick, cardamom pods, and fennel seeds to a simmer in a large saucepan over medium-high heat, stirring until the sugar dissolves.

3. Add the pears stems up, cover, reduce the heat to low, and simmer under tender but not mushy, 20 to 40 minutes depending on the ripeness and exact size of the pears.

4. Transfer the pears to a bowl. Boil the remaining liquid in the saucepan over high heat until thick and syrupy, about 5 minutes. Strain the liquid through a fine-mesh sieve and over the pears in the bowl, then refrigerate for at least 6 hours, covering tightly after the first hour.

5. To serve, smear about 2 tablespoons cream on each plate, set a pear stem up on top, and drizzle the remaining syrup over them.

▶ AHEAD

- Make the mascarpone cream and pears up to 3 days in advance. Store separately but covered in the refrigerator.

▶ GARNISH

Sprinkle two or three candied violets around the plate. To go all out, serve with Almond/Cardamom Biscotti (page 238).

▶ NOTES

- For even cooking, pick similar pears: about the same shape, weight, thickness, and firmness.

- Use a melon baller to core a pear from the bottom. Start by making a circular indentation into the flesh just where the blossom was, then slowly and carefully work your way up into the flesh, removing the seeds and the fibrous material around them. Remember that a pear's core is much smaller than an apple's. The seeds are near the bulbous end; it will only take one or two scoops of the melon baller to get them all. Peel after coring, not before.

Fig Galette, Honey Cream

1 TART/6 OR 8 SERVINGS

This free-form tart demands the best fresh figs you can find, not dull and hard, certainly not squishy and soft. In other words, you may well need to make a trip to a farmers' market in the summer. The crust is fairly short so it offers lots of crunch under this rather luxurious final plate.

¾ cup all-purpose flour, plus more for dusting

½ cup whole wheat pastry flour

½ teaspoon salt

4 tablespoons (½ stick) cold unsalted butter, cut into little pieces

3 tablespoons solid vegetable shortening, preferably expeller-pressed

About 3 tablespoons ice water

¼ cup ginger jam

1¼ pounds fresh Black Mission figs, stemmed and halved lengthwise

2 tablespoons packed light brown sugar

¼ teaspoon ground cardamom

¼ teaspoon ground cinnamon

1 cup heavy cream

3 tablespoons honey

1. Whisk both flours and the salt in a large bowl. Use a pastry cutter or a fork to cut the butter and shortening into the flour mixture until the whole thing resembles coarse sand. Add 3 tablespoons ice water, then stir to form a dough, adding more ice water a little bit at a time, as needed to make it cohere without getting sticky.

▶ AHEAD

● Bake the tart up to 8 hours in advance. Store, uncovered, at room temperature.

▶ NOTES

● Arrange the figs in a decorative pattern over the tart, spiraling them toward the center or making straight lines that transverse the circle.

● Use a flavorful honey—perhaps true orange blossom (not just honey flavored with orange extract), star thistle, or even eucalyptus.

2. Dust a clean, dry work surface with flour, then gather the dough into a ball and set it on top. Dust a rolling pin with flour and roll the dough into a 14-inch round about ⅛ inch thick, moving the round occasionally on the work surface to make sure it's not sticking. (Add more flour underneath if it is.)

3. Position the rack in the center of the oven and heat to 400°F. Line a large baking sheet with parchment paper or a silicone baking mat.

4. Transfer the dough to the baking sheet (parts may hang over the edges). Spread the center of the dough with the jam, leaving a 2-inch border around the perimeter. Place the figs cut side up on the jam. Combine the brown sugar, cardamom, and cinnamon in a small bowl and sprinkle over the figs and jam.

5. Fold the clean border of the crust up and over the galette. The border will not, of course, cover the entire thing but will leave a rustic, misshapen hole in the center. Bake until the crust is browned, the figs are soft, and the jam is bubbling, about 35 minutes. Transfer to a wire rack to cool for at least 30 minutes.

6. Set a large bowl and the beaters of an electric mixer or a large whisk in the refrigerator for at least 2 hours. Pour the cream into the bowl, then use an electric mixer at high speed (or the whisk) to beat the cream into soft peaks. Beat or whisk in the honey.

7. To serve, slice the tart into 6 or 8 wedges, then top each on serving plates with the cream.

▶ **POUR**

A 6-Puttonyos Tokaji, gloriously rich with that unique floral-and-oak perfume

Banana Shortbreads, Peanut Cream, Grape Granita

8 SERVINGS

This dessert may well be the best PB&Js adults could have: a crunchy banana cookie, some soft whipped cream scented with peanuts, and a spiky grape ice crystals. It's a little bit retro and a little bit insane, just like a modern dessert should be.

AHEAD

- Make the granita up to 4 days in advance. Store, covered, in the freezer.

- Steep and strain the cream without beating it up to 1 day in advance. Store, covered, in the refrigerator.

- Bake the cookies up to 1 day in advance. Once cooled, store in a sealed plastic bag at room temperature.

2 cups roasted peanuts in their shells

2 cups heavy cream

2 cups unsweetened Concord grape juice

8 tablespoons (1 stick) unsalted butter

1 overripe small banana, thinly sliced

1 cup whole wheat pastry flour

2 tablespoons all-purpose flour

6 tablespoons packed light brown sugar

⅓ cup finely chopped pecans

½ teaspoon ground cinnamon

¼ teaspoon salt

2 tablespoons water

1 teaspoon vanilla extract

1. Crush the peanuts and their shells under a rolling pin on a big cutting board. Scrape everything into a large saucepan and stir in the cream. Warm gently over low heat—do not let the mixture simmer, bubble, or even fizz. Cover and set aside to steep at room temperature for 2 hours. Strain through a fine-mesh sieve into a bowl. Cover tightly and refrigerate for at least 6 hours.

2. Pour the grape juice into a 9 x 5-inch loaf pan. Set on the floor of the freezer and chill for 2 hours. Scrape with a fork to form crystals, then put the pan back on the floor of the freezer.

3. Position the rack in the center of the oven and heat to 350°F. Line a large rimmed baking sheet with parchment paper or a silicone baking mat.

4. Combine the butter, banana, both flours, brown sugar, pecans, and cinnamon in a large food processor and process until well blended. Add the water, salt, and vanilla through the tube, pulsing to form clumps of dough.

(continued)

5. Turn the dough out onto a clean, dry work surface and gather together as a coherent mass. Lightly flour the work surface, then press and roll the dough into an 8-inch square. Trim it so it's indeed a perfect square. Cut into eight 2 x 4-inch rectangles (that is, one cut in the center horizontally, then three equidistant cuts vertically). Poke holes in the rectangles with the tines of a fork, then pull them apart and set on the prepared baking sheet with at least 1 inch between them.

6. Bake until browned and firm, about 22 minutes. Cool on the baking sheet for 1 minute, then transfer to a wire rack to cool completely.

7. Use an electric mixer at high speed to whip the cold peanut cream into a very thick sauce, not like a meringue, softer and more luxurious.

8. To serve, set a cookie on a small plate. Dollop generously with the cream and sprinkle the granita crystals on the cream.

▶ NOTE

● Because the cream has been warmed for steeping, it can no longer be beaten into peaks. It'll be soft but thick, like a rich sauce.

Chocolate Pots de Crème

8 SERVINGS

These smooth, silky custards will be just the thing after a substantial meal. And after melting the chocolate, there's no cooking to be done! The tofu will set up as the chocolate cools completely, turning them into soft, luxurious fare. Who says you need cream to make a pot de crème?

6 ounces bittersweet chocolate (at least 60% cacao)

18 ounces soft silken tofu

6 tablespoons unsweetened cocoa powder

¾ cup sugar

1½ tablespoons vanilla extract

1. Set up a double boiler over about 1 inch of simmering water or set a heatproof bowl over a saucepan with a similar amount of simmering water. Chop the chocolate and add it to the top of the double boiler or the bowl. Reduce the heat so the water simmers slowly, then stir until about three-quarters of the chocolate has melted. Turn off the heat and remove the top half of the double boiler or the bowl. Continue stirring until all the chocolate melts. Cool for 10 minutes, stirring occasionally.

2. Place the tofu, cocoa powder, sugar, vanilla, and melted chocolate in a large food processor and process until smooth, scraping the inside of the bowl at least once. Divide among eight ¾- to 1-cup ramekins or dessert dishes. Chill in the fridge for at least 4 hours before serving.

▶ AHEAD

● The recipe can be completed up to 2 days in advance. Store the ramekins, covered, in the refrigerator.

▶ GARNISH

Serve with Chocolate Chip Cookies, Maple, Tahini, Dates (page 236).

▶ NOTES

● Escaping steam can condense into chocolate and cause it to seize—that is, break into a watery liquid and little chocolate threads. Make sure the heat is low enough that the simmering water is not causing much steam around the double boiler or bowl.

● Instead of ramekins, use old-fashioned teacups.

▶ POUR

A nonvintage ruby port for sharp, plummy extravagance against the chocolate

Coconut Crepes, Passion Fruit Cream

8 SERVINGS

Tropical flavors end a large meal with present, bright notes, mitigating the deeper tastes that have come before. Here, the sour pop of the modified pastry cream brings the tender coconut crepes to an enticing finish. You'll need patience to make them, but the job goes faster than you might imagine once you get the hang of it. And you can indeed make them in advance.

CREAM

- 8 large egg yolks, at room temperature
- ½ cup sugar
- ⅓ cup cornstarch
- 2½ cups whole or low-fat milk
- ⅓ cup strained passion fruit juice (about 5 ripe passion fruits), the seeds reserved
- 1 teaspoon vanilla extract

CREPES

- 2¾ cups regular or light coconut milk
- 1 cup plus 2 tablespoons whole or low-fat milk
- 4 large eggs, at room temperature
- 2 cups all-purpose flour
- 1½ tablespoons sugar
- ½ teaspoon salt
- ½ cup unsweetened shredded coconut
- Unsalted butter, for the skillet

1. To make the cream: Use an electric mixer at medium speed to beat the yolks and sugar in a large bowl until thick and pale yellow, scraping down the inside of the bowl occasionally, about 4 minutes. Beat in the cornstarch until smooth.

> **AHEAD**
> - Make the cream up to 1 day in advance. Store, covered, in the refrigerator.
> - Make the crepes up to 4 hours in advance. Keep them on the plate under the towel.

> **LESS**
> Instead of making pastry cream, stir the sugar, passion fruit juice, and vanilla into 3 cups Greek yogurt.

> **MORE**
> Turn this whole dessert into a crepe cake: Smear a small amount of pastry cream on each crepe, stacking them up on top of each other on a cake plate or serving stand (you will not be able to move the cake once it's built). Top with a plain crepe and dust it with confectioners' sugar. The trick is to smear the cream as evenly as possible in each layer so the cake does not mound in the middle. Cut into wedges with a sharp knife, not a cake server.

> **GARNISH**
> Diced kiwi would also be beautiful on the crepes with the passion fruit seeds.

2. Heat the milk in a large saucepan over medium heat until puffs of steam rise from its surface (but it has not yet bubbled). Beat about half this hot milk into the egg yolk mixture until smooth, then scrape the warmed egg yolk mixture into the remaining milk in the saucepan and beat until smooth.

3. Reduce the heat to low and whisk until thick and bubbling, about 2 minutes. Whisk in the passion fruit juice and vanilla. Scrape the cream into a large bowl and refrigerate for 30 minutes. Press plastic wrap against the cream in the bowl to seal it, then refrigerate for at least 4 hours.

4. To make the crepes: Whisk the coconut milk, milk, and eggs in a large bowl until very smooth and rich. Whisk in the flour, sugar, and salt until smooth. Whisk in the coconut.

5. Set a 10-inch *nonstick* skillet over medium heat. Add a little bit of butter, just to coat the skillet when melted. Pour about ¼ cup of the batter into the skillet and swirl the skillet vigorously to coat its bottom with the batter. Cook for 1 minute, then flip the crepe, picking it up at one edge with a fork or a nonstick-safe spatula. Cook until set, about 1 minute longer, maybe less. Transfer to a large plate and cover with a clean kitchen towel. Continue making more until you've made 24 crepes, stacking them one on top of each other and keeping them lightly covered.

6. To serve, lay the crepes out on a large, clean, dry work surface. Spread each crepe with 2 tablespoons cream. Fold them up and set three on each plate. Top with the reserved passion fruit seeds.

NOTES

● Passion fruits are ripe when they are deeply wrinkled, sort of like prunes but not so deflated. Some varieties actually turn black as they wrinkle. However, despite its desiccated appearance, you should hear juice inside the fruit when it's shaken.

● To make the passion fruit juice: Slice about ½ inch off the top of each passion fruit, then use a serrated grapefruit spoon to scrape the inside pulp and seeds into a fine-mesh sieve set over a small bowl. Wipe the passion fruit pulp against the mesh with the back of a wooden spoon or a rubber spatula, catching the juice below. Pick out and reserve the seeds for later. Store in a covered bowl in the refrigerator.

Pumpkin Pie Tamales

16 TAMALES

Dessert tamales are a Mexican tradition—and a wonderful way to offer a comforting, rather homey dessert. The sweet masa dough accents the dried spices to give these a distinctly autumn feel. It's a big, hearty dessert, vaguely savory thanks to so much masa in the mix. If you've planned a meal with more than three courses, make this full recipe but freeze half the batch for another event in the months ahead, serving only one tamale per person on the night of your dinner party.

6 ounces corn husks

Boiling water

1¾ cups canned solid-pack pumpkin puree (see Note)

1 cup canola oil

1 cup warm tap water

1 cup packed light brown sugar

3½ cups masa harina

1 teaspoon ground cinnamon

1 teaspoon ground ginger

1 teaspoon salt

½ teaspoon ground cloves

¼ teaspoon freshly grated nutmeg

Warmed maple syrup, for garnish

1. Set the corn husks in a large roasting pan or baking dish, separating the husks gently so they can soak evenly. Pour boiling water to submerge them, then soak for 30 minutes, using a plate to weight them down in the hot water.

2. Meanwhile, mix the pumpkin, oil, warm water, and brown sugar in a big bowl until creamy. Whisk the masa, cinnamon, ginger, salt, cloves, and nutmeg in a second bowl. Stir the masa mixture into the pumpkin mixture to make a soft, uniform batter.

3. Remove a husk from the water and lay it smooth side up on your work surface. Spread ¼ to ⅓ cup pumpkin mixture into the center of the husk. Fold the sides over the filling, then fold the top and bottom over the filling to enclose it. Tie shut with butchers' twine. Continue making more tamales.

4. Set up a large vegetable steamer over 2 inches of simmering water (or several tiers of a bamboo steamer over a pot of simmering water). Add the tamales, cover, and steam for 1 hour 30 minutes. Cool for 10 minutes.

5. To serve, set the tamales on plates, then untie and unwrap them in the kitchen, leaving the husk on the plate as a "bed" for the tamale. Drizzle with maple syrup just before serving.

AHEAD

● Make the tamales through step 3 up to 8 hours in advance and store in the refrigerator before steaming. Or freeze in a sealed plastic bag for up to 3 months; steam directly out of the freezer for 1 hour 45 minutes (not 1½ hours).

MORE

Making a choice based on whether you want a vegetarian or vegan dessert, serve anything with these tamales that you'd serve with pumpkin pie: whipped cream, ice cream, frozen vanilla yogurt, chopped nuts, or squares of dark chocolate. Or go simpler and drizzle melted butter over the unwrapped tamales before adding the maple syrup.

NOTES

● The husk is merely to flavor the dough. You discard it once opened.

● You'll want many more than 16 husks, since some will tear or shred as you soak them or fill them.

● Use unsweetened pure solid-pack pumpkin, not pumpkin pie filling (which has sugar and spices in it).

Walnut/Honey Semifreddo, Pomegranate Molasses

8 SERVINGS

Look no further for the absolutely creamiest and best fro-zen dessert. Our technique for semifreddo is a three-part fandango in the kitchen: whipped cream, zabaglione, and Swiss meringue, all folded together. You'll dirty every bowl you own, but the results are a marshmallow-like frozen wonder, a texture that can't be matched. We balance all that sweet richness with streaks of sour pomegranate molasses, a Middle Eastern condiment that's available in many high-end grocery stores and certainly from all sorts of grocery purveyors on the Web.

1 cup walnut pieces

⅔ cup heavy cream

3 large eggs, separated, plus 1 large egg yolk

¼ cup honey

1 cup sugar

½ teaspoon cream of tartar

¼ teaspoon salt

1½ tablespoons pomegranate molasses

1. Toast the walnuts in a dry skillet over medium-low heat until lightly browned and fragrant, about 5 minutes, stirring occasionally. Pour into a mini food processor and grind until powdery like sand.

2. Line the inside of a 9 x 5-inch loaf pan with plastic wrap, leaving long pieces over the edges that you will be able to fold over the pan once the semifreddo is inside it.

3. Use an electric mixer at medium speed to beat the cream in a chilled large bowl to soft peaks, about 3 minutes.

4. Clean and dry the beaters. Set up a double boiler over 1 inch of slowly simmering water or set a heatproof bowl over a saucepan of simmering water. Add the 4 egg yolks and honey. Beat with an electric mixer at medium speed until thick and foamy, almost doubled in bulk, about 4 minutes. Thick ribbons will fall off the turned-off beaters when it's the right consistency.

(continued)

AHEAD

● Complete the recipe up to 3 days in advance. Store, covered, in the freezer.

GARNISH

Sprinkle pomegranate seeds and toasted walnut halves around the plates.

NOTES

● If you don't have a mini food proces-sor to grind the walnuts, do so in batches in a cleaned and dried spice grinder.

● The mixer's beaters must be cleaned and dried after each step. Any water droplets or other gunk can impede the chemical processes needed to make the components.

5. Clean and dry the beaters again. If you've used a double boiler, scrape the egg yolk mixture into a bowl. Clean and dry the top of the double boiler. Otherwise, set a second, clean heatproof bowl over the simmering water in the saucepan. Beat the 3 egg whites, sugar, cream of tartar, and salt over the simmering water with an electric mixer at medium speed until thick and marshmallowy, about 5 minutes. Remove the bowl from the heat, add the ground walnuts, and continue beating at medium speed for 2 minutes to cool.

6. Fold the egg white mixture into the egg yolk mixture until smooth, then fold the whipped cream into this combined mixture.

7. Drizzle the pomegranate molasses onto the combined mixture, then use a large rubber spatula to fold two times, creating streaky ribbons. Pour and spread this mixture into the prepared loaf pan. Fold the plastic wrap over the semifreddo to seal it. Freeze on the floor of the freezer for at least 8 hours. Even when fully frozen, the semifreddo will be soft and creamy.

▶ POUR

A Canadian ice wine from the Niagara region for a sweet, smooth, almost lubricious bit of syrupy perfection

Porter Pie,
Graham Cracker Crust, Meringue

8 SERVINGS

This pie has an intriguing edge, like a digestif in dessert form. The porter will offer its distinctly bitter sweetness, mellowed by both chocolate and coconut milk, but never muted. The crunchy crust will give it a necessary, textural contrast. The pie is best while still warm, perhaps the last thing you make before you take a shower in the late afternoon before the party.

▶ NOTES

● Add the meringue to the pie while the filling is warm to allow the meringue to cook from both sides, bottom and top, while in the oven.

● Daub the meringue onto the pie, then spread it gently. Use your cleaned fingers to seal it to the crust—and make sure there are no holes in the meringue across the pie.

CRUST

1¾ cups graham cracker crumbs

3 tablespoons granulated white sugar

¼ cup roasted pecan or walnut oil

1 tablespoon regular coconut milk (do not use light)

FILLING

1 cup porter

1 cup regular coconut milk (do not use light)

2 ounces dark chocolate (60% to 70% cacao), chopped

¼ cup packed dark brown sugar

3 tablespoons cornstarch

1 teaspoon vanilla extract

½ teaspoon salt

2 large eggs, separated, plus 1 large egg white

½ teaspoon cream of tartar

6 tablespoons confectioners' sugar

1. Position the rack in the center of the oven and heat to 350°F.

2. To make the crust: Stir the graham cracker crumbs, granulated sugar, nut oil, and coconut milk in a large bowl until well moistened. Press this mixture into a 9-inch pie plate to form an even, compact crust. Bake for 10 minutes, then cool on a wire rack while you make the filling. Leave the oven on but increase the temperature to 400°F.

3. To make the filling: Whisk the porter, coconut milk, chocolate, brown sugar, cornstarch, vanilla, and salt in a large saucepan over medium heat until the sugar dissolves. Keep whisking until the mixture begins to bubble and thicken, about 4 minutes. Remove from the heat.

4. Whisk the 2 egg yolks in a large bowl until uniform. Whisk the hot porter mixture into the yolks in three additions until smooth. Spread this mixture into the baked crust.

5. Use an electric mixer at high speed to beat the 3 egg whites and cream of tartar in a large, scrupulously dry bowl until quite foamy. Beat in the confectioners' sugar 1 tablespoon at a time, then continue beating until soft peaks can be formed when the turned-off beaters are dipped into the meringue, about 5 minutes in all.

6. Use a rubber spatula to spoon and spread this mixture over the warm filling in the pie, taking extra care to seal it to the edge of the crust all around. Dip the spatula quickly but gently into the meringue to make peaks all over it. Bake until the meringue is lightly browned, about 8 minutes. Cool on a wire rack for at least 1 hour before slicing.

Apricot No-Cheese Cake

8 SERVINGS

Here's an exception to our no-fakes rule: a vegan cheese-cake. If it weren't so delightful, if the pop of the apricots didn't bounce off the savory almond butter, if the texture wasn't perfectly smooth and rich, we might skip it and go for the traditional recipe. But we wouldn't dare. It's that good. Plus, as a boon to nerves in the kitchen, it's more forgiving than a traditional cheesecake. There's a lot to be said for that on the day of a dinner party.

Solid vegetable shortening, for greasing

1 cup California dried apricots (about 3 ounces)

Boiling water

2 cups graham cracker crumbs (do not use honey graham crackers)

¼ cup almond oil

¼ cup maple syrup

1¾ pounds silken tofu

⅔ cup sugar

¼ cup almond butter

2 tablespoons finely grated orange zest

1 tablespoon vanilla extract

⅓ cup all-purpose flour

1. Position the rack in the center of the oven and heat to 350°F. Grease the inside of a 9-inch springform pan with some shortening on a wadded-up paper towel. Put the apricots in a small heatproof bowl and cover with boiling water. Set aside to soak for 20 minutes.

2. Mix the graham cracker crumbs, almond oil, and maple syrup in a medium bowl. Pour into the prepared pan. Press the mixture evenly across the bottom and 1 inch up the sides of the pan.

3. Drain the apricots in a colander set in the sink, then put them in a large food processor. Add the tofu, sugar, almond butter, orange zest, and vanilla. Process until smooth, scraping down the inside of the bowl at least once. Add the flour and pulse until absorbed.

4. Pour and scrape the batter into the prepared pan. Bake until lightly browned and definitely set but slightly jiggly at the center when the pan is tapped, about 45 minutes. Transfer in the pan to a wire rack and cool for 1 hour. Run a knife around the edge of the cake to loosen it from the pan, then unlatch the sides and remove it. Set the cheese-cake in the fridge and chill for at least 4 hours before serving.

AHEAD

• Make the cheesecake up to 3 days in advance. Once chilled, cover tightly with plastic wrap and store in the refrigerator.

NOTE

• Dried California apricots are darker, richer, and tarter than Turkish apricots.

POUR

A chilled Muscato d'Asti for apricot-inflected luxury

Summer Pudding, Black Currants, Blackberries

8 SERVINGS

If you're a fan of bread and jam, then this is the dessert for you. A summer pudding is a long-forgotten and easy dessert that's much in need of a comeback. The pectin in the berries melds with the bread to turn the whole kit and caboodle into a chilly bombe that can be turned out of the bowl and sliced into wedges to serve. If you're not concerned about its being a vegan dessert, you'll also need some sweetened whipped cream at the table. When it happens, you'll know why.

6 cups blackberries

2 cups black currants

1½ cups sugar

2 tablespoons crème de cassis

¼ teaspoon salt

1½-pound loaf sliced vegan country-style white or oat bread, crusts removed

1. Mix the blackberries, currants, sugar, crème de cassis, and salt in a large saucepan. Bring to a simmer over medium-high heat, stirring often, until the berries break down, about 5 minutes.

2. Line a 2-quart soufflé dish with plastic wrap (see Note). Dip a slice of bread in the berry mixture, then place it on the bottom of the soufflé dish. Dip a few more slices of bread, using them to coat the bottom of the dish in an even layer. You'll need to tear or cut the slices to fit.

3. Spoon about one-third of the berry mixture into the dish. Place a second layer of bread over the berries, again tearing and slicing pieces to make an even fit. Add half the remaining sauce, then make another layer of bread, add the rest of the sauce, and top with a layer of bread.

4. Seal the top with plastic wrap, then set the soufflé dish on a rimmed baking sheet. Set a small plate on top of the dish, then weight it down with a large can (say, a 28-ounce can of tomatoes). Refrigerate for at least 8 hours.

5. To serve, remove the can, plate, and top layer of plastic wrap. Turn the soufflé dish upside down on a serving platter or cutting board. Remove the dish, holding on to the plastic wrap at the sides. Peel off the plastic wrap, then slice into wedges to serve.

▶ AHEAD

● Make the recipe through step 4 up to 1 day in advance. Refrigerate on the baking sheet.

▶ NOTES

● Although a summer pudding is usually made in a large mixing bowl, we prefer it in a straight-sided soufflé dish because it then comes out more like a cake—and looks more impressive at the table.

● Spread the plastic wrap evenly in the baking dish so there are few creases or wrinkles.

● There's no need to dip the second and further layers of bread in the berry mixture; they'll become soaked and coated as they sit in the refrigerator.

▶ POUR

A slightly chilled, late-harvest Zinfandel with pronounced cassis and blackberry accents

Olive Oil/Vin Santo Cake, Pine Nuts, Dried Apples

8 SERVINGS (MAYBE MORE)

There are more dried apples than flour in this cake, a way to get the maximum amount of moisture into the batter without its turning gummy or soupy. Those apples combine with the fragrant pine nuts and the sweet vin santo to make an irresistible cake. Use the highest-quality olive oil you can comfortably afford, a bottling that will lend its full aroma to the cake.

1½ cups chopped dried apples

1 cup all-purpose flour (see Note), plus more for dusting

½ cup toasted pine nuts, chopped

5 large eggs, separated, plus 2 large egg whites, at room temperature

½ teaspoon cream of tartar

½ teaspoon salt

¾ cup sugar, divided

½ cup highly flavored, fruity olive oil, plus more for greasing

½ cup vin santo

1. Position the rack in the center of the oven and heat to 375°F. Grease the inside bottom and sides of a 9-inch springform pan with a little olive oil on a wadded-up paper towel. Add a little flour, then tip and tilt the pan to coat the inside. Tap out any excess flour.

2. Mix the apples, flour, and pine nuts in a medium bowl.

3. Beat the 7 egg whites, cream of tartar, and salt with an electric mixer at high speed in a large bowl until droopy peaks can be formed when the turned-off beaters are dipped into the mixture. Beat in ¼ cup of the sugar until you can feel no sugar grains between your fingers, about 3 minutes.

4. Clean and dry the beaters. Use the mixer at medium speed to beat the 5 egg yolks and the remaining ½ cup sugar in a separate large bowl until thick and pale yellow, about 4 minutes.

5. Scrape down and remove the beaters, then fold in the oil with a rubber spatula. Once smooth, fold in the wine. Add the flour mixture and fold gently, just until there are no dry, white bits left in the batter. Fold in half the beaten whites until incorporated, then fold in the remaining whites just until they disappear. Pile the batter into the prepared pan.

6. Bake for 10 minutes. Reduce the oven temperature to 325°F and continue baking until set when tapped, about 40 minutes. Cool on a wire rack for 10 minutes. Run a thin knife around the sides of the cake. Unlatch and loosen the sides of the pan without removing it. Continue cooling to room temperature.

AHEAD

- Bake the cake up to 8 hours in advance. Store, uncovered, at room temperature.

GARNISH

Dust the top of the cooled cake with confectioners' sugar.

NOTES

- Vin santo ("holy wine" in Italian) is a dessert wine, originally from Tuscany, but now produced more generally (and even in some locales outside Italy). It's quite sweet, a little herbaceous, and often amber, although the color can range from pale brown to neon orange.

- Make sure the springform pan is well oiled and floured, even down in the crevice between the sides and the bottom.

- To get the egg whites and yolks to room temperature, separate the whole eggs into one bowl for the whites and a second for the yolks. Set the two bowls out on the counter for 15 to 20 minutes.

- Don't stint on beating the egg yolk mixture. It should fall off the turned-off beaters in thick ribbons.

- The flour needs to be lightly packed into the measuring cup. Scoop up the cup of flour, tap the measuring cup on the counter to compact the flour, and spoon in more until full and level.

- To remove the cake from the bottom of the pan, invert the cooled cake onto a cutting board. Run a long, thin, sharp knife between the cake and the pan bottom. Pull it off and reinvert onto a serving platter. However, if the springform pan you've used has a nonstick surface, you'll want to forgo this step and use a nonstick-safe knife to cut wedges from the cake still sitting on its metal bottom.

POUR

The same vin santo used in the cake

Espresso/Chocolate Bundt, Ginger/Whisky Sauce

8 SERVINGS (MAYBE MORE)

We've long loved to bring out a dark chocolate bar and some whisky as the ending salvo for a dinner party. But with this fairly straightforward but rich cake, we can have our cake *and* our chocolate *and* our whisky, too. The cinnamon and coffee in the batter mitigate some of the sweetness, offering spicy and bitter notes against the otherwise sweet sauce.

2¼ cups all-purpose flour

1¼ cups granulated white sugar

½ cup unsweetened cocoa powder

1 teaspoon baking soda

½ teaspoon ground ginger

½ teaspoon ground cinnamon

½ teaspoon salt

¼ teaspoon baking powder

1 cup cooled, very strong coffee, preferably espresso

½ cup roasted walnut oil, plus more for greasing

¼ cup molasses

1 tablespoon vanilla extract

⅔ cup packed light brown sugar

⅓ cup water

1½ tablespoons minced crystallized (or candied) ginger

3 tablespoons whisky, preferably a blended whisky

> AHEAD
>
> • Complete the recipe up to 6 hours in advance. Once cooled, cover, and store at room temperature.

> NOTE
>
> • You shouldn't waste a fancy single malt here, but you do want a flavorful whisky without much peat or smoke. Or substitute bourbon for a sweeter glaze.

1. Position the rack in the center of the oven and heat to 350°F. Grease the inside of a 10-inch Bundt pan thoroughly with some walnut oil on a wadded-up paper towel.

2. Whisk the flour, granulated sugar, cocoa powder, baking soda, ground ginger, cinnamon, salt, and baking powder in a large bowl. Stir in the coffee, walnut oil, molasses, and vanilla until there are no dry pockets in the batter. Pour and scrape into the prepared pan.

3. Bake until a toothpick inserted into the center of the cake comes out clean, about 35 minutes. Cool in the pan on a wire rack for 5 minutes, then unmold onto the rack and continue cooling for 15 minutes.

4. While the cake is still slightly warm, set it on a serving platter or cake stand. Stir the brown sugar, water, and crystallized ginger in a small saucepan over medium heat until the sugar dissolves. Bring to a boil, stirring very frequently. Boil for 2 minutes, stirring all the while. Remove the pan from the heat. Stir in the whisky until smooth, then bring back to a boil. Boil for 1 minute, stirring all the while. Spoon this sauce over the cake so that it soaks into the cake but also runs down into the center well.

Orange/Coconut Bundt

8 SERVINGS (MAYBE MORE)

Bundt cakes have indentations to hold their glazes. But since this cake is so flavorful, we kept the glaze very simple, just a sweet orange finish. This cake is moist and delicate but with a sturdy crumb, a surprising change from often overly heavy and overly sweet vegan cakes.

1¾ cups regular or light coconut milk

1 cup granulated white sugar

⅔ cup coconut oil, plus more for greasing

½ cup packed light brown sugar

2 teaspoons vanilla extract

¼ cup plus 1 tablespoon finely grated orange zest (see Note)

¾ cup orange juice, preferably freshly squeezed, divided

3 cups all-purpose flour

2 teaspoons baking powder

1 teaspoon baking soda

1 teaspoon salt

1½ cups shredded unsweetened coconut, toasted

2 cups confectioners' sugar

1. Position the rack in the center of the oven and heat to 350°F. Melt a little coconut oil in a small bowl in the microwave on high, then brush the oil on the inside of a 10-inch Bundt pan.

2. Place the coconut milk, granulated sugar, coconut oil, brown sugar, vanilla, ¼ cup of the zest, and ½ cup of the orange juice in a large food processor. Process until smooth, scraping down the inside of the bowl once.

3. Add the flour, baking powder, baking soda, and salt and pulse repeatedly to combine. Scrape down the inside of the bowl one more time. Add the coconut and pulse just to combine without grinding the coconut.

4. Scrape and smooth the batter into the prepared pan. Bake until a toothpick inserted into the center of the cake comes out clean, 45 to 50 minutes. Cool in the pan on a wire rack for 5 minutes, then unmold onto the rack to cool to room temperature, about 1 hour.

5. Glaze the cake by mixing the confectioners' sugar with the remaining ¼ cup orange juice and 1 tablespoon zest in a large bowl until the sugar has dissolved. Set the cake on a serving platter and drizzle the glaze over the cake.

AHEAD

● Bake the cake and glaze it up to 8 hours in advance. Store, covered, at room temperature.

NOTES

● Make sure the zest is very finely grated, preferably with a Microplane or the smallest holes of a box grater. Take off only the orange zest, none of the white pith underneath. You'll need about 3 large oranges for this much zest.

● If you don't want the glaze puddling around the cake on the platter, set paper towels under the wire rack that holds the cake, then drizzle the glaze over the cake in a very small, steady stream. (The paper towels will make counter cleanup easier.) Let stand about 15 minutes to harden the glaze, then transfer the cake to a serving platter.

Pecan/Coconut Cake, Orange Marmalade

8 SERVINGS (MAYBE MORE)

This tall layer cake may be the most deceptive recipe in the book. It looks gorgeous, like a fine bakery item, yet it's so easy to make. Because purchased marmalade stands in for any icing, you'll have this dessert put together in no time. The crumb is so moist and light with the tofu and coconut milk that there's no call for a sauce or even a frozen concoction on the side.

AHEAD
- Make the cake up to 8 hours in advance; when cooled, store, covered, at room temperature.

NOTE
- Although we prefer this cake with orange marmalade, you could substitute other marmalades—like lemon or lime—and even other nuts, like walnuts or skinned hazelnuts.

2½ cups all-purpose flour, plus more for dusting

1½ cups ground pecans

1 tablespoon baking powder

½ teaspoon salt

½ cup solid vegetable shortening, preferably expeller-pressed, plus more for greasing

1½ cups sugar

½ cup soft silken tofu (a smidge more than 4 ounces)

1 tablespoon vanilla extract

1½ cups regular or light coconut milk

1¼ cups orange marmalade

Confectioners' sugar, for dusting

1. Position the rack in the center of the oven and heat to 350°F. Grease the insides of two 9-inch round cake pans with a little shortening on a wadded-up paper towel. Dust with little flour, coating the sides and bottom before tapping out the excess.

2. Whisk the flour, pecans, baking powder, and salt in a medium bowl.

3. Use an electric mixer at medium speed to beat the shortening and sugar in a large bowl until fluffy and light, about 3 minutes. Beat in the tofu and vanilla until smooth.

4. Add half the flour mixture and beat at low speed until combined. Add half the coconut milk and beat until smooth. Scrape down the inside of the bowl. Beat in the remaining half of the flour, then beat in the remaining coconut milk. Split the batter between the prepared pans.

5. Bake until lightly browned and a toothpick inserted into the centers of the cakes comes out clean, about 25 minutes. Cool in the pans on a wire rack for 5 minutes, then unmold onto the rack to cool to room temperature, at least 1 hour.

6. Invert a layer on a cake stand so the flat bottom is now facing up. Spread the marmalade over the cake, then top with the second layer, this one with its flat bottom facing down. Dust with confectioners' sugar before serving.

Strawberry/Black Pepper Cake, Chocolate Balsamic Glaze, Vanilla Gelato

8 SERVINGS

Because this cake and its glaze are so strongly flavored—with enough black pepper that you'll even get a little burn after several bites—a fairly plain gelato is the best accompaniment, just a creamy mix of eggs and milk. True Italian gelato has no cream in the mix. However, American whole milk has a lower fat content than Italian milk, so we've added a little cream to make up the difference. We're sure you won't mind.

▶ AHEAD

● Make the gelato up to 2 weeks in advance. Store, covered, in the freezer.

● Bake and glaze the cake up to 8 hours in advance. Store, uncovered, at room temperature.

GELATO

- 7 large egg yolks, at room temperature
- ½ cup plus 2 tablespoons sugar
- 2¾ cups whole milk
- ¼ cup heavy cream
- 2 tablespoons vanilla extract
- ¼ teaspoon salt

CAKE AND GLAZE

- 1½ cups all-purpose flour, plus more for dusting
- 2 teaspoons freshly ground black pepper
- ½ teaspoon baking powder
- ½ teaspoon baking soda
- ½ teaspoon salt
- ½ cup plus 1 tablespoon sugar
- ⅓ cup canola oil, plus more for greasing
- 1 cup strawberry jam
- 2 large eggs, at room temperature
- 1 teaspoon vanilla extract
- 2 tablespoons balsamic vinegar
- 3 ounces bittersweet chocolate, preferably 60% to 70% cacao, chopped

1. To make the gelato: Use a whisk or an electric mixer at medium speed to beat the egg yolks and sugar in a medium bowl until thick and pale lemony yellow but still gritty, about 2 minutes.

2. Heat the milk and cream in a medium saucepan until small bubbles pop up along the pan's inner rim. Do not boil but adjust the heat to keep the mixture hot.

3. Whisk about one-quarter of the hot milk mixture into the egg yolk mixture until smooth, then whisk this combined mixture back into the saucepan with the remaining hot milk mixture. Immediately reduce the heat to low—if you're using an electric stove, move the pan to a second burner just now set on low. Cook slowly, stirring all the while, until the mixture thickens to the consistency of wet cake batter

and coats the back of a wooden spoon, about 7 minutes. Strain through a fine-mesh sieve into a clean bowl to remove any extraneous bits of cooked egg. Stir in the vanilla and salt. Refrigerate until cold, at least 4 hours, or overnight.

4. Just before you make the gelato, place the vanilla custard and your ice cream machine's dasher, if possible, in your refrigerator's freezer, just to assure they're very cold, but for no more than 10 minutes. Freeze the custard in your ice cream machine according to the manufacturer's instructions. Scrape into a plastic container, seal, and transfer to the floor of your freezer to freeze completely, about 8 hours.

5. To make the cake and glaze: Position the rack in the center of the oven and heat to 350°F. Grease the inside of a 9 x 5-inch metal loaf pan thoroughly with some oil on a wadded-up paper towel. Add a little flour, then tilt and tip the pan so that it films the sides and bottom. Tap out any excess.

6. Whisk the flour, pepper, baking powder, baking soda, and salt in a medium bowl.

7. Use an electric mixer at medium speed to beat ½ cup of the sugar and the oil in a large bowl until well blended and most of the sugar is dissolved. Beat in the jam until smooth, then beat in the eggs one at a time, scraping down the inside of the bowl after each addition. Beat in the vanilla until smooth.

8. Scrape down and remove the beaters. Fold in the flour mixture just until there are no spots of dry flour in the mix. Pour and scrape the batter into the prepared pan.

9. Bake until browned and a toothpick inserted into the center of the cake comes out clean, about 45 minutes. Cool in the pan on a wire rack for 5 minutes (it may collapse in the center), then unmold onto the rack to cool to room temperature, about 1 hour.

10. Set paper towels under the wire rack (to make cleanup easier). Whisk the vinegar and the remaining 1 tablespoon sugar in a small saucepan over medium heat until the sugar dissolves. Continue whisking until bubbling. Remove the pan from the heat and whisk in the chocolate until melted. Pour this mixture over the top of the cake and spread with a rubber spatula so it drips down the sides of the cake.

11. To serve, soften the gelato on the counter for 5 minutes, slice the cake into wedges, and scoop gelato on the side.

❭ NOTES

● Coating the back of a wooden spoon is a tricky marker for a gelato custard. If you want to be perfectly accurate, clip an instant-read deep-frying thermometer to the inside of the pan and cook until 170°F, stirring almost constantly.

● Glass loaf pans can overbake the sides and bottoms of delicate batters. We prefer metal pans.

Coconut Cheesecake Flan

8 SERVINGS

We have to thank Juli Hernandez-Roberts, the head of the test kitchen at *Fine Cooking* magazine, for introducing us to a version of this coconut-rich dessert. She offered it at a glorious Cuban dinner party: dish after dish of astounding flavors and textures. At the end, she sat the flan on the table and some seriously full guests dove in without looking back. It's extraordinarily light and creamy with a hint of the velvety texture of cheese.

½ cup unsweetened shredded coconut

1 cup sugar

⅓ cup water

4 large eggs plus 8 large egg yolks, at room temperature

3 cups regular coconut milk (do not use light)

2½ cups sweetened condensed milk (do not use low-fat or fat-free)

2 tablespoons dark rum, such as Myers's

2 teaspoons vanilla extract

1. Position the rack in the center of the oven and heat to 350°F. Spread the coconut on a large rimmed baking sheet and bake, stirring often, until lightly browned and toasted, about 10 minutes. Transfer the pan to a wire rack to cool. Leave the oven on and increase the temperature to 375°F.

2. Combine the sugar and water in a medium saucepan over high heat. Stir until the sugar dissolves, then cook until the mixture is dark amber, 3 to 4 minutes. Pour into a 9-inch cake pan. Swirl the hot pan to coat the bottom and about 1½ inches up the sides. Set on a wire rack to harden while you complete the recipe.

3. Whisk the whole eggs, egg yolks, coconut milk, condensed milk, rum, and vanilla in a big bowl until creamy and smooth. Pour into the caramel-lined pan. The caramel may crack and shatter. Cover tightly with foil.

4. Set a large roasting pan on a pulled-out oven rack. Set the cake pan in the roasting pan. Pour in hot tap water to come halfway up the sides of the cake pan. Bake until the center jiggles like set Jell-O when tapped, about 1 hour 30 minutes.

5. Remove the pan from the water bath and cool on a wire rack for 2 hours. Set the covered pan in the fridge for at least 24 hours. Uncover and run a thin knife around the edge of the pan. Set a lipped serving platter over the cake, then invert. Remove the pan, letting the caramel run down the cake. Sprinkle with the toasted coconut.

> AHEAD
- Make the flan up to 3 days in advance. Refrigerate the covered cake without unmolding.
- Toast the coconut up to 2 days in advance. Once cooled, store in a sealed plastic bag at room temperature.

> NOTE
- Take care that you do not burn the mixture in step 2 by turning it black with an acrid, sharp smell.

Steamed Pudding, Chocolate Sauce

8 SERVINGS (MAYBE MORE)

Don't wait for the winter holidays to steam a dessert pudding, sort of a textural cross between a cake and a flan but with more complex, darker flavors. Here, the combination of almonds and dates actually yields an exceptionally light version of the more standard dessert. Despite that, it's also got great crumb, the better to soak up the decadent chocolate sauce made with coconut milk.

▶ AHEAD

● Make the cake through step 4 up to 3 hours in advance. Store, uncovered, at room temperature.

● Make the sauce up to 3 hours in advance. Store, covered, in its saucepan.

PUDDING

1¼ cups whole wheat pastry flour

1 cup ground almonds

1 cup chopped pitted dates

½ cup fresh breadcrumbs (see Note)

1 teaspoon baking powder

1 teaspoon baking soda

½ teaspoon salt

1 cup sugar

1 cup banana puree (about 3 small bananas)

½ cup unsweetened almond milk

¼ cup almond oil, plus more for greasing

1 teaspoon vanilla extract

SAUCE

1 cup regular coconut milk (do not use light)

6 tablespoons unsweetened cocoa powder

⅓ cup sugar

2 ounces bittersweet chocolate, preferably 60% to 70% cacao, chopped

1 teaspoon vanilla extract

¼ teaspoon salt

1. To make the pudding: Generously grease the inside of a 2-quart soufflé dish with almond oil on a wadded-up paper towel.

2. Whisk the flour, almonds, dates, breadcrumbs, baking powder, baking soda, and salt in a big bowl. Whisk the sugar, banana puree, almond milk, almond oil, and vanilla in a second bowl until creamy.

3. Fold the wet ingredients into the dry with a rubber spatula until there are no dry pockets of flour mixture, then spoon and spread this mixture into the prepared soufflé dish. Lay a piece of parchment paper over the top of the soufflé dish; fold down and secure in place by knotting butchers' twine around the outside of the dish.

4. Set up a large steamer over about 2 inches of simmering water. Set the prepared soufflé dish on the steamer rack, cover the steamer, and steam for 1 hour 30 minutes. Check the water occasionally to make sure it hasn't boiled away. Transfer the hot baking dish to a wire rack to cool for 1 hour. Invert onto a cake plate or serving platter and remove the soufflé dish.

5. To make the sauce: Whisk the coconut milk, cocoa, sugar, chocolate, vanilla, and salt in a medium saucepan over medium heat, whisking all the while until just beginning to bubble and thicken slightly. Cool to room temperature, whisking occasionally, about 1 hour. To serve, slice the pudding into wedges and spoon the sauce on top.

NOTES

● Whole wheat pastry flour is not the same as whole wheat flour. The former has a much finer grind, capable of creating the tender crumb of this steamed pudding.

● Not all breadcrumbs are vegan. Read the label to be sure. Or buy a plain, vegan loaf and grind your own breadcrumbs from 1-inch pieces in a food processor.

● Although you can make a steamed pudding in a variety of molds, we found the round, high-sided soufflé dish helped the dessert keep a very dense, chewy texture and gave it a shape about like a cake (that can then be cut into wedges).

Lemon Cream Donuts

8 DONUTS

You won't believe the reactions when you end a dinner party with donuts. In fact, the crew at the photo shoot for this book couldn't believe it. They all hung around the set during this shot, nobody off doing their respective tasks, until we called it a wrap—and then there was a general frenzy in the room. Some of them also had a hard time believing these were vegan donuts. At least that's what we think they were saying. Their mouths were full. And some of their shirts were messy. Make sure you give your guests a warning: These donuts are stuffed full. They're for forks and plates. If people try to bite into them, they're inviting wardrobe (and upholstery) disaster.

▶ **AHEAD**

● Make, fill, and glaze the donuts up to 4 hours in advance. Once cooled, store, loosely covered with wax paper, in a cool spot. If it's summer and there's no cool place, store, loosely covered, in the refrigerator but allow to come back to room temperature for 1 hour.

▶ **NOTES**

● If the yeast doesn't activate in step 2, you'll need to start over.

● A 3-inch round cookie cutter or ring mold is the best tool for cutting the rounds of dough.

● A Bismarck tip (for a pastry bag) is a thin pointed tip designed specifically for filling donuts.

▶ **POUR**

Shots of bracing, sweet, iced limoncello

CREAM

8 ounces silken tofu

8 ounces soy cream cheese (1 cup)

¾ cup confectioners' sugar

2 teaspoons finely grated lemon zest

1 teaspoon lemon extract

½ teaspoon vanilla extract

DONUTS

¾ cup unsweetened almond milk, at room temperature

2 teaspoons active dry yeast

¼ cup plus 1 teaspoon granulated white sugar

¼ cup almond oil

2½ cups all-purpose flour, plus more for dusting

½ tablespoon salt

Refined canola oil, for deep-frying and for greasing the bowl

GLAZE

1 cup confectioners' sugar

2 to 3 tablespoons fresh lemon juice

1. To make the cream: Place the tofu, cream cheese, confectioners' sugar, lemon zest, lemon extract, and vanilla in a large food processor and process until creamy, scraping down the inside of the bowl at least once. Scrape into a bowl, cover, and refrigerate for at least 6 hours.

2. To make the donuts: Whisk the almond milk, yeast, and 1 teaspoon of the granulated sugar in a large bowl. Set aside to proof for 5 minutes, until foamy.

(continued)

3. Whisk in the almond oil and remaining ¼ cup sugar until the sugar dissolves, then stir in the flour and salt to form a firm dough. Dust a clean, dry work surface lightly with flour. Turn the dough out onto it. Knead for 10 minutes. Oil the inside of a large bowl, then gather the dough into a ball and set it in the bowl. Cover with a clean kitchen towel and set aside in a warm, dry place until doubled in bulk, about 2 hours.

4. Lightly flour a clean, dry work surface, then turn the dough out onto it. Lightly flour the dough, then roll to a large sheet between ¼ and ½ inch thick. Cut this sheet into as many 3-inch rounds as you can. Remove the rounds, gather the excess dough together, press it into a mass again, dust with as little flour as possible, and roll once more, doing this operation until you have 8 rounds.

5. Line a large rimmed baking sheet with parchment paper or a silicone baking mat. Set the rounds on it, loosely cover with a clean kitchen towel, and set aside in a warm, dry place until risen and relaxed a little, about 30 minutes.

6. Pour about 3 inches oil into a large pot or Dutch oven. Clip a deep-frying thermometer to the inside of the pan and heat the oil over medium heat to 375°F. Add two or three dough rounds. (They should float on one level.) Fry, turning once, until puffed and brown, about 4 minutes. Transfer to a wire rack and continue frying more, adjusting the heat so the oil's temperature remains at a (near) constant 375°F. Cool the fried donuts for at least 30 minutes.

7. Fit a pastry bag with a Bismarck tip (see Note) and fill the bag with the cream. Insert the tip into a donut and pipe in about ¼ cup. A little cream may ooze back out of the hole, a sign it's stuffed right. Set aside and continue filling more donuts.

8. To make the glaze: Mix the confectioners' sugar with 2 tablespoons lemon juice in a shallow soup bowl. Stir with a fork until a thick glaze, adding additional lemon juice in dribbles, to make the glaze just thin enough to coat without being runny. Dip the top of each slightly warm donut in the glaze to coat, letting any excess run off. Place on a rack glaze side up for 15 minutes to firm up.

Fleur de Sel Caramels

45 CARAMELS

Although these caramels make a wonderful after-dinner treat in the living room around a fire, you could certainly let them stand as a dessert in their own right at the table. They're a perfect balance of sweet and salty. And, surprisingly, vegan to boot. Have coffee on hand. And relax. The meal's over.

- 2 cups regular coconut milk (do not use light)
- 6 tablespoons demerara sugar
- 2 tablespoons coconut oil, plus more for greasing
- 2 teaspoons vanilla extract
- ½ tablespoon flaked sea salt
- 1¼ cups plus 2 tablespoons granulated white sugar
- ¾ cup light corn syrup
- ¾ cup water

1. Line a 9 x 5-inch loaf pan with parchment paper, pressing it to fit the sides and angles. Microwave a little coconut oil in a small bowl on high until melted and brush over the parchment paper, coating it evenly. Reserve extra for oiling the knife later in step 5.

2. Stir the coconut milk, demerara sugar, coconut oil, vanilla, and salt in a large saucepan over medium-low heat until warmed but not simmering, about 3 minutes.

3. Meanwhile, stir the granulated sugar, corn syrup, and water in a medium saucepan until the sugar dissolves. Clip a candy-making thermometer to the inside of the pan and continue cooking until 310°F without disturbing.

4. Remove the candy thermometer from the pan. Whisking all the while, pour the hot caramel into the coconut mixture, taking care to work efficiently but carefully since the mixture will roil up in the pan and can burn you. Whisk until smooth, then clip the candy-making thermometer to the inside of this pan and cook until 242°F, 8 to 12 minutes. Pour the mixture into the prepared loaf pan. Cool on a wire rack until set and firm, about 4 hours.

5. Pull the parchment paper out of the pan with the candy block attached. Place on a cutting board parchment side down. Slip the parchment paper out from under the candy. Oil a large chef's knife with some of the coconut oil, then slice the block widthwise into 1-inch-wide strips. Cut these strips into 1-inch pieces. Store on a plate with wax paper between the layers at room temperature for up to 4 hours, or cover and store in the fridge for up to 1 week. Allow chilled caramels to come back to room temperature for a couple of hours before serving.

▶ MORE

Rather than serving these caramels as a dessert, you could offer them as a take-away gift, a little party favor for the evening. Wrap each caramel in a 3½-inch square of wax paper or in a small, purchased, candy wrapper, available from baking supply stores.

▶ GARNISH

Sprinkle the caramels with more flaked sea salt.

▶ NOTES

- Demerara sugar is a coarse-grained, raw sugar with characteristic, slightly bitter notes in the sweetness. Do not substitute brown sugar.

- For the richest caramels, search out Vietnamese or Thai brands of coconut milk specifically labeled "for dessert," such as those sold under the Aroy-D label. These are loaded with coconut fat. But do not use sweetened cream of coconut.

- The caramels will show every fingerprint. Once cooled, touch the candy as few times as possible. If you want no fingerprints, wear latex surgical gloves when cutting (and wrapping) the candies.

▶ POUR

A budget-busting Sauternes, with all the honey and stone-fruit accents imaginable, because every dinner party deserves it

UNTIL NEXT TIME

At the end of an evening, we always have a little treat to send home with our guests, a gift that can carry the party into the next day. Yes, we've sent people away with Fleur de Sel Caramels. But we find that a little bag of granola may be the best gift of all. What's better than waking up the next morning, knowing that breakfast is made?

Our granola is multigrained, loaded with dried cranberries and flavored with maple syrup. It'll keep for at least a month at room temperature if it's well sealed. We've even been known to bring a bag or jar of this granola as a host gift to the dinner parties we've attended. It's our way of saying "thanks for dinner—we've got your breakfast covered tomorrow."

And it's our way of thanking you, too. We hope you now see that you can prepare and enjoy a vegetarian dinner party without sacrificing flavor or texture, that you can take vegetables for their own worth without gussying them up to become fake meats, and that you can craft a coursed celebration that's one of the best gifts you can give to your friends.

We wish you hours around your table with much laughter and conversation. Here's to the best of food and life, made better with friends. Here's to dinner parties. They're not coming back into vogue. They were always here, waiting for the right moment.

Kitchen-Sink Granola

MAKES ABOUT 2½ QUARTS

4 cups rolled oats (do not use quick-cooking or steel-cut)

1 cup wheat flakes

1 cup barley flakes

½ cup toasted wheat germ

½ cup finely chopped walnuts

½ cup unsweetened shredded coconut

½ cup instant nonfat dry milk

¼ cup packed dark brown sugar

1 tablespoon ground cinnamon

1 teaspoon salt

⅔ cup maple syrup

⅔ cup roasted walnut oil

1 tablespoon vanilla extract

¾ cup dried cranberries

1. Position the racks in the top and bottom third of the oven (or do the best you can dividing your oven into thirds) and heat to 350°F. Mix the oats, wheat flakes, and barley flakes in a very large bowl. Divide between 2 large rimmed baking sheets, spreading the mixture into even layers. Bake for 10 minutes. Leave the oven on.

2. Meanwhile, stir the wheat germ, walnuts, coconut, powdered milk, brown sugar, cinnamon, and salt in the same very large bowl.

3. Scrape the hot oat mixture into the bowl and toss well.

4. Stir the maple syrup, walnut oil, and vanilla in a small saucepan over medium heat and cook until small bubbles fizz around the inside edge of the pan, about 3 minutes. Pour this mixture over the oat mixture. Toss very well to coat all the dry ingredients with the liquids.

5. Divide this mixture between the two baking sheets. Bake for 10 minutes. Stir the mixture on the baking sheets well, then reverse the sheets top to bottom and rotate them back to front. Bake until irresistible and golden brown, about 10 minutes.

6. Transfer the baking sheets to a wire rack. Sprinkle the dried cranberries on top. Toss well, then cool to room temperature, about 2 hours.

7. Spoon and pour into cellophane bags that can be tied with raffia, or into canning or decorative jars that can be sealed well. Store, tightly sealed, at room temperature for up to 1 month.

ACKNOWLEDGMENTS

A book is like a wedding cake: You plan for it for a long time, its appearance is a cause for celebration, but the beautiful frosting hides the work. Specifically, from these people:

- Elissa Altman caught our vision from the get-go: that two omnivores believe vegetables encompass the widest range of culinary possibilities. She saw it—and didn't flinch.

- Dervla Kelly took over and championed the book as it neared its publication. She is our steady advocate for its success.

- Chris Gaugler's design is beyond, as always: hip without being irritating, cool without being dim. We'd do every book with her if we could.

- Jeffrey Batzli is its brilliant creative director. Through him, all this work became the book in your hands.

- Susan Turner has stoked its PR fires with an even-handed and honest openness. Her hard work is never heard, only seen.

- Eric Medsker's photography captured and even elevated our vibe. His enormous talent lofted the book higher than we could have hoped.

- Kate Slade is hands-down one of the finest copy editors around. We beg for her to help us with our boos. Um, books.

- Paige Hicks' whimsy and sophistication are found in every prop: every plate, linen, glass, and fork. She intuited our style and made it chic.

- Thanks, too, to her great assistant, Mike Hurst. Who knew you'd be a hand model?

- Eric's assistant, Sean Lippy, did everything quickly and well except blot out the sun. And he was asked to.

- Barrett Washburn was invaluable at the shoot, calmly prepping ingredients and preparing dishes as Bruce cooked like a fiend. If he lived closer, he'd be out of the kitchen and at our table for many dinner parties.

- Many thanks—the twenty-third time!—to Susan Ginsburg, our agent for every book we've written. We're clearly a winning team, the kind writers dream about.

- And thanks, too, to Stacey Testa at Writers House, a calm voice in the daily Sturm und Drang.

- During the ridiculously long shoot, Jan and Jerry Rathbun walked the dogs and Jean Millard did a grocery run all the way to Hartford on her birthday! Wow, we owe you all many more dinner parties.

- Emily Forrest generously provided us with the fabulous OXO tools. Behind every recipe in this book lies at least one OXO product.

- And then there are the dinner party guests who have tasted these recipes over the past year at our New England home: Fayette Reynolds, Rich Rosenfeld, Robin and Allen Cockerline, Denise and Bill Mickelson, Jerry Webman, Greg Millard, Sylvia and Jay Abbott, Sylwia Orczykowska and Adam Zieminski, Tara Blyth, Virginia Watkins, Julie Weinstein and Mike Lewis, Debbie Weinstein Rome, and Paul and Esther Lou Scarbrough. Hurry back to our table. We miss you by the time you're halfway up the driveway.

INDEX

Boldfaced page references indicate photographs.